NINE BAGS OF GOLD

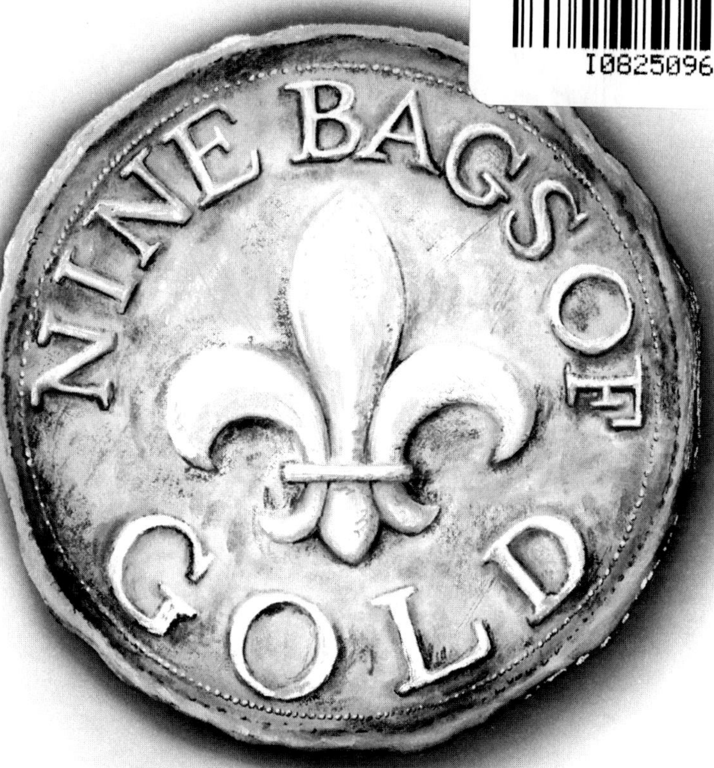

The Real-Life Hunt for the Lost Treasure of Acadie

STÉPHANE LEBLANC-RAINVILLE

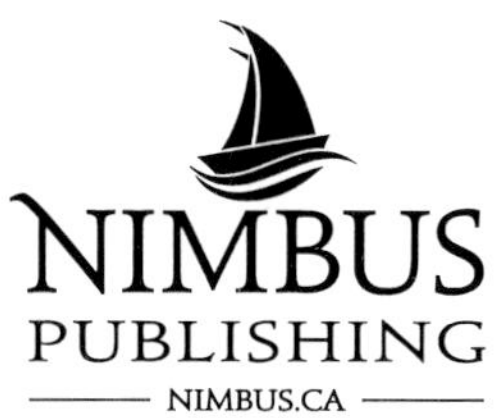

Nimbus Publishing Limited
3660 Strawberry Hill Street, Halifax, NS, B3K 5A9
(902) 455-4286 nimbus.ca

Nimbus Publishing is based in Kjipuktuk, Mi'kma'ki, the traditional territory of the Mi'kmaq People.

Printed and bound in Canada

NB1791

Editor: Marianne Ward

Editor for the press: Angela Mombourquette

Cover and interior design: Bee Stanton

Library and Archives Canada Cataloguing in Publication

Title: Nine bags of gold : the real-life hunt for the lost treasure of Acadie / Stéphane LeBlanc-Rainville.
Other titles: Real-life hunt for the lost treasure of Acadie
Names: LeBlanc-Rainville, Stéphane, author.
Description: Includes bibliographical references and index.
Identifiers: Canadiana (print) 20250333058 | Canadiana (ebook) 20250335115 | ISBN 9781774715314 (softcover) | ISBN 9781774715321 (EPUB)
Subjects: LCSH: Treasure troves—New Brunswick—History. | LCSH: New Brunswick—History.
Classification: LCC FC2471.9.T7 .L43 2026 | DDC 971.5/101—dc23

Nimbus Publishing acknowledges the financial support for its publishing activities from the Government of Canada, and the Canada Council for the Arts.

Pour ma Farah, ma Gabrielle et mon Olivier.

Et aussi pour mes parents, mon Moncton et mon Acadie.

Contents

Introduction

Time flies over us, but it leaves its shadow behind.
– Nathaniel Hawthorne

Age-old legends, elusive protagonists, deathbed confessions, mind-bending plot twists, purported treasure maps, large-scale digs, and tantalizing cliffhangers—this late 1800s saga seems to have it all. In 1937, Sherman Blakeny revealed to the press his prior involvement in the search for nine leather bags of gold buried in mid-eighteenth-century Acadie by French troops on the run. But how accurate are his words? And how much more might there be to them? *Nine Bags of Gold* dedicates itself to finding answers. Still, the book would be remiss not to relay the story of its own origins. Blakeny and I, it turns out, share something of a link.

There are moments when past, present, and future coalesce. Locking the door of one's childhood home for the final time represents such a moment: Memories rush back, the here and now pauses, and destiny beckons. Melancholy surfaced in 2018 as my aging parents prepared to sell the family residence. The house of my youth lies nestled in Sunny Brae, a sleepy neighbourhood in Moncton, New Brunswick. It stood both as a pillar of constancy and a marker of passing years. The domicile at 58 Peter Street hailed from the nineteenth century and appeared shrouded in mystery. I gave in to my curiosity, stirred by nostalgia and homecoming. I would pore over stories of the old walls over the next few months, both literally and figuratively. Soon, I got more than I bargained for.

Fifty-eight Peter Street has undergone several transformations since its construction in 1888. Demolitions, additions, and a possible quarter turn of the original section have created an odd jumble. My back-of-the-envelope doodles struggled to capture the architectural puzzle, and I developed a 3-D computer model instead. To my surprise, putting myself at a child's eye level and walking through the virtual replica awakened dormant memories. I also found that, by peeling away the house's newer layers, I could reverse the arrow of time and travel through the last 130 years of this one spot on Earth. History came alive. Before long, my focus drifted toward the people who had roamed the century-old hallways. I began forging a bond with a past more distant than my own. And what rich tales these former fifty-eighters have to tell.

The ghosts of 58 Peter have worn many a hat: artificial limb–maker, mother, ice- and coal dealer, First World War soldier, homemaker, excavator, maritime entrepreneur, church leader, gravel miner, musician, oil distributor, hardware store owner, politician, doctor, judge, architect, and university professor, to name only a few. The residence's storybook is replete with anecdotes of trivia, tragedy, and triumph. I grew fond of the abode's forerunners, thanks to the wealth of material available from a multitude of sources. But Sherman Blakeny—the larger-than-life character whose sixty-year tenure spanned from 1889 to 1949—sticks out from the lot. His reputation as a born

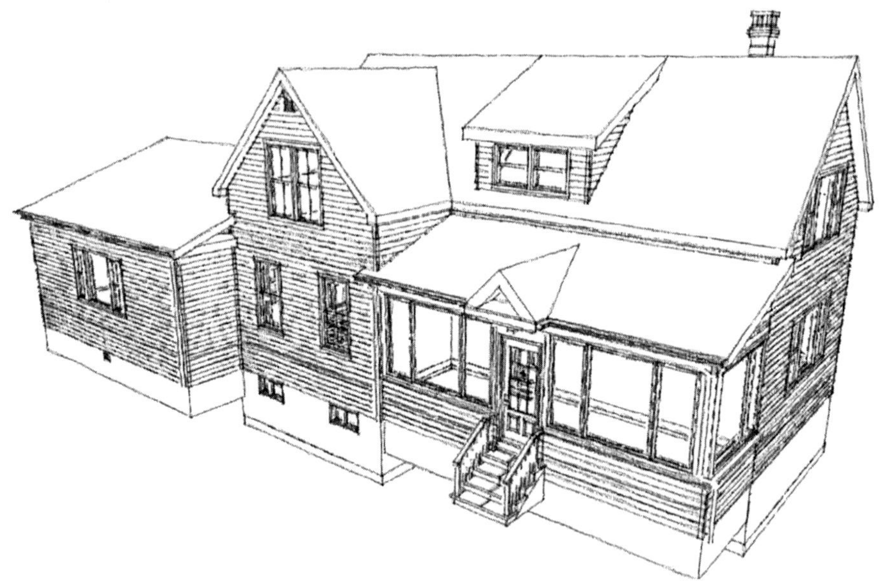

A sketch of 58 Peter Street as it appeared in 2015. [Author]

raconteur is perhaps what prompted journalist Ian Sclanders to feature him in the 1937 Saint John *Telegraph-Journal*'s travel series This New Brunswick—A Parade of People and Places.

And boy did Blakeny ever deliver.

The story on the front page of the paper on July 24, 1937, the nineteenth instalment of Sclanders's travel series, reads unlike any other and sowed the seed of *Nine Bags of Gold.* Here is the full transcription:

Another Story of a Treasure Hunt For Gold Now Thought Buried Beneath a Moncton Reservoir

by Ian Sclanders, Moncton, Westmorland County

Charles Sherman Blakeny pointed to the crook in the Petitcodiac which caused Moncton in the early days to be known as The Bend.

"Right down there," he said, "the English crossed the river on the bodies of the French they killed. They marched across, using the dead Frenchmen for a bridge.

"When I was a boy"—he admits 72 years but looks far younger—"the foundation of the old sugar refinery was being dug. I remember how the workmen turned up skeletons. It was an appalling sight to see the bones coming out of the ground, skulls and jawbones and teeth imbedded in the salt mud. The authorities took over and made the contractors bury them.

Mr. Blakeny guessed it must have been a very bloody battle to leave such grim relics behind, that long ago encounter that ended in defeat of the French troops and gave control of Acadia to the British.

But the battle is incidental, just background for this piece.

It figures only because it deposited another buried treasure in Westmorland County, where the woods seem to be full of them.

Mr. Blakeny looked for the treasure, looked for it on a grand scale.

With from 20 to 30 men working for him on the job, and six or seven teams of horses, he plowed seven acres of land at Irishtown to a depth of five feet.

But this is getting ahead of the story.

Bags of French Gold

Now, ever since the oldest residents of Moncton can remember, and long before that again, the legend has been that at Irishtown there are buried nine big leather bags of French gold.

"This," Mr. Blakeny related, "was sent out from France to pay the army. The country was over-run with the British at the time and the French were taking every precaution."

Realizing it was useless to try to get their ship up the river past the British guns they left it at Grindstone Island, at the mouth, and transferred to dories.

Even the small boats were sighted, however, and the French, pursued by a large force, had to take to the woods. The going was difficult, as it led through rocky, densely wooded country. And the gold was heavy.

They despaired of evading capture so long as they were burdened by the nine leather bags that contained the fortune that was the army payroll, so they buried it, making a chart to show where it was hidden.

They reached the French army safely but before a party could return to get the gold the British had started a mass attack—the battle that lost Acadia for France and gained it for England. They retreated with the other soldiers and doubtless some of them were killed.

One, the tale goes, was captured, and under duress revealed that the nine bags of gold had been buried.

But he could not, or would not, lead his captors to the exact location, and he did not have the chart.

Government Search

"There's no doubt about the story—no doubt that the treasure is there," Mr. Blakeny said. "Back 70 or 80 years ago the government itself had convincing enough evidence to finance a search. The government had men working in the area for two years, a couple of miles from where we searched later. I don't know how many thousands of dollars it spent."

The government finally abandoned its effort.

Talk of the treasure died down.

Then, 45 years ago, there came to Moncton an old man named Simpson, whose home was in Quebec.

His story was that a man whom he had helped had given him a chart—the chart—which had been made by those who buried the payroll.

There was a romantic tale attached to it—how a French soldier had secretly preserved it hoping to return himself and reclaim the treasure and how, wounded and on his deathbed, he had given it to a friend, and how, at last, it had fallen into the hands of the man who gave it to Mr. Simpson.

Mr. Simpson had in the bank a little money which he had saved against his old age—a few hundred dollars.

He decided to gamble it on the chances of finding a fortune, and he drew it all out of the bank—every last cent of it.

With his chart and his money he came on to Moncton.

"That chart," said Mr. Blakeny, "was the oldest document I ever saw. It was all in French."

Formed Company

"People got interested and they went in with Mr. Simpson and formed a treasure company to finance the search. Havelock Warman took some stock, and Theopolus LeBlanc, the hotel-keeper, and the two McSweeneys. I took a little stock myself. About $1,000 was put up altogether.

"They gave me the contract for digging up the land.

"We had to get the engineers to work on the chart to find out the spot it indicated and I have always claimed that that is where our trouble was. No two of them would agree. One fellow would say 'There is the spot,' and another would indicate a place half a mile away and say the same thing. We had the best engineers we could get, too.

"We did find landmarks shown on the chart—a south running stream and a spring. It showed the treasure as being buried behind a big rock but a lot of building stone had been taken out of the place and the rock was gone, so that wasn't any help.

"So we decided to dig over seven acres in the approximate location. We used horses and plows and scrapers—there weren't any [mechanical] shovels in those days—and turned the ground over to a depth of five feet. When you get down that far, you can tell from the look of things whether the earth has ever been dug up before. We worked there for about two months, then the money was all gone and the engineers still couldn't agree.

"Poor Simpson was broken-hearted. He had spent his last cent and had been certain that he would find the treasure and be able to spend the rest of his life in comfort."

Mr. Blakeny smiled as he thought of something else.

His Dreams

"I slept out there at Irishtown one night. I had a beautiful big black team of horses then. I dreamed that they were pulling the plow along and that I saw the plowshare cut through a leather bag and that gold coins burst out of it.

"It was so real that I woke up shouting, 'We've found it—we've found it.'

"Well, that was the closest I ever came to seeing the treasure. But I'm just as certain as I am that I'm standing here that the treasure is there."

"Do you think it will ever be found?" we asked him.

"No, I don't think it will ever be found now. And the reason I don't think so is that I'm afraid Moncton's water reservoir at Irishtown—that's just a quarter mile from where we worked—is built right on top of it."

That is Mr. Blakeny's opinion—that the treasure is covered by the Irishtown reservoir. And he knows more about the old chart and the opinions of the engineers than anybody else living, for he himself directed the digging operations.

It is almost a shame to put it in print.

Because it would be too bad indeed to detract from the pleasure of the week-end treasure hunters who have pick-marked the Irishtown area with their garden spades and who haunt the place from Saturday noon until Sunday night through the summer with all manner of weird and wonderful divining rods.

But then, there are so many buried treasures in Westmorland County that they can always try another. The woods are full of them in Westmorland—the buried treasures and the treasure hunters both.[1]

My reaction to Blakeny's account of his search for nine bags of French gold interred in my native Acadie was one of surprise and disbelief. The little-known story is worthy of a novel. And yet, for Blakeny, a fairy tale this was not. Rather than recall vague hearsay, he offered specifics from events he had participated in himself. My personal connection with him only heightened my thirst for answers. Over the next several years, I would strive to understand his story to the fullest. But I also needed to remain clear-eyed.

In all honesty, I have always been of two minds about Blakeny's interview. A map pointing to buried treasure strikes the imagination because it just *might* be possible. Could fantasy align with reality just this once? Wishful thinking goes against the no-nonsense adult in me. My inner child holds other ideas. Curiosity sidestepped—or at least postponed—the resolution of my internal conflict. Above all, I wanted to find out more. And so, rather than seek out the improbable motherlode, my book would aim to uncover the truth, whatever it turned out to be. In contrast with the more typical lost-riches genre, my default stance would be one of restraint and doubt, not one of hope and belief. I trusted my scientific background would keep my search honest. The final product could receive no better accolade than approval by bona fide historians, whose standards I have strived to emulate.

Nine Bags of Gold chronicles the natural evolution of what one might describe as a historico-forensic inquiry into a late-nineteenth-century treasure hunt. The investigation also grapples with Blakeny's conviction that an old French document—one he held in his hands—pointed to buried gold in southeastern New Brunswick. To this end, bits of historical context covering the early 1600s to the mid 1700s intersperse the chapters. These short texts, which concentrate on New France, and Acadie more specifically, offer sobering counterpoints to images of wealth concealed in this part of North America. As such, they provide an essential backdrop to Blakeny's story.

Acadie does not feature on any modern map. Yet, as far back as the early seventeenth century, this part of New France spread across much of Atlantic Canada. The 1713 Treaty of Utrecht left the colony of Acadie a geopolitical patchwork: France kept Isle Saint-Jean (Prince Edward Island) and Isle Royale

(Cape Breton). Britain, meanwhile, gained peninsular Acadie (mainland Nova Scotia). Continental Acadie (New Brunswick, the Gaspé Peninsula, and eastern Maine) remained in dispute but under de facto French control. Britain claimed continental Acadie in 1763, along with several of France's other North American colonies, at the conclusion of the Seven Years War.

Acadie's shifting boundaries and changing place names make period references somewhat of a minefield. One case in point is the so-called North Shore, a term that, in the eighteenth century, referred to the coastline of today's New Brunswick and Nova Scotia, opposite Prince Edward Island, along the Northumberland Strait. Most important to remember, though, is the military tension between French-held continental Acadie and British-held peninsular Acadie during the first half of the eighteenth century. *Nine Bags of Gold* retains the distinction throughout.

Indigenous Peoples in Canada are reappropriating their own appellations. *Nine Bags of Gold* uses *Mi'kmaq* for the group and *Mi'kmaw* for the adjectival form and single individuals. It also employs *Kanien'kehá* over Mohawk, *Wαpánahki* over Abenaki, and *Wolastoqiyik* over Maliseet.

Transcriptions of English texts and normalized translations from eighteenth-century French are mine alone, as are any and all errors. On the monetary front, today's Canadian-dollar equivalent accompanies references to period currencies.

Why write in English when I could have done so in my native French? My choice may raise eyebrows in circles—many close to my own—dedicated to promoting Acadie's interests. At its core, *Nine Bags of Gold* revolves around protagonists whose English-speaking heritage lends itself less naturally to French prose. Just the same, this book contains an important Acadian element, and it may thus introduce the Acadian story, as told by an Acadian teller, to a new audience. As of this writing, I am working on a French adaptation, which, I hope, will resonate with those more versed in the language of Molière.

Finally, we live in an age increasingly driven by polarization, inward-looking reflexes, and tribal tendencies. The challenge is to open our hearts and souls to the realities of others. Twain noted that "travel is fatal to prejudice, bigotry, and narrow-mindedness." *Nine Bags of Gold* represents an invitation to undertake such a voyage. I take from my own writing journey that curiosity for history with a small "h"—say, the 58 Peter Street of my youth—inevitably translates into curiosity for History with a big "H." Learning about the past, I discovered, has the potential not only to thrill, but also to inform our collective present and guide our joint future.

In the end, all history is shared history.

Chapter 1
The Call of the Unknown

Mystery creates wonder and wonder is the basis of man's desire to understand.
– Neil Armstrong

TALL TALES ABOUND IN EAST COAST FOLKLORE: SWASHBUCKLING PIRATES, ghostly spirits, phantom sailing ships, and lost riches. The yarn Sherman Blakeny told Ian Sclanders in 1937—nine leather bags of gold buried in Acadie by mid-eighteenth-century French troops on the run—appears too outrageous to merit serious consideration. But that did not deter a shadowy adventurer from trying his luck.

In the late 1800s, an elderly man named Simpson travelled from Quebec to Moncton and knocked on Blakeny's door. He owned a purported French treasure map from the mid-1700s and hired Blakeny for his expertise as an excavator. The chart, it seemed, pointed to a fortune concealed near Le Coude (present-day Moncton) in New France's colony of Acadie.[2] Simpson was both unfamiliar with the region and short on money; he needed help finding the booty he believed awaited him.

It is one thing to dismiss Simpson's quest as one man's delusion. It is another to question the judgment of those whose sanity was never in doubt. Blakeny contributed money of his own after he signed an excavation contract with Simpson. Four Monctonians—LeBlanc, Warman, and the "two McSweeneys"—also sponsored the project. The group raised upward of $1,000, or about $35,000 in today's dollars. Dozens of labourers and six or seven teams of horses plowed seven acres of land to a depth of five feet over a span of two

Eighteenth-Century Acadie. The Petitcodiac River's characteristic elbow gave Moncton its former name of Le Coude and later of The Bend. [LIBRARY OF CONGRESS GEOGRAPHY AND MAP DIVISION, MAPS OF NORTH AMERICA, 1750-1789, 312]

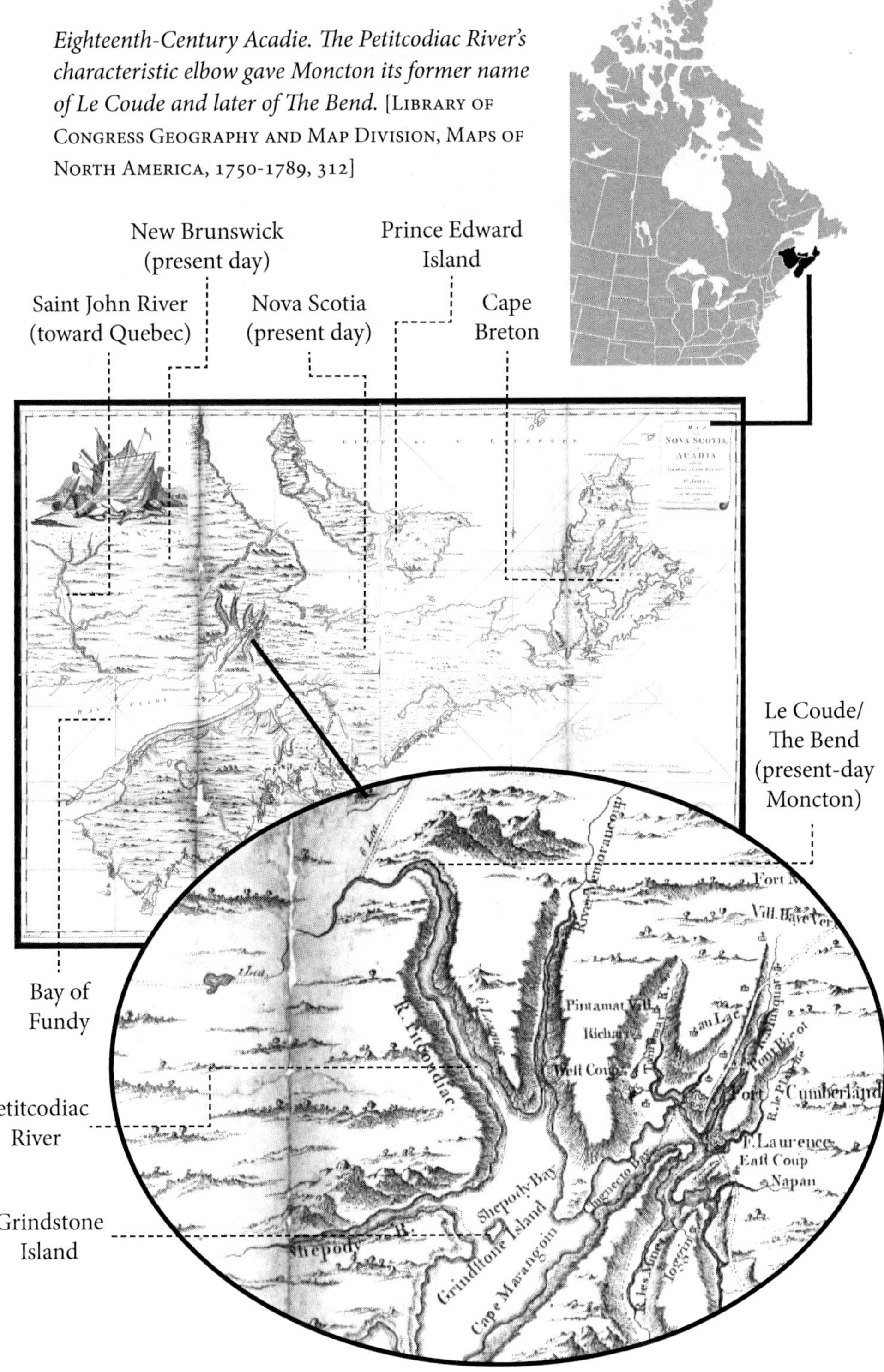

months in Irishtown, a small locality on Moncton's northern outskirts. Diggers failed to find anything. Had Simpson's map deceived him? Or did French gold still lie buried mere metres from where he abandoned his operation? Blakeny, for his part, never doubted the treasure's existence. Authorities, he recalled, had launched a recovery attempt in the area decades before.

Should we dismiss Blakeny's story as an elderly man's flight of fancy? His narrative includes dates, names, places, and other specifics that folk tales usually lack. If we are to believe him, Blakeny described nothing less than New Brunswick's greatest search for lost riches, bar none. Simpson's quest would also rank as Canada's most significant were it not for efforts to dig on Nova Scotia's fabled Oak Island. The Oak Island mystery, often qualified as the world's longest-running treasure hunt, began in 1795 with the discovery of a strange depression in the ground.[3] Enthusiasts expect the hole, dubbed the "Money Pit," to guard anything from gold to priceless artifacts. Ever more ambitious attempts have probed the site, although little hard evidence points to anything meaningful.[4] During the last decade or so, the reality TV series *The Curse of Oak Island* has chronicled the saga's current incarnation and enduring appeal.

Blakeny's tale is no less remarkable. But Sclanders's interview, it would seem, has not seen the light of day in its original form for the better part of a century. Partial retellings derived from Blakeny's own account have appeared in print.[5] Such rehashes are incomplete at best and wrong at worst. With each iteration, old information is lost and nothing new is added. As the echoes of Blakeny's story fade away, so too does our ability to remember and celebrate a striking piece of Canadiana. This book hopes to remedy the situation.

But it also aspires to do much more.

A Mystery in the Making

No matter how emphatically he recounted his tale, Blakeny did not support his claims with documents, photographs, artifacts, or other testimonies. His reminiscences are detailed and layered, but so too are good works of fiction. His story's complexities, while welcome, fail to prove anything. Which bits—all, some, or none—are accurate? The just-so narrative hangs on one man's word and appeals to faith alone. To be sure, unsubstantiated does not mean untrue. It is only that Blakeny's assertions, if they are legitimate, should hold up to scrutiny.

Blakeny also leaves readers wanting more. Could we unmask Simpson and tell his story? Did the treasure seeker travel to Moncton by himself, and did he journey there only once? When and where did the Irishtown dig take place, and did the excavation leave traces on the ground or in local lore? How did Blakeny learn of the incredible legend he tells, and how did it square up with a would-be French treasure map? How did Simpson acquire the chart, and what made him so confident about its authenticity? In short, how did the two men come to believe in the unbelievable?

Blakeny's tale triggers an avalanche of questions, irrespective of whether it elicits faith or doubt in the reader's mind. In the end, the multi-tiered enigma screams for—and deserves—a complete and detailed investigation. *Nine Bags of Gold* constitutes such a deep dive into a most intriguing past.

A Skeptical Inquiry

To be very clear, this book cannot be about finding buried riches that probably never were. In light of Acadie's past, chances are remote that French troops interred nine leather bags of gold near Le Coude. Treasure maps are also firmly rooted in popular fiction. Indeed, history appears to record no instance of an old chart ever leading to concealed valuables.[6] That alone casts a dark cloud over Simpson's operation. It should also give pause to anyone intent on trying their luck in Irishtown. In a word, there is much to bet that Simpson was on a wild goose chase. Our search for solid evidence, in contrast, is as sensible as they come. Still, we can draw parallels between Simpson's quest and our own. Both pursue something of value. Their respective objectives—gold for one and truth for the other—are all that separate them. But whereas most treasure seekers begin from a stance of belief, mystery solvers start from a standpoint of doubt. Or so they should.

Plausibility is the first casualty of a literary subgenre claiming to explain the origins of yet-to-be-discovered treasure. The Oak Island riddle, for one, has inspired countless works promoting outlandish theories about what could be buried on the site and why. Some include the safekeeping of the Holy Grail by the Knights Templar, the hiding of Inca wealth stolen by Spanish conquistadores, the burying of ill-gotten loot by Caribbean pirates, the preserving of Shakespeare's manuscripts in mercury, and the depositing of Marie Antoinette's crown jewels.[7] Other, less far-fetched accounts still commit the cardinal sin of vaulting from flimsy findings to improbable interpretations.[8]

Not so here.

Should *Nine Bags of Gold* end up rubbing covers on the lost-treasure bookshelf, it will stand out as the odd duck of the lot. The recovery of vanished fortunes may conjure up dreams of wild adventure, but we should summon our inner sleuths instead. Think Sherlock Holmes, not Indiana Jones. Getting to the bottom of Blakeny's story poses a daunting challenge. We will don our proverbial deerstalkers on more than one occasion. Our investigation will sometimes border on the wonkish, especially since we do not have the luxury of clues appearing as if by magic. Let us also subscribe to Holmes's standard method: Take little for granted, support conclusions with evidence (not vice versa), treat information as distinct from speculation, and favour simpler, more sensible explanations. Such an approach will sidestep obvious hazards. It will also help us peer behind the curtain of Blakeny's words.

One last heads-up. This book makes use of the participative "we" to signal that both reader and author are embarking on a journey of co-discovery. Our tussle with Blakeny's narrative will follow twists and turns as it tells its own story. But there is also something to be said for choosing the scenic route. In fact, we cannot hope to understand Simpson's saga to its fullest without marvelling at how seemingly unconnected individuals from different times and places became interlinked through a most peculiar chain of events. So, let us delight in learning about people whose unique lives get a new shot at remembrance.

Blakeny and Sclanders no doubt knew they were conveying a compelling narrative. Both men were natural-born storytellers. The two raconteurs must have sensed that Simpson's quest would work its vicarious magic by tapping into the reader's imagination. Just this once, they must have thought, truth could be stranger than fiction.

Simpson certainly met his share of people who challenged the legitimacy, feasibility, or even sanity of his endeavour. But so too did countless late-nineteenth-century adventurers. To be sure, Simpson was no trailblazing hero. He may well, in fact, have contracted a severe and misguided case of gold fever. He may also have come under the same romantic spell as many of his Victorian contemporaries. But did his curiosity, like our own, get the best of him?

"Mystery creates wonder and wonder is the basis of man's desire to understand." Neil Armstrong's quote encapsulates humanity's drive for exploration. It also implies that discovery requires effort. We should strive to unravel Simpson's treasure hunt for what it was, not for what we might wish it to be. Not all questions will find answers. More will arise still. Readers fearful that a solved enigma amounts to a spoiled one can also rest easy: The allure of Simpson's saga will endure. If anything, it will only deepen. This book's revelations—including those of a ninety-four-year-old Irishtown farmer—will test the resolve of even the most hardened of skeptics.

But this, as Sclanders put it, is getting ahead of the story.

The Ballad of Captain Kidd

My name was William Kidd; God's laws I did forbid,
And so wickedly I did, As I sailed...
I spied three ships from France, to them I did advance,
And took them all by chance, As I sailed...
I spied three ships from Spain, I looted them for gain,
I'd ninety bars of gold, And dollars manifold...
– Traditional broadside ballad

In 1701, authorities hanged William Kidd *twice* at London's Execution Dock. The hangman's rope snapped on the first try. The second attempt did the trick. A third-rate Scottish freebooter who later moved to America, Kidd had been unfairly convicted of piracy, among other crimes. But while unremarkable in life, he became notorious in death.

Kidd apprenticed as a seaman in New York. He soon found his calling under Jean Fantin, a French buccaneer who marauded the Caribbean and West African shores. Kidd then turned to privateering—or state-sponsored plunder of enemy vessels—after he commandeered his own ship. He had success initially. His actions caught the eye of Lord Bellomont, New York's governor, who, in 1695, commissioned him to attack French interests.[9] The expedition would be Kidd's downfall.

In 1698, Kidd intercepted the 350-ton *Quedagh Merchant* off the coast of India. The Armenian boat, which cruised under a French safe conduct, carried gold, silver, silk, and opium. It seemed a legitimate target at first. Pressured by his mutinous crew, Kidd claimed the vessel as a prize. Only, the *Quedagh Merchant*'s voyage had been brokered by the English East India Company. Moreover, much of the cargo belonged to a courtier of the Moghul emperor, who, in turn, demanded restitution from London. England showed Kidd little mercy and declared him an outlaw. Kidd sailed back to Boston, aware of the price on his head. Before reaching his destination, he hid part of his loot on Gardiners Island, near New York. The treasure, he believed, would give him leverage in seeking clemency. The plan backfired. Lord Bellomont, the colony's governor, feared his own implication in potential conspiracy charges. He arrested Kidd and confiscated the trove. Kidd spent a year in a New York prison. Bellomont then sent him to England for summary trial, sentencing, and execution. Kidd's body was gibbeted next to the Thames Estuary. The gruesome display served as a potent warning to those who would dare run afoul of England's 1698 Piracy Act.[10]

However undeservedly, the name Captain Kidd has become synonymous with piracy. The outlaw owes his notoriety to legends attesting that he deposited gold and jewels along North America's eastern seaboard, possibly even in Acadie on the Bay of Fundy's rocky coast.[11] Broadside ballads did much to spread the word.[12] Rumours swirled despite the fact that New York's governor immediately recovered the Gardiners Island loot in full.[13]

The life of Captain Kidd has inspired countless works of fiction, including an 1852 romanticization by Washington Irving, the short story "Kidd the Pirate." Ralph Paine remarked in his *Book of Buried Treasure*, "Many years ago a pamphlet was published, purporting to be true, which was entitled, 'An Account of Some of the Traditions and Experiments Respecting Captain Kidd's Piratical Vessel.' In this it was soberly asserted that Kidd in the *Quedagh Merchant* was chased into the North River [the lower Hudson] by an English man-of-war, and finding himself cornered, he and his crew took to the boats with what treasure they could carry, after setting fire to the ship, and fled up the Hudson, thence footing it through the wilderness to Boston."[14]

A treasure ship under threat of British capture. The transfer of loot onto smaller boats. An escape upriver, a speedy landfall, and an overland hike to friendly territories. It is difficult not to see here the seeds of Blakeny's tale of French gold buried in present-day southeastern New Brunswick.

Chapter 2
The Teller's Tale

Let the buyer beware.
– Sherman Blakeny

On a fair-weather morning in 1932, Sherman Blakeny stood on the dock at Point Wolf, NB (now Fundy National Park), to greet his namesake scow, the *Sherman B*. The flat-bottom barge, piloted by Captain Sidney Merriam, belonged to a small fleet that ferried sand and gravel up the Petitcodiac River from quarries in Albert County. Blakeny, by then sixty-six years old, still enjoyed trucking from Moncton in the middle of the night over muddy roads to oversee loading operations in person. But, on that day, things did not go as planned.[15]

The *Sherman B* sprang a leak after it took onboard a full load of gravel. Captain Merriam rushed to release the vertical, hinge-mounted sideboards that secured the freight in place. Much of the cargo spilled into the water. The manoeuvre saved the listing craft and lightened it enough for repairs to be effected on the fly. Soon, the *Sherman B* was back on its way.

Years later, Merriam recalled that Blakeny had raced ahead in his truck to await the *Sherman B* at its Moncton wharf. There, Blakeny had been in the habit of measuring the gravel load by first planting an iron rod through the heap until it reached the deck. He would then slide his fist along the rod and meet the top of the pile to judge its height. On more than one occasion, the boat's skipper caught Blakeny plunging his hand deep into the gravel. The sly manoeuvre excluded a portion of the load from the tally and reduced

Above: The Sherman B *(1930). Right: Sherman Blakeny* [COURTESY RICK DESBRISAY]

Merriam's pay accordingly. But on the day the *Sherman B* was nearly lost, Blakeny insisted on paying only one-third of the agreed fee. Merriam quit in disgust, disgruntled by the recent events and aggrieved by his employer's longstanding tactics. Blakeny, he remarked, was "a nice man, but greedy."[16]

What light, if any, does Captain Merriam's testimony shed on the extraordinary tale Blakeny recounted to Sclanders in 1937? Blakeny's narrative is free of self-contradictions. It also aligns with the broad strokes of Moncton's history, at least those a layperson might have offered at the time. In short, Simpson's treasure hunt resists assessment because we lack external evidence. Somehow or other, we need to widen our scope. And what better way than to learn about the storyteller himself? Because, it would seem, there is more to Blakeny than meets the eye.

Sherman Blakeny

Charles Sherman Blakeny was born on December 14, 1865, in Elgin, New Brunswick, a small hamlet south of Moncton, in Albert County. While Blakeny was still a boy, he and his family resettled in the Tankville district of Irishtown, a small community north of Moncton. The reasons for the move remain murky, but conditions on the new homestead were no upgrade over the old. The Blakenys first needed to clear the land of trees and rocks before farming could supply the most basic of foodstuffs. The lifestyle there was reportedly primitive. The budding youth endured backbreaking work. Such a toilsome upbringing no doubt shapes one's character.[17]

Though the Blakenys improved their Tankville property, it was not to last. The City of Moncton purchased the lot in 1878 and incorporated it as part of the watershed that surrounds the city's reservoir in Irishtown. The basin, it turns out, is also the one under which Blakeny claimed that French gold would forever lie buried. The former Blakeny farm has now reverted to a state of wilderness, and no visible traces of it remain. The reservoir no longer provides fresh water for the city. Together with its encircling floodplain, it currently forms the bulk of the Irishtown Nature Park.[18]

Blakeny left Tankville an aspiring young man and headed to Moncton. He wed Alice Humphrey Warman in 1888. The very next year, the two settled in Sunny Brae, then a small village across from Moncton on the opposite bank of Halls Creek. Several children were born from their union. From modest beginnings, first as a horse trader and trucker, Blakeny followed his calling as an entrepreneur. In turn excavator, ice cutter and dealer, coal prospector and distributor, gravel miner and supplier, scow owner, and concrete-block manufacturer, he reinvented himself many times over. He also served on the Sunny Brae council. He ultimately earned an enviable reputation as a respected citizen, businessman, public official, benefactor, patriarch, devout Baptist, and member of the Masonic order.[19] Blakeny Fuels, a descendant of Blakeny & Son Ltd., still operates today.

Changing market forces contributed to Blakeny's frequent self-renewal. Profits always remained slim. In 1912, he failed in his bid to move his family to Alberta. The Blakenys were never affluent, yet they wanted for nothing. On occasion, they even managed to purchase luxury items, including a Mason & Rich house organ and a Ford Model T.[20]

Tragedy did not spare the Blakenys. Three children did not reach their first birthday. A teenage son, George, died in 1917 from a bicycle accident. Another son, Ronald, was killed in action during the First World War. In 1922, after thirty-four years of mariage, Blakeny's spouse, Alice, succumbed to cancer at the age of fifty-two. A daughter, Edith, lost her life to respiratory illness in 1923. All told, the Blakenys raised three boys and six girls. In 1924, Blakeny took Daisy Mary O'Donnell (née Norton), herself a widow, as his second wife. He passed away on July 24, 1949, at eighty-three, still the owner of 58 Peter Street, the Sunny Brae property—and my childhood home—he had acquired sixty years before.[21]

On the surface, Blakeny's biography reads as rather conventional. But that would be discounting the man's multilayered personality.

A Resourceful Man

A born trader, "ever ready to enter into new ventures and try out new ideas," Blakeny proved resourceful.[22] He received a poor grade-school instruction but made up for it with initiative. Family lore tells of a twelve-year-old Blakeny travelling barefoot to neighbouring Kent County with a calf worth between two and three dollars. The story goes that he returned three weeks later with a horse, a buggy, and $28.30 in cash. He also displayed a flair for problem-solving. The ability eventually served him well in often unusual side-profit endeavours. In one case, he set up a large horse-driven circular saw in his home's backyard. The contraption helped him win a contract to pave Moncton's Main Street with cedar logs.[23]

In another case, Blakeny acquired a five-horse carryall outfitted with upholstered cushions, a high covered top, and canvas curtains. The four-wheel carriage, nicknamed "The Barge," shuttled revellers on group outings or to country dances. The vehicle was a forerunner in the city for its use of electric lamps. In yet another first, Blakeny mounted an old Ford engine onto one of his gravel-hauling scows. He experimented with towing multiple boats to increase speed and shipping volume. He even repurposed his fleet for sightseeing excursions and live-music moonlight cruises. A near-fatal mishap put an end to such riverboating entertainment.[24]

Blakeny also had compassionate qualities. He once rushed a boy to a doctor after his sled hit a hay wagon.[25] One time, at the age of seventy-four, he volunteered to help extinguish a chimney fire.[26] He earned the gratitude of an entire community in 1934 when an early winter storm destroyed the bridge between Moncton and Leger's Corner (now Dieppe). His ice-cutting business responded by erecting an ingenious traverse with wire cables. Large frozen blocks could quickly reach the other side of Halls Creek rather than travel along a long and wasteful detour. Soon, pedestrians used the jury-rigged sluice to get across.[27]

A Colourful Character

Moncton circles would have known Blakeny for his colourful character. Anecdotes praise his trading acumen. His relationships, though, were sometimes adversarial. He once drove over a pair of scales and was condemned to a fine of $35 (~$1,225). He and his business partners faced a $2,528 (~$52k) lawsuit in 1932 over a boat collision on the Petitcodiac—two men lost their lives in the accident. The court initially awarded partial compensation, but the defendants won on appeal.[28]

Importantly for our story, fair dealing did not represent Blakeny's only approach to business. We previously alluded to his miserly practices, as witnessed by his employee Captain Merriam. Moral compromises were perhaps necessary during lean Depression years in the dog-eat-dog world of scowing on the Petitcodiac. But other accounts depict Blakeny in similarly unfavourable light. For example, Captain Bedford Cook piloted the *Sherman B* when the craft overturned and had to undergo costly repairs. The skipper asked Blakeny to be rehired the following spring. The latter answered frigidly, "I wouldn't have cared if you had broken up all my other scows. But not the *Sherman B*. I'm sorry I haven't got a job for you."[29]

Blakeny's eldest son, Hanford, himself describes his father's early dealings as questionable. The senior Blakeny, he recalled, was "an astute horse-trader and horse-dealer, one of the now vanished type whose motto was:

'Let the buyer beware'—or 'everything's fair in love, war, or a horse-trade.'"[30] Hanford remembered driving his father's dump cart during the excavation of a Presbyterian manse's cellar. Perched on the high seat, he could smell the stench of asafetida, a pungent, resinous gum that Blakeny had applied to a rag strapped to the mare's bridle bit so that its vapours would mask the horse's chronic heaving. No sooner did the symptoms subside than he hoodwinked an unsuspecting dealer into swapping the worthless animal for a healthy replacement.

Blakeny also enjoyed horse-trading humour in which naive customers invariably lost out to unscrupulous merchants. He believed it important "to get the better end of the bargain if possible."[31] Win-win scenarios, it seems, were not always at his mind's forefront.

And some skulduggery was not off the table either.

Modern and old-school. Visionary and narrow-minded. Philanthropist and cheapskate. Compassionate and indifferent. Trustworthy and suspect. We cannot reduce Blakeny to a convenient two-dimensional caricature. Still, his elastic scruples raise troubling doubts, and his personality cannot help but colour our investigation. Indeed, did Blakeny manufacture a fake treasure map out of thin air? Did he create a fictional Simpson as a front? And did he sell investors on a futile but lucrative excavation contract?

Simply put, is the Irishtown dig just a fraud?

It is unclear whether the Moncton partners ever met the sphinxlike Simpson. If Blakeny posed as a middleman, a counterfeit chart vindicating local legend could have persuaded potential backers. Recountings of the failed search would overcome any suspicions so long as the origins of the deception remained secret. Blakeny's precarious finances in the late 1800s would have given him the motive. His expertise, ingenuity, and gyrating moral compass would have given him the means. And his well-heeled Moncton acquaintances would have given him the opportunity. In short, was Blakeny's interview with Sclanders the smug and cocky showing off of someone who got away with it?

We must again broaden our scope and reach beyond the storyteller himself. Our first lead comes from a familiar source. Blakeny's tale constitutes this book's initial stroke of lightning, but an extraordinary footnote by his own son, Hanford, represents its trailing thunderclap.

Acadie

HISTORICAL • CONTEXT •

In 1604, merchant Pierre Dugua de Monts and cartographer Samuel de Champlain led France's first successful attempt at colonizing the New World. The choice fell on Acadie—a vast stretch of territory Italian explorer Giovanni di Verrazzano had named Arcadia. Buildings went up on Isle Sainte Croix, an islet between today's Maine and New Brunswick. A harsh winter ensued. Thirty-five men—half the expedition's party—died of scurvy. Survivors relocated across the Bay of Fundy the next spring.[32]

Founded in 1605, the new settlement of Port Royal, in present-day Nova Scotia, represented a marked improvement over the old. The Mi'kmaq tolerated the incursion and provided vital support. The harbour enjoyed protection from the northwesterly winds. There was fresh water, fish, game, and fertile soil. L'Ordre de Bon Temps (The Order of Good Cheer) and *Le Théâtre de Neptune* kept up health and morale. Despite inauspicious beginnings, Acadie was off to a promising start.[33]

In 1607, France's King Henry IV revoked Dugua de Monts's fur-trade monopoly. Port Royal resumed its activities soon after, but it would henceforth answer to Quebec. Competing interests—political, religious, economic, and private—shaped Acadie's development. France's rivals periodically eyed the territory. Battles for possession weighed on its first eighty years of existence. A civil war between 1640 and 1645 added to its troubles. Franco-British hostilities would further plague it over the next century.[34]

From the 1630s onward, French emigrants chanced a one-way trip to Acadie. The self-reliant settlers reclaimed coastal salt marshes with dikes and aboiteaux—tide-driven sluice valves that allow seawater out but not in.[35] Acadians spread across the Bay of Fundy mostly through organic outgrowth. They founded Beaubassin (near Amherst, NS), Grand-Pré (near Wolfville, NS), and Chipoudie (near Hopewell, NB) around 1670, 1680, and 1695, respectively. No longer French in the European sense, they forged a distinct identity. They also proved innovative in self-governance and loyal to their way of life. France and Britain, for their part, tended to view the peace-seeking Acadians as mere pawns on the geopolitical chessboard.[36]

An Anglo-American force captured Port Royal in 1710. The defeat of the Acadian capital had repercussions in Europe. The transfer of peninsular Acadie (mainland Nova Scotia) to British rule as part of the 1713 Treaty of Utrecht profoundly impacted its inhabitants. Pressure grew on the Acadians to switch allegiance as plans for British colonization took shape. They refused. Some remained and threaded the political needle of defiant neutrality. Others managed to quit for territories still under French control. By the 1730s, Acadians with surnames such as Aucoin, Babineau, Blanchard, Breau, Landry, Sonier, and Thibodeau had founded Le Coude on the site of present-day Moncton.[37]

To stay or to go: The choice proved illusory for the war-weary Acadians. As subsequent events would show, they would pay dearly for making their homes on North America's doorstep. But crisis also implies opportunity. Blakeny's legend, while likely apocryphal, unfolds in a time and place rife with social upheavals and military tensions. Mid-eighteenth-century Acadie, it appears, constitutes fertile ground in which tales of buried treasure easily take hold.[38]

Chapter 3
An Extraordinary Footnote

Every man is the son of his own works.
– Miguel de Cervantes

IN 1929, BLAKENY'S ELDEST SON, HANFORD, BECAME MONCTON'S NEWEST mayor. A moment during the Dirty Thirties would epitomize his tenure. A crowd of angry men demanded work, food, and shelter. He confronted the mob. Nervous and alone on a City Hall stage, he said, "I promise you that as long as I am Mayor of the City of Moncton no man, woman or child will go hungry, without clothing or a place to sleep. Tomorrow morning I want every person who is in need of assistance to come to the Mayor's Office. Help will be given, I promise you." That same night, the Moncton City Council approved expenditures for necessities, rent subsidies, and jobs programs.[39]

Our investigation into Simpson's treasure hunt is in dire need of corroborating Blakeny's story with another source. Hanford inspires trust. Any mention of his father's involvement in Simpson's quest would strengthen our case. A footnote in his autobiography appears to do just that. And then some.

An Extraordinary Footnote

In 1960, Hanford self-published his autobiography, *The Story of Business and Its Founders*. Almost as an afterthought in the book's last pages, he retold his father's treasure-hunt story through a verbatim transcription of W. F. Robb's 1950 column in the *Moncton Transcript*. Robb's rehash borrowed liberally—even literally—from Sclanders's 1937 article and contributed no new information.[40] But Hanford offered the following footnote as a personal addendum:

> (NOTE. – I definitely remember the night Mr. Simpson came to our home in Sunny Brae. He and my father gathered about the table in the kitchen, in the dim light of the oil lamp, to examine the map. It was an old and faded parchment with compass inscriptions written in French. I recall the marks indicating the location of the big rock which was supposed to have the picture of a frog carved on the bottom. After they had talked about it for hours, Mr. Simpson made a contract with my father to excavate on the Bishop property on the Irishtown Road. Later I went out and saw where the digging had been done. Needless to say, the treasure never was found. – C. H. Blakeny).[41]

An eyewitness to Simpson's meeting with Blakeny. Another description of Simpson's prized treasure map. Compass indications penned in French. A large boulder engraved with the likeness of a frog. A whittling down of Simpson's operation to the Bishop property on Irishtown Road. Hanford's account, should it prove accurate, stands not only to back up his father's claims, but also to reveal additional clues. Yet validating one uncertain story with another is risky business. First, though, a quick foray into Hanford's life and a vetting of his character are in order.

Hanford's Youth

Charles Hanford Blakeny was born in Moncton on December 2, 1888. By his own account, his childhood in Sunny Brae was a happy one. Standards of living had increased and allowed for play. He recalled tobogganing with his dog and jumping into the hay from the barn's rafters. Other memories involved flinging sand-filled paper bags, sliding in the nude on Halls Creek's muddy banks, improvising steam cannons, and journeying to family picnics aboard "The Barge."

Hanford's entrepreneurial spirit, like his father's, was on early display. Get-rich-quick schemes struck his imagination. He peddled subscriptions, buttons, pens, and flowers door to door. He once sold hundreds of soap boxes in return for a writing desk. In another venture, he and his friends ferried passengers over Moncton's snow-covered roads. Their odd vehicle—a pair of hand-pulled sleds mounted with a large piano box decked with upholstered seats, signal bell, headlights, small windows, and a door—perhaps drew inspiration from The Barge. Rides cost two cents. A rotund woman once caused the contraption to tip over on its side. She lay imprisoned for some time, jammed against the exit, before rescuers arrived on the scene.

Hanford worked as a water boy on construction sites. Ever the optimizer, he used a carrying pole to double his load. He also delivered papers, tended to family chores, and helped out with his father's business.[42]

An Awakening

The words "Great is the Glory of Achievement," written in gold letters on the Blakenys' organ, impressed the young Hanford. He later confided the inscription had challenged him to "achieve, create and accomplish something in life." He apprenticed at Moncton's *Daily Transcript* under the tutelage of brash owner and editor John T. Hawke. But he knew that a grade-seven education limited his prospects.

Hanford entered Mount Allison University in 1909. There, he led the *Argosy* student newspaper and relied on the three-dollar-a-week stipend he received from his brother. He also worked odd jobs as assistant librarian and as gun cleaner to the University's Officer Training Corps. He served as president of his class, president of the student council, and president of the Eurhetorian Debate Society. He also found time to run a private magazine. He earned his BA in 1915.

Hanford's hopes of becoming a lawyer evaporated due to his father's floundering business. His family's precarious finances forced him to delay then abandon plans for more studies. He "reluctantly but dutifully" teamed up with his father to form Blakeny & Son Ltd. in 1915.[43] The first of many prudent decisions, he insisted on equal partnership. He does not claim for himself the credit of having rescued the Blakenys' fortunes. Still, the evidence speaks for itself: He operated a much-needed turnaround of the business, took on personal debt, and sought new opportunities. As his father pulled back from day-to-day management, Hanford ultimately steered the company toward oil delivery, concrete manufacturing, and hardware retail.[44]

A Higher Calling

Success in the business world did not quench Hanford's thirst for accomplishment. He entered politics out of frustration and served as Moncton's mayor for five years. In 1935, he tried his luck at the provincial level and won a seat in New Brunswick's legislature. He became Speaker of the House in 1939 and was named Minister for Education, Federal and Municipal Relations in 1940. He reformed New Brunswick's school system and provided French children with books in their language. He also pooled and redistributed education funding on the basis that students from poorer counties deserved better opportunities. His vision helped pave the way for the province's later renaissance.[45] Hanford retired in 1949, the year of his father's death. He inherited his childhood Sunny Brae home, 58 Peter Street, and moved back in. (The property changed hands several times before my parents acquired it in 1979.)

Left: Charles Hanford Blakeny; Right: Blakeny & Son Ltd. oil delivery truck and storage tanks (c. 1952). [COURTESY RICK DESBRISAY]

Hanford wrote what would be an apt epitaph: "To me, there has always been an objective to be reached—a desire to accomplish, a wish to achieve.... But this I know, something within spurred me on to the task, to struggle, to attain, to be of service to others—call it ambition or instinct, or what one may."[46] He passed away in 1961 at age seventy-two.[47] Tributes were uniformly praiseworthy. New Brunswick's premier, Louis J. Robichaud, proclaimed at the time that Hanford "was one of New Brunswick's most outstanding and valued citizens."[48]

Driven and caring. Dutiful and independent. Energetic and affable. Cerebral and contemplative. Assertive and open-minded. Even when pitted against one another, Hanford's character traits embody harmony. The temperaments of the junior and senior Blakenys offer a study in contrasts; it appears the younger Blakeny inherited his mother's calmer, more thoughtful spirit.[49] Still, both men did much with the cards they drew. Let us also not forget that, despite Blakeny's vagaries, Hanford's parents provided an environment in which their son could thrive.

A Story's Stress Test

Previously, we expressed concern that Simpson's quest could have been a charade invented by Blakeny himself to win a large though futile excavation contract. Our rediscovery of Hanford's extraordinary footnote therefore takes on outsized significance. We vetted Blakeny's son and found that he was categorically unimpeachable.[50]

In the Blakenys' combined accounts, we now have the embryo of a verified search for nine bags of French gold guided by an alleged treasure map. But do we dare hang our hats solely on the hook of Hanford's moral rectitude? Could deceit still explain the material at hand? By playing devil's advocate, we can stress-test our case.

One possible interpretation is that the two Blakenys were pranksters in cahoots. Did the duo push an inside joke in the local press? It would be out of character. The family's reputation would suffer should the truth leak. Another possible interpretation is that the father duped the son. But Hanford wrote that he attended his father's meeting with Simpson and watched the two men pore over the chart. If Hanford witnessed a hoax, then Blakeny staged a one-act drama with a fake document and an elderly actor posing as an imagined treasure-seeker. A mere boy at the time, Hanford could have served no useful role in such shenanigans.

We need more facts before we can hook our wagon to the Blakeny tandem, but our stress test suggests that Blakeny's tale has solid foundations on which we can build. That is not to say that the legend of buried gold must be true or that Simpson's alleged treasure map was genuine. Simpson, let alone the Blakenys, could not have been certain himself. The point is simply that the Blakeny father and son intended their narratives as authentic depictions of reality, at least as each man understood it to be.

For our investigation, that spells progress.

Statements by the junior and senior Blakenys, while separated by twenty-three years, agree point for point. Hanford's character bolsters his own testimony. His extraordinary footnote, in turn, lends credence to his father's more fleshed-out account. In a word, the broad strokes of Simpson's treasure hunt appear accurate.

Let us not forget that Hanford passed on additional clues:

- Simpson's document was a faded parchment with compass inscriptions.
- It specified that a frog-carved rock marked the gold's location.
- Simpson's dig site—somewhere on the Bishop property fronted on Irishtown Road—is also coming into view.

We will pursue these exciting leads in due time. But first, we should pick the low-hanging fruits. As we again widen our scope, Simpson's four financial backers—LeBlanc, Warman, and the two McSweeneys—begin appearing on our radar.

Simpson and Blakeny, we already know, did not act alone.

Le Chameau

HISTORICAL CONTEXT

In 1725, the forty-four-gun *Le Chameau* left the port of La Rochelle on the western coast of France. The six-hundred-ton flute ferried dignitaries, various cargo, and gold, silver, and copper coins to sustain France's colonies in the New World. The ship never reached its destination.

On the night of August 27, near Isle Royale (Cape Breton, NS), a storm battered *Le Chameau* and swept it onto rocky shoals. The vessel broke apart. Everyone onboard—over three hundred souls—perished. It is unclear whether the passengers anticipated their demise before disaster hit. The sleep garments worn by most of the recovered bodies suggest the catastrophe struck suddenly and unexpectedly. Difficulty in establishing longitude may have contributed to the crew's disorientation. Period maps often put today's Nova Scotia several degrees west of its true position for the same reason. *Le Chameau* sank only a few nautical miles from the safety of Louisbourg, the fortress France built in 1713 on Isle Royale's south-eastern tip.[51] In 1734, authorities erected Canada's first lighthouse at Louisbourg in a bid to prevent similar disasters in the future.[52]

The treasurer general of New France estimated the specie lost in the *Le Chameau* tragedy at 28,853 French livres (~$613,000).[53] Quebec dispatched experienced divers—Antoine Frustier *dit* "sent-le-vent" and Pierre Poittevin nicknamed "Tempête"—to retrieve the payload. The two men, fuelled by chocolate and lathered in animal fat to ward off hypothermia, braved Cape Breton's frigid waters.[54] Poor conditions doomed the salvage operation.

In 1965, Alex Storm and two others searched for the wreck of *Le Chameau* off the Cape Breton coast. They eventually located the sunken ship with their makeshift underwater metal detector. The trio lifted over five hundred louis d'or gold coins, four thousand silver coins, and several unique artifacts from the ocean floor. The question of ownership devolved into a protracted dispute that ultimately called on Canada's Supreme Court. The sale of the treasure at a New York auction netted the equivalent of several million dollars in today's currency.[55]

Cape Breton lore kept alive memories of the *Le Chameau* tragedy for two hundred and fifty years. The rediscovery of the vessel in 1965 no doubt emboldened those who, like Simpson before them, believed in legends and dreamed of recovering New France's lost riches.[56] Only, looking for treasure at sea is not the same as on land.

Le Chameau's story is noteworthy, but retrieving valuables from under the waves is nothing new. Shipwrecks were not only commonplace at the time, but also unrivalled at putting vast sums of money out of reach. In contrast, no force of nature is so powerful on terra firma. It follows that large caches end up underground not by accident but by design. In a word, buried booty presupposes intent. Nineteenth-century fiction authors, such as Edgar Allen Poe, James Fenimore Cooper, Washington Irving, and Robert Louis Stevenson, exploited the premise to full effect.[57] More than anyone else, these writers introduced the treasure-map meme into popular culture.

Chapter 4
The Four Financiers

A bank is a place that will lend you money if you can prove you don't need it.
– Bob Hope

BLAKENY IDENTIFIED HAVELOCK WARMAN, THEOPOLUS LEBLANC, AND THE two McSweeneys as the Moncton well-to-dos who sponsored Simpson's quest. The naming of these individuals constitutes perhaps the most specific aspect of Blakeny's entire story, but is it accurate? It would be a black eye on Blakeny indeed if his recollections involved someone who was either deceased, unborn, or worse, never existed at all. The four financiers should have left corresponding traces in Moncton's history books and should contribute several clues to our investigation.

And they will also have us solve a few mysteries of their own.

Théophile B. LeBlanc

"Theopolus LeBlanc, the hotelkeeper" can only be Théophile B. LeBlanc.[58] He was born in 1842 in Saint-Anselme, NB. Of Acadian descent, he ran his namesake guesthouse on Moncton's Duke Street. Hotel LeBlanc, not as upscale as the Brunswick or the American, welcomed travellers on a budget.[59] Centrally located in the Atlantic provinces, Moncton featured easy rail connections to the continent and river access to the eastern seaboard.[60]

LeBlanc—no immediate relation to me—formed part of a small but growing French-speaking minority in Moncton's business landscape.[61] Reportedly, his "word was as good as his bond."[62] He was also one of Moncton's racehorse owners and highest taxpayers.[63] The Moncton *Daily Times* wrote at length in 1898 about a rare-coin collection held by his son, Blair. The precious artifacts, it said, lay behind "fifteen very large and handsome antique oak and walnut cases with glass fronts."[64]

LeBlanc's hotel also doubled as a saloon.[65] Authorities repeatedly sanctioned the innkeeper for violating Canada's 1878 Temperance Act, known as the Scott Act, which curbed the sale of alcohol.[66] They fined LeBlanc in 1886 and 1889, among several other instances. They accused him of "illegally selling intoxicants" in 1890.[67] He played cat-and-mouse with Moncton law enforcement for the better part of the ensuing decade. He was once suspiciously nowhere to be found when officers came to serve him his papers in 1899.[68] Surprisingly, his establishment stood immediately next door to Moncton's police headquarters.

Scott Act fines did not disqualify individuals from serving in honourable capacities. LeBlanc performed jury duty, advised city council on procurement, and dabbled in local politics.[69] His wife, Osithe Surette, shouldered the hotel's day-to-day and freed him to pursue other opportunities.[70] For one, he was a sought-after contractor who had helped erect a Presbyterian church and build Moncton's so-called "City Hall and Market Building."[71] He also once worked as a stone cutter on the lower dam of the Moncton reservoir.[72] His knowledge of the reservoir area and his fluency in French may have proved useful in interpreting Simpson's map.

In 1898, LeBlanc purchased the Humphrey farm in Sunny Brae. The land later became the Université de Moncton's seed property. LeBlanc retired from the hospitality industry around 1901 and joined his son Blair in part-time construction jobs.[73] He passed away on July 4, 1904, after a stroke had left him paralyzed the previous year.[74]

Kathleen Borlase (née White), a fourth-generation descendant, extensively researched her family's past. When I reached out to her, she informed me that word of Simpson's treasure hunt had not survived in LeBlanc family lore.

Left: Osithe Surette, wife of innkeeper Théophile B. LeBlanc [Regis Brun]; Above: Moncton police enforcing Canada's 1878 Temperance Act, or Scott Act (c. 1907). [MONCTON MUSEUM COLLECTION]

Havelock Warman

Havelock Herbert Warman was born in Molus River, NB, in 1863. He began his working life as a sales representative for a merchandizing store in nearby Newcastle. In 1896, he moved to Moncton, where he founded Lounsbury, which still exists today. The concern deals in furniture, construction, farming equipment, and automobiles across much of New Brunswick.[75] Warman led the company's incorporation in 1918 and worked as its general manager until his retirement in 1925.[76]

Active in municipal and party politics, Warman served as alderman-at-large for the City of Moncton. Like LeBlanc, he owned racehorses.[77] He also supported Prime Minister John A. Macdonald's National Policy, an 1878 program advocating high-tariff protectionism, westward immigration, and expansion of the Canadian Pacific Railway.[78]

Warman was a well-known philanthropist and member of the Wesley Memorial United Church, the Masonic Lodge, and the Order of the Elks. At the time of his death in 1934, he worked as a local representative for the New York Life Insurance Company.[79]

Warman's move to Moncton in 1896 suggests that Simpson's treasure hunt took place after 1892, the date implied by Blakeny's "45 years ago." But a suggestion remains just that. A consummate salesman, Warman travelled extensively.[80] Maybe he ran into Simpson during a Moncton business trip and invested in the venture on the spot. His company sold agricultural machinery—a potential asset on the digging front.[81] Perhaps he also met Simpson through Alice Warman, his second cousin and Blakeny's first wife.[82]

The Two McSweeneys

From Blakeny's 1937 vantage point, the "two McSweeneys" needed no further introduction. The knowing reference hints at one of Moncton's most prominent families, which had six sons.[83] City directories list no one else with the McSweeney surname at the time, other than immediate members of that one family.[84] More difficult to sort out is which two McSweeneys helped finance Simpson's quest.

Herbert Havelock Warman, manager of Lounsbury Co. Ltd. [MONCTON DAILY TIMES]

Peter McSweeney Jr. [Topley Studio/Library and Archives Canada/PA-033773] *ran a dry goods and clothing store on Moncton's Main Street.* [Moncton Museum Collection]

We can eliminate Peter McSweeney Sr.—the Moncton merchant, landowner, and patriarch—from the outset. His death in 1884 preceded the birth of Blakeny's eldest son, Hanford, in 1888; the latter's recollection of Simpson's visit to his Sunny Brae home rules out any involvement of McSweeney Sr.[85] But a treasure hunt in want of cash would have welcomed any of the patriarch's six enterprising sons.

One son, William, moved to Halifax around 1875 and passed away in 1896.[86] Five others, Edward, Peter Jr., Thomas, John, and George, remained in Moncton and became affluent businessmen in their own right. Edward and John formed McSweeney Bros. Peter Jr. and Thomas specialized in dry-goods retail. George purchased the future Brunswick Hotel in 1884.[87]

John died in April 1890, and Thomas passed away the following November. Hanford was only a year old at the time; he could not have remembered Simpson's quest from such a young age. Edward died in 1893.[88] It does not

George McSweeney [Moncton Museum Collection] *owned Moncton's Brunswick Hotel, advertised as "the finest east of Montreal."* [Provincial Archives of New Brunswick photo P256-205]

seem that he gained enough notoriety to eclipse one of his two surviving Moncton brothers.[89]

The remaining two McSweeney siblings grew in Moncton's collective consciousness. George expanded his Brunswick Hotel. Like LeBlanc, he received several fines for Scott Act infractions.[90] He also served on the Moncton town council and worked as US consul delegate on trade matters.[91] He died in 1912.

Peter Jr., for his part, felt the pinch of competition as larger retail players began setting up shop. By that point, though, he had made the jump to politics. He sat on the city council (Moncton incorporated as a city twice, in 1855 and again in 1875). In 1899, he was appointed to the Senate of Canada, where he served until his death in 1921. His estimated fortune at the time amounted to approximately $500,000 ($7.3 million).[92]

Changing times ensured the McSweeney family would never again dominate Moncton society as it once did, but George and Peter Jr. both outlasted and outshone their brothers. They would have stood out to anyone looking back on the McSweeneys in 1937. Thus, I feel certain, based on my own research, that the "two McSweeneys" are Peter Jr. and George. Moncton-born historian Dan Soucoup reached the same verdict in 2000.[93]

A Small World

Moncton was a small world in the late nineteenth century. Business circles were smaller still. The collapse of the shipbuilding industry in the 1860s threatened the community's very existence. A decade later, the Intercolonial Railway (ICR) breathed new life into the local economy when it selected the municipality as the location for its headquarters.[94] Still, in the early 1890s, Moncton covered only a few square kilometres and comprised fewer than ten thousand souls.[95]

Proximity between Blakeny and Simpson's four investors was unavoidable given Moncton's small size. Surviving evidence points to both business and personal links between Simpson's partners. For instance, Blakeny and LeBlanc both contributed to the construction of a Presbyterian church. Blakeny began excavating the Higgins Block at the intersection of Main and Botsford in May 1901, and Peter McSweeney Jr. contracted LeBlanc less than two weeks later to work on his new retail store, just kitty-corner from Blakeny's dig.[96] LeBlanc and the McSweeneys all attended Moncton's only Catholic house of worship at the time. George McSweeney and LeBlanc also no doubt interacted as fellow hotelkeepers. Warman and the two McSweeneys all served on the city council. Blakeny and Warman belonged to the Masonic order. LeBlanc and Warman both owned racehorses and likely fraternized at the track. In short, in the rarified air of Moncton's small, late-nineteenth-century business world, people could count on one thing: Everyone knew everyone.

The Ties That Bind

In his 1937 interview with Sclanders, Blakeny made use of corporate language to describe his association with Simpson and the four Moncton financiers: "People got interested and they went in with Mr. Simpson and formed a treasure company to finance the search. Havelock Warman took some stock, and Theopolus LeBlanc, the hotelkeeper, and the two McSweeneys. I took a little stock myself. About $1,000 was put up altogether."

Expressions such as "company" and "stock" had clear connotations even at the time. We would expect a businessman such as Blakeny to fully understand their meanings. At face value, then, Blakeny's jargon suggests a legal framework codifying how Simpson and his partners would pool resources, manage interactions, divide profits, and resolve disputes. But was Blakeny employing mere figures of speech?

Simpson's quest raised about $1,000, the equivalent of about $35,000 today. Each of the four sponsors therefore invested $8,750 on average, or somewhat less, depending on how much Blakeny and Simpson contributed to the pot. The sums are not insignificant. Well-heeled stakeholders would demand assurances in return. Simpson's group could choose among several alternatives to make its ties official.

One possibility is a gentleman's agreement. That, however, would imply a certain naiveté. Simpson had everything to lose as an outsider. He would have been foolish to place all his trust in a handshake. A minor transaction this was not. In fact, a treasure hunt is much like a lottery, or the purchase of a chance to win a large but improbable prize. The deep-pocketed backers were savvy entrepreneurs who knew how to lock in rewards ahead of time. In other words, they would have insisted on putting details in writing.

A deal couched on paper constitutes a legal step up. Still, it might not prove ironclad. For instance, an IOU (short for "I owe you") can formalize spur-of-the-moment decisions without binding legalities. A contract, in comparison, not only ties parties in the eyes of the law, but also offers judicial recourse. Blakeny himself mentioned that Simpson and the four partners gave him "the contract for digging up the land." But even such paperwork can be stillborn if terms are unclear, unsound, or unlawful. Without the assistance of an attorney, Simpson and his associates would risk operating under an unenforceable agreement.[97] But there were other options.

Simpson may have considered a limited partnership. The structure would protect the personal assets of passive investors, such as the four financiers, should a lawsuit materialize against the group. The next rung up the legal ladder would have been incorporation. Such a framework would shield all

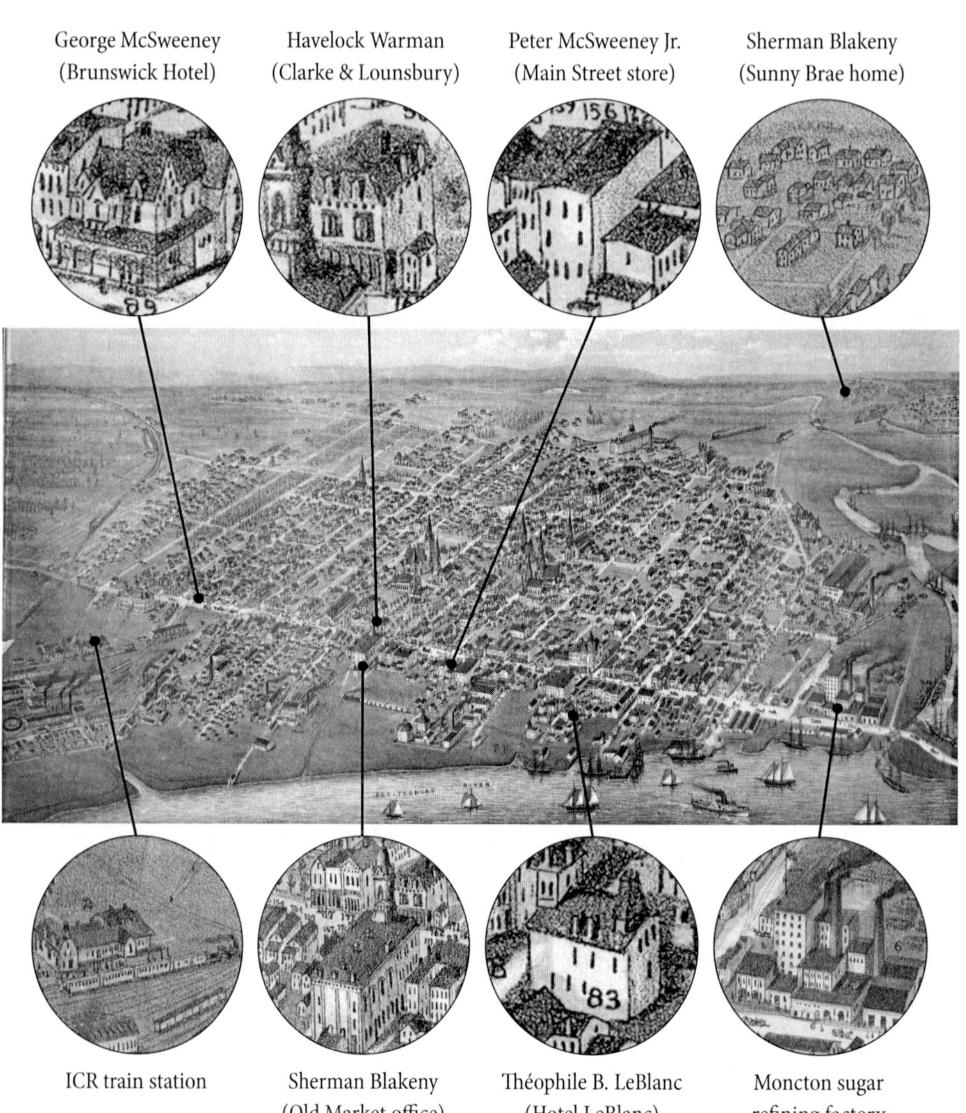

D. D. Currie's 1888 panoramic map depicts Moncton much as it appeared to Simpson. Medallions show some locations associated with Simpson's financiers. [Library of Congress Geography and Map Division, G3434.M6A35 1888.D4]

stakeholders—including Simpson himself—from potential lawsuits. But it would be unwieldy, time consuming, and expensive, not to mention complete overkill.[98] Critically, however, limited partnerships and corporations had to register with the Province. An entry from Simpson's party in the government's ledgers would represent a spectacular breakthrough for our investigation. Sadly, I have found nothing of the sort in the records. Yet as the saying goes, absence of evidence is not evidence of absence. Muddying the waters is the fact that limited partnerships often filed petitions either improperly or not at all. Also missing from provincial archives, for instance, are some—though not all—of Blakeny's ventures. Some lawyers, it seems, were content for the documentation to sit in their cabinets rather than in the public central repository.[99]

A written agreement between Simpson and his associates would not only confirm the involvement of LeBlanc, Warman, and the two McSweeneys, but would also stand to reveal Simpson's elusive identity. Such a document may persist in family papers or in the dusty drawers of a Moncton law firm, though the outlook is grim. My own investigative efforts in this regard—including a rummage through Hanford Blakeny's posthumous records preserved by one of his grandsons, Brian Rattenbury—have proven fruitless. Richard DesBrisay, Hanford's other grandson, was unable to add anything.

The four financiers were already dead by 1937, the year of Blakeny's interview. Still, a surviving friend, colleague, or family member could have pointed out any misrepresentations. Also, Moncton had a limited footprint, businesses were few, and owners tended to know each other personally. Even decades later, Blakeny had little opportunity to confuse Simpson's backers with other people.

I only managed to reach a handful of descendants from Simpson's likely sponsors. None was aware of their ancestor's involvement. It was a long shot anyway. The Irishtown quest currently lies 120 years in the past, and we are probing the fading memories of fourth and fifth generations. The four financiers are now silent. But a single clue—Havelock Warman's move to Moncton in 1896—suggests that the treasure hunt may have unfolded after 1892.

The timeline of Simpson's visit is critical to our story. A date—or at least a time interval—would also help us better target our research efforts. Such is our very next order of business. And a good thing too. Because in saying Simpson's search took place "45 years ago," Blakeny was more than a little off.

The Paris Meridian

HISTORICAL CONTEXT

Founded in 1666, the French Académie des Sciences filled a need for objectivity in governance. It commissioned the Observatoire de Paris the very next year. The institution stands today as one of the largest astronomical centres in the world.[100] And, importantly for our story, it also revolutionized French mapmaking.

The Observatoire had earthly functions, in addition to its task of understanding the heavens. The problem of measuring east–west position on the globe remained vexing, particularly at sea. The Ferro meridian had been in use for five hundred years. But the Paris-based meridian engraved on the Observatoire's very floor would henceforth serve as the new standard. The Cassini family oversaw France's study of longitude. It published an account of its observations in 1740. In practice, however, cartographers—and therefore the French navy—adopted the Paris reference soon after its inception in 1667.[101]

Britain implemented similar innovations. The kingdom inaugurated the Greenwich meridian in 1721. Several more European countries established their own version. It was perhaps a matter of both pride and convenience for European nations to view themselves as the arbitrary centre of the world. It was also second nature for eighteenth-century navigators to consult maps from various origins; converting from one coordinate system to another was a necessary skill.[102] Would treasure hunters from the late-nineteenth century, such as Simpson and Blakeny, have been so chart savvy?

In 1884, at the urging of Canadian Sanford Fleming, several countries met at the International Meridian Conference in Washington, DC. There, they partitioned the globe into twenty-four time zones. Delegates also agreed that the Greenwich longitude would become the universal standard. France abstained and held out for a few decades more. Today, the Paris meridian remains a historical curiosity that matters only for interpreting old French maps. Relative to Greenwich, it lies 2° 20' 14.03" to the east—a difference capable of throwing off unsuspecting seafarers by more than a hundred nautical miles. *Red Rackham's Treasure*, the twelfth album from Hergé's The Adventures of Tintin, brilliantly illustrates the potential for confusion. In the book, the protagonists hope to recover treasure from France's three-masted *La Licorne*, an imaginary, late-seventeenth-century ship said to have sunk near an unnamed Caribbean island. They sail to the coordinates indicated on three ancient scrolls. But only when Tintin realizes that the documents reference Paris—not Greenwich—do the explorers backtrack to the correct spot.[103]

Did Simpson commit a similar rookie mistake when trying to pinpoint mid-eighteenth-century French gold buried in Acadie? His chart, after all, was "an old and faded parchment with compass inscriptions written in French." If he based himself on the Greenwich system and searched near the Moncton reservoir, then the location specified on his map lies to the east, close to a deserted islet—Boughton Island—in Prince Edward Island's Georgetown Harbour. France first settled the area in 1732 and named it Trois-Rivières.[104]

Modern-day seekers tempted to scour Boughton Island should be mindful that "compass inscriptions" are indications of heading, not of position. Moreover, offsetting the Moncton reservoir's coordinates by the Paris meridian puts us near but not on Boughton Island. Even if granted some leeway, Simpson's document led not to a small island but to a "south running stream." No major brook exists on Boughton Island, nor would we anticipate one on such a low-lying islet.

Treasure or not, it seems Simpson was looking in the right spot.

Chapter 5
Dating the Search

For time is the longest distance between two places.
– Tennessee Williams

In 1937, Blakeny proclaimed that Simpson came to Moncton "45 years ago." This would put the Irishtown treasure hunt in 1892. Had the Sunny Brae excavator intended to pin down the exact year of the search, he could have done so easily, as in the statement, "In 1892…." Instead, his choice of words could have been a way for him to convey a date *range*. Indeed, if he could neither recall nor infer the operation's precise time frame, he may well have hedged his bets. The key, then, is to coax Blakeny's affirmation into a better estimate of when Simpson set foot in Moncton. For this, we need our thinking caps.

Cue the deerstalkers.

Fuzzy Dates

We all use shorthand to express fuzziness when dating the past. The phrase "five hundred years ago" can be code for anything between four hundred and six hundred. Likewise, "fifty years ago" can mean sometime between forty and sixty. Call this the uncertainty rule.[105]

So entrenched is the uncertainty rule that we occasionally need to override it. For example, we would have to specify "*exactly* five hundred years ago" to remove all ambiguity. It appears, then, that Blakeny's statement of "45 years ago" hinted at a date range. And the uncertainty rule enables us to guess at what period he had in mind.

Blakeny's words have a give-or-take of about five years. Accordingly, they place Simpson's visit between 1887 and 1897. The intent behind, say, "47 years ago" would have been clearer: that is, whereas 45 naturally divides by 5, no intuitive number does so for 47. Had Blakeny said "35 years ago," we would put Simpson's quest between 1897 and 1907. But we know from LeBlanc's death in the spring of 1904 that the search took place before then. If Blakeny had said, "40 or 50 years ago," it would have blurred the timeline even more; he used that very pattern—"back 70 or 80 years ago"—to signal several decades of leeway while commenting on a previous government-sponsored effort in Irishtown.

Perhaps Blakeny could have found more accurate wording to express the period he had in mind. But that would be asking much of the seventy-two-year-old, whom Sclanders put on the spot to recall events from long ago. The precise time frame may also not have seemed particularly essential to the two men.

The crux of the issue is this: Dating an uncertain past is tricky. Blakeny's "45 years ago" could be an imperfect—or "fuzzy"—choice, given his limited options, time, and incentive. His statement implies a span of "1892 plus or minus five years," or from 1887 to 1897. And this, surely, represents a better starting point than just 1892. Can we refine the date range further?

Dating Evidence

We argued that Warman's move to Moncton in 1896 pushes Simpson's quest to a later date. What do other clues say? Previously, we used Hanford Blakeny's birth in 1888 to home in on the "two McSweeneys." In similar fashion, Hanford's early life shaves off two years from our possible timeline. The junior Blakeny was only a month old in December 1888—much too young to remember Simpson's visit to their Sunny Brae household. The memory also excludes the first half of 1889; Blakeny bought 58 Peter Street from Archibald Blake on June 12 that year.[106]

Hanford's childhood favours the upper half of the 1887–1897 range because he was not yet four in 1892. Additional events from Hanford's past will help us narrow things down further.

The Moncton Hiatus

While Hanford was in his "growing boyhood" (his words), the Blakeny family moved from Sunny Brae to Moncton and then back to Sunny Brae again. Hanford attended Moncton's Aberdeen School "for about four years" during this hiatus.[107] Critically, the four-year period excludes a visit by Simpson to Blakeny's Sunny Brae home. Dating it should yield a clue.

According to the 1901 Canadian census, the Blakenys lived in Moncton, not Sunny Brae. However, the 1891 and 1911 surveys show them in Sunny Brae, not Moncton.[108] Clearly, the Moncton hiatus straddled 1901.

Hanford also recalls that he abandoned school "at the end of Grade 7" in 1902 to work at the *Moncton Transcript*.[109] Luckily for us, the new Aberdeen School opened in the fall of 1898.[110] We can therefore work out that Hanford spent at most four school years there: 1898–99, 1899–1900, 1900–01, and 1901–02. But while he is adamant about leaving at the end of the 1902 spring semester, he is unsure whether he stayed in Moncton for a full four years.[111] In other words, he may only have enrolled at Aberdeen in 1899 or after.

One of Hanford's sisters, Jean, was born on April 17, 1897. Her birth certificate lists both her birthplace and address as Sunny Brae, not Moncton.[112] Another sister, Dorothy, was born on September 25, 1899. Her birthplace and address show Moncton, not Sunny Brae.[113] Evidently, the Blakenys quit Sunny Brae for Moncton between April 1897 and September 1899.

Moncton city directories appeared for 1899 and 1903. The 1903 edition reveals the Blakenys resided at 29 Steadman Street. The 1899 version notes that the dwelling was "unoccupied."[114] But information gathered during the previous summer or fall rapidly became stale. Canvassing for the 1899 compilation, it turns out, started on October 19, 1898.[115] The Blakenys could not have moved to the "unoccupied" house before then. Likewise, they must have lived in Moncton well into 1902 for the 1903 release to include them as such.

Property deeds add a last piece to the puzzle. Blakeny purchased 29 Steadman for $1,425 (~$50,000) on March 25, 1899.[116] Buying a home and inhabiting it are two separate things. But one bit of trivia also puts the Blakenys in Moncton before the fall of 1899: A newspaper column from September 7 wrote that a fire near 29 Steadman gave off cinders that "communicated with stables occupied by Sherman Blakeny."[117]

Sunny Brae (above) and Moncton (below). Photographer C. E. Northrup shot the two scenes minutes apart from McKay's Tower (1891). [PANB P211-15422; PANB P256-208]

In summary, the Blakeny's Moncton hiatus began sometime between March and September 1899 and ended not before late 1902. At issue, then, is whether Simpson's visit in Sunny Brae preceded or followed the interlude

Our dating of Simpson's search has evolved from 1892, the year intimated by Blakeny. Thanks to the uncertainty rule, we estimated that Blakeny's "45 years ago" spans a period ranging from 1887 to 1897. Key events in Hanford's life have further refined the picture, which simplifies considerably if presented in graphic form.

From the figure, we can rule out the lower end of Blakeny's range because Hanford was either too young or unborn. Other clues further limit Simpson's visit to two windows of opportunity—one from 1896 to 1899 and a second from 1902 to 1904. The latter window is shorter. And, unlike the former, it sits outside Blakeny's implied range. All told, evidence suggests that our treasure seeker travelled to Moncton between 1896 and 1899.

Our task now is to prove it.

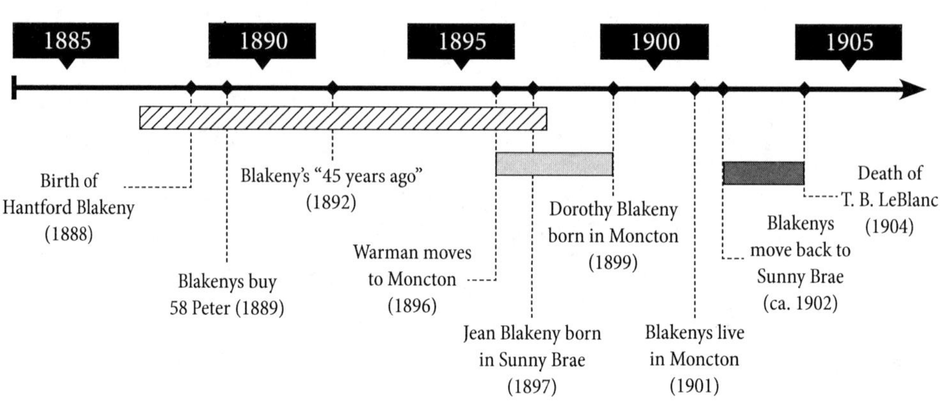

Timeline of key events. Blakeny puts Simpson's treasure hunt between 1887 and 1897 (▨) (1892 ± 5 years). Evidence narrows down the quest to one of two possible windows: 1896 to 1899 (▭) and 1902 to 1904 (▬). [AUTHOR]

The Duc d'Anville's Expedition

HISTORICAL • CONTEXT •

In 1746, sixty-four French ships carrying eleven thousand men set sail from Île d'Aix for the other side of the Atlantic. The expedition, led by Admiral Jean-Baptiste-Louis-Frédéric de la Rochefoucauld de Roye, Marquis de Roucy, duc d'Anville, boasted a list of ambitious objectives: protect Quebec, recapture Louisbourg, reconquer peninsular Acadie, retake Newfoundland, and ravage New England. The operation, despite its resolve, would prove a tragic and costly failure.[118]

A storm in the Bay of Biscay hampered progress. Doldrums near the Azores brought the boats to a standstill. Lightning reportedly hit a gunpowder magazine and killed dozens. After two months at sea, the squadron remained seven hundred nautical miles out from present-day Nova Scotia. Food and water were rationed. Scurvy and other diseases ran rampant. Yet the voyage's troubles had only just started.

Lead ships arrived at Sable Island only to be dispersed by a furious gale. Damaged vessels had to turn back. After a long journey during which hundreds of sailors and soldiers perished and hundreds more fell ill, the battered fleet finally dropped anchor in Chebucto (now Halifax).[119] D'Anville, sick and weakened himself, died from a stroke.[120] His second-in-command, Rear-Admiral Constantin-Louis d'Estourmel, in a fit of despair, drew his sword and attempted suicide.[121] He survived his wounds and relinquished control to Rear-Admiral Jacques-Pierre de Taffanel, Marquis de La Jonquière, New France's governor-general-in-waiting.[122]

Fresh supplies from nearby Acadian villages helped shore up the ailing men. Meanwhile, La Jonquière still planned on retaking Port Royal. Quebec had dispatched a land party to Acadie to join the mission. The thirteen hundred–strong militia led by Jean-Baptiste-Nicolas-Roch de Ramezay, unaware of how contagion spreads, contracted the disease that plagued d'Anville's crew.

Undeterred, La Jonquière set sail to recapture Port Royal. Only when headwinds dashed all hopes of success did he call off the raid and order the fleet back to France. Storms and strikes by British warships marred the voyage home. Tattered vessels from the once-proud expedition limped into French ports, one by one or in small groups. A stunned witness reportedly said, "There is the *coup de grâce* for our navy." Some estimates put casualties as high as eight thousand, or nearly three-quarters of d'Anville's original complement.[123]

The French armada never brought the fight to its enemy. To be sure, it encountered its share of bad luck. But the demise of d'Anville's force was less a cause than an effect of the French navy's dilapidation. Inefficient patronage, ossified hierarchies, antiquated technology, disorganized outfitting, ill-trained crews, and uncertain leadership doomed the enterprise from the start. The endeavour exemplifies how France struggled to support its colonies. It also highlights the dangers of equating nobility titles with hard-earned seamanship.

The failure of d'Anville's mission dashed Acadian hopes of one day returning under French rule. But the Indigenous Peoples of peninsular Acadie, who lacked immunity against European-bred diseases, would suffer the most. Up to half of the Mi'kmaw population perished during the winter of 1746–47 after sickness from the French expedition spread to its ranks. D'Anville's campaign, while hard hit itself, left a trail of human misery in its wake.[124]

Mid-eighteenth-century France lay bankrupt after years of fighting in Europe. It could no longer stand in the way of the British navy. Blakeny's story is correct on this point: French ships cruising along the Acadian coast had everything to fear from a British encounter. Maritime archives document several such clashes. Still, I have found none matching the circumstances of Blakeny's tale.

Chapter 6
A Revelation

Buried treasure and hidden knowledge have a lot in common. You have to dig for both.
– Anonymous

INDEPENDENT AND CONVERGING ACCOUNTS HAVE NOW PUT BLAKENY'S UNVERified story through its paces. Arguably, much of the narrative has moved from the plausible to the proven. We have vetted witnesses, scrutinized accomplices, and narrowed down dates. We have every reason to press on. The question is how. We can no longer interview first-hand memories. No new evidence has come to light. In effect, the trail has gone stone cold for the better part of seven decades.

But here is a thought. If Blakeny's tale warranted retelling in 1937 and after, it did before, too. Simpson's operation was no minor affair. The large-scale project would have piqued curiosity in a small community like Irishtown. Nothing routine or practical could explain it. Blakeny's dozens of labourers could not have mistaken the treasure hunt for anything else. Tongues no doubt wagged. Word surely spread. And newspapers of the time may well have caught wind of it.

The Nineteenth-Century Press

Scouring newspapers from the late nineteenth century is an experience unto itself. British colonies whipped themselves into a patriotic fervour during the lead-up to the Boer Wars. The Dreyfus Affair exposed antisemitic fault lines. The Klondike gold rush reached its zenith. Politics were nakedly hyper-partisan. Advertisements shamelessly peddled cure-all medicines. Personal intelligence columns—gossip that documented hotel comings and goings—rivalled today's social media. The telephone constituted a novelty. Broadcast radio had yet to invade living rooms. Steam-powered trains and ships had become hallmarks of progress. Horses, carriages, and sailboats remained in use, though one could already sense their days were numbered. Motorized flight was still years away, as was the Ford Model T, the world's first mass-produced car.

But everything screeches to a stop when the eye stumbles on this:

> The search for the alleged hidden money on the Bishop farm by a man named Simpson still continues with unabated vigor. He has secured the assistance of several Monctonians and Bishop's land in which the money is supposed to be is being all plowed up to the depth of three or four feet.[125]

The thrilling revelation—all of two sentences in Moncton's *Daily Transcript* of October 5, 1899—could not be more rewarding of our efforts. The column's implications are profound.

An independent witness—a reporter no less—attested to Simpson's quest. Moreover, the journalist chronicled the operation as it unfolded. We cannot overstate the value of contemporary accounts. If the year of Blakeny's 1937 interview means rather little, the date of the *Daily Transcript* article is as good a time-stamp as we could hope for. Simpson, we now know, looked for treasure in 1899, not in 1892, as Blakeny intimated. Gratifyingly, the search falls within the 1896–1899 range we deduced beforehand. Hanford's recollections turned out to be highly accurate. His father's, in contrast, were a whopping seven years off.

The 1899 piece is in keeping with the Blakenys' combined testimonies. The excavation took place on the "Bishop farm." Simpson recruited the assistance of "several Monctonians," whose names remain unspecified. The operation plowed the earth to a depth of "three or four feet," roughly in line with Blakeny's stated five-foot limit. Bishop, the Irishtown landowner, gave Simpson his blessing to dig on his property.

Intriguingly, the reporter writes that the search "still continues." The words leave little room for interpretation—the piece can only be an *update* to an earlier article fresh in the minds of readers.

Still on the Hunt

If it exists at all, the earlier article remains strangely elusive. We can find no signs of it in the *Daily Transcript* for the days, weeks, and months before October 5. What the update column may have been alluding to, though, is this:

> Still on the Hunt
>
> Simpson, an elderly man who was referred to last spring as being in search of a hidden treasure near the Moncton reservoir, is still on the hunt for the booty which he claims is buried in that section. Mr. Simpson is so enthusiastic over the search that he has succeeded in interesting two or three Moncton men, who are said to be putting up money for expenses in connection with the search. The scene of the operation is on the bank of the brook leading from the reservoir on John Bishop's farm, where the work of digging was commenced last spring. Recently the idea of plowing up the hillside has been conceived and greater progress is being made in turning over the sod. Mr. Simpson follows the plot, scanning the earth very closely, and persists in the belief that the treasure will yet be unearthed. And his charts, he claims, assure him that the treasure is buried in the locality where he is at work.[126]

Why this piece from September 25, 1899, exists in the *Daily Times* instead of the *Daily Transcript* is a puzzle. Perhaps the journalist who reported on Simpson's quest freelanced for both newspapers. Or maybe it was customary for dailies to update stories they had not broken themselves. Regardless, the *Daily Times*'s column is an eye-opener.

The text describes Simpson as "an elderly man," in keeping with Blakeny's own impression of "an old man." By our count, this is the fourth mention that omits the treasure seeker's given name. Did Simpson employ an alias? It would make little sense for him to hide something so important from Blakeny. The

Sunny Brae excavator, in turn, had no reason to conceal the truth decades after the fact. There is also a step between being guarded and using a false identity; matters of money and law can become especially problematic in the latter case.

The September 25 article offers new clues to the site of the search. We now know that Simpson targeted the "John Bishop" farm and operated on "the bank of the brook leading from the reservoir." This information will serve us well. The text also mentions that "the work of digging began last spring." This is unexpected for a piece dating from the fall. Blakeny remarked that he laboured "for about two months." Altogether, then, Simpson could have been toiling for anywhere between four and seven months by the time October 5 rolled around. His initial plan, surely, did not involve exhuming seven acres of land. If he came from far away, as Blakeny claimed, a reconnaissance effort in the spring of 1899 may have been in order. Perhaps he spent the summer in Moncton orchestrating Blakeny's more ambitious assault.

The use of horse-pulled equipment fits in well with the account that "*recently* the idea of plowing up the hillside has been conceived" (emphasis mine). Blakeny said engineers could not agree on where to excavate. In the end, he decided "to dig over seven acres in the approximate location." If two separate attempts took place, then Blakeny's two-month operation could not have started much earlier than August to be still ongoing in October.

The reporter tells us that "two or three Moncton men" bankrolled the "money for expenses in connection with the search." This is consistent with Blakeny's story, although the number of financiers is on the low side. Unfortunately, the piece fails to name anyone. Indirectly, however, it confirms that George and Peter Jr. were indeed the "two McSweeneys." By 1899, all the other McSweeney brothers were long dead. Peter McSweeney Jr., freshly appointed to the Senate of Canada, left Moncton for Ottawa on May 15, 1899. He returned on July 22—enough time for Simpson to approach him between mid and late summer and for Blakeny to begin his work.[127]

The article presents Simpson as enthusiastic and confident. "His charts," it stresses, underlie his assurance. King among these was no doubt *the* chart—the document Blakeny and his son Hanford had marvelled at in their Sunny

Brae home. The article adds that the bank of the brook, which leads from the reservoir and intersects John Bishop's farmstead, was likely the site indicated on the map.

Finally, the article appears to be yet another update. The reporter wrote that Simpson "was referred to last spring." There is again no mistaking the word choice: The *Daily Times*—or perhaps the *Daily Transcript*—published an earlier piece in the spring of 1899. Sadly, we may never know the information it contains. The editions of the *Daily Times* between January and June 1899 seem irretrievably lost.[128] As for the *Daily Transcript*, I could find no allusion to Simpson's quest in the months before September 25.

We have now confirmed that an elderly man by the name of Simpson came to Moncton to look for gold on the Bishop farm in Irishtown, near the Moncton reservoir. He shopped around his purported treasure map and recruited several Monctonians to finance his quest. Horses and plows worked the earth to depths averaging between three and five feet.

We have also learned much more. The search unfolded in 1899 on the property owned by *John* Bishop. The site itself was on the bank of the brook leading away from the reservoir. Although Blakeny's operation lasted about two months, Simpson was active both in the spring and in the fall that year. Simpson perhaps conducted a small, targeted effort before Blakeny took charge of a larger, brute-force attempt by the late summer. Our story has established characters and a definite time frame. What it needs now is a better sense of place.

The location of Simpson's dig presents us not with one mystery but two.

Halifax

HISTORICAL CONTEXT

In 1748, France reclaimed Louisbourg without firing a shot. Where the duc d'Anville's expedition failed, French diplomacy succeeded. Britain ceded the fortress for territories in the Austrian Netherlands as part of the Treaty of Aix-la-Chapelle. News of Louisbourg's restitution provoked outrage in New England.

Louisbourg had been a thorn in Britain's side for decades. It also offered haven to French privateers preying on New England shipping during times of war.[129] An Anglo-American force captured the stronghold in 1745, and deciders in Boston believed the matter settled. Three years later, the United Kingdom nullified the victory with the stroke of a quill. Resentment in the American colonies fed growing revolutionary sentiments. Henceforth, Britain would favour the sword over the pen. And, to do so, it would need its own Louisbourg.[130]

In 1749, Edward Cornwallis arrived in Chebucto with 2,500 emigrants and founded Halifax. The town counteracted Louisbourg's influence and signalled a fresh offensive.[131] British fortifications erected throughout peninsular Acadie worked at subjugating defiant Acadians and Mi'kmaq.[132]

France, meanwhile, remained overextended militarily, financially, and geographically, and it feared Britain's buildup. New France's commandant general, Roland-Michel Barrin de La Galissonnière, opted for a containment strategy rather than fight an unwinnable war.[133] He made his stand at the Missaguash River, the natural boundary on the Isthmus of Chignecto that divides peninsular and continental Acadie. He adopted a scorched-earth policy of relocating peninsular Acadians to the continental side. There, he believed, a Nouvelle Acadie would legitimize French claims of sovereignty and form a bulkhead against further British incursions.[134]

The British allowed Catholic priests into peninsular Acadie to minister for the Acadian and Mi'kmaw faithful. Chief among these was Abbé Jean-Louis Le Loutre, a zealous French missionary who laboured covertly to promote France's interests. He incited Indigenous Peoples and Acadians to take up arms. He also spared no efforts to resettle Acadians to regions still under France's protection. Both reviled and revered at the time, he remains a controversial figure to this day.[135]

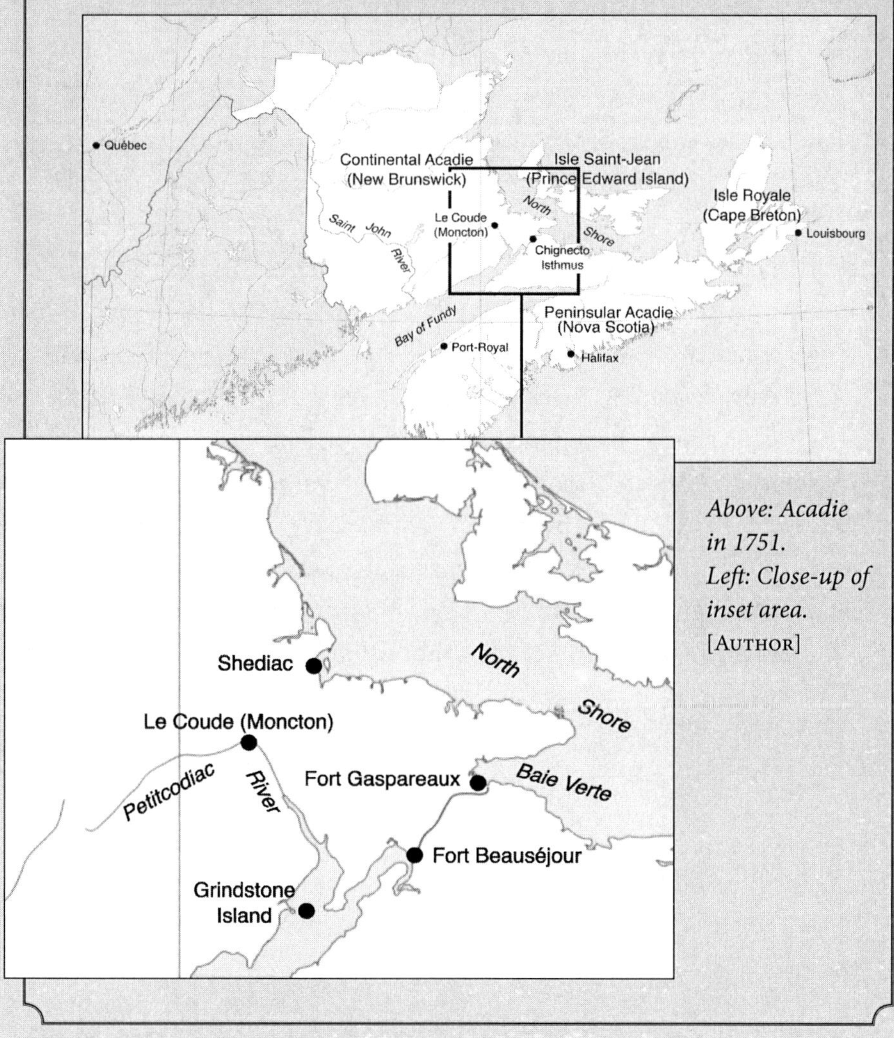

Above: Acadie in 1751.
Left: Close-up of inset area.
[AUTHOR]

In 1750, Major Charles Lawrence campaigned in Chignecto.[136] There, he met opposition near the Acadian village of Beaubassin from Louis Chevalier de La Corne, a French-Canadian officer tasked with blocking British progress.[137] Abbé Le Loutre, with La Corne's tacit approval, applied La Gallissonière's policy to the letter and burned Beaubassin to the ground. The manoeuvre denied the enemy local supplies and forced three thousand peninsular Acadians to retreat to the continental side. With France and Britain still nominally at peace, Lawrence withdrew.[138]

Lawrence appeared again in Chignecto five months later. Mi'kmaw and Acadian irregulars resisted to no avail. The British built Fort Lawrence next to the ashes of Beaubassin. La Jonquière, by now New France's governor, countered in 1751 by commissioning Fort Beauséjour, New France's largest fortification on the Atlantic seafront after Louisbourg. He also ordered the construction of Fort Gaspareaux, a fortlet near Baie Verte on the North Shore. Together, the two bastions formed a defensive cordon across the narrow isthmus. War was no longer a matter of if but of when.

Blakeny's legend, while unsubstantiated, evokes the Franco-British struggle for Acadie during the mid-eighteenth century. The founding of Halifax in 1749 and Lawrence's military operations in 1750 precipitated events. Chignecto, because of its strategic location, saw the first shots in the North American theatre of the Seven Years War. With landmarks such as Grindstone Island, the Petitcodiac River, and Le Coude, Blakeny's tale takes place within a stone's throw of the action.

Chapter 7
X *Marks the Spot*

Mr. Sniff: What are you looking for?
Mr. Snoop: A five-dollar bill.
Mr. Sniff: Are you sure you lost it on this street?
Mr. Snoop: Oh no! I lost it in the next block, but I'm lookin' up here because the light is better.
– "Think and Grin: Bright Idea"
(edited by F. J. Rigney)[139]

Blakeny's references to a water reservoir, a spring, and a south-flowing stream are tantalizing. Still, were they all we had, the location of Simpson's dig site would remain a mystery. Only marginally more helpful is Hanford's 1960 footnote, which recalled "the Bishop property on the Irishtown Road." A common surname and vast farmlands on a busy roadway can only do so much to narrow down options.[140]

If we can hope to pinpoint ground zero, it is because the *Daily Times* wrote on September 25, 1899: "The scene of the operation is on the bank of the brook leading from the reservoir on John Bishop's farm." The indications, while still rough, are good enough. With these clues in hand, we have a shot at rediscovering *where* it all unfolded. However, we also stand a chance of understanding *why* Simpson searched where he did. Mr. Snoop's gem of a reply in the chapter's introductory quote alerts us to a distinct possibility. Simpson did hunt for gold on John Bishop's land, but he may, in fact, have preferred to look elsewhere.

X Marks the Spot

We still lack key information before we can walk the grounds of Simpson's dig. Rather than fumble about a map of Irishtown, let us begin at a coarse scale and zoom in progressively.

As a starting point, Blakeny's clues are as good as any. Irish immigrants displaced by the Industrial Revolution in the 1820s settled in present-day Irishtown, a few kilometres north of Moncton. The Great Irish Famine of the 1840s brought over many more. New Brunswick's timber industry proved attractive, as did vast forests that could be turned into farmlands.[141]

The Moncton reservoir, Blakeny's most identifiable hint, sits in Tankville, in Irishtown's most southerly reaches. From 1878, it served as the city's only large water supply until 1914, when the more dependable McNutt Reservoir—a few kilometres to the west—came online.[142] The Moncton reservoir has an odd, golf-club shape due to its position on the edge of an east–west plateau.[143] Its wide, shallow floodplain to the northeast gives way to a narrower basin to the southwest.[144] There, a dam offers a six-metre drop, sufficient elevation for gravity to pressurize kilometres of pipeline to Moncton. The decommissioned reservoir forms the bulk of Irishtown Nature Park.[145]

Lynch's Brook, the inlet stream that feeds the reservoir, is also the only outlet.[146] Its source sits a few kilometres north of Tankville near the headwaters of the Shediac River.[147] From there, Lynch's Brook—otherwise known as Black Mill Brook—flows roughly south until it reaches the reservoir. From the dam's spillover, it then heads due south for about two kilometres before merging sharply with the westerly Ogilvie Creek. There can be no doubt: Since there is no other "brook leading from the reservoir," Lynch's Brook must be the tributary referenced by the *Daily Times*. Moreover, only it can be the "south running stream" mentioned by Blakeny.

As for John Bishop, his land first belonged to his parents, Eunice and Jack. The couple homesteaded the lot in 1860 and later passed it on to their son.[148] The province's cadastral map shows that the original deed to "E. Bishop" (Eunice Bishop) consists of an elongated, east–west, fifty-acre tract fronted on Irishtown Road.[149] The farmstead lies approximately four hundred metres—or about a quarter-mile—south of the reservoir. If we are correct, the Bishop property and Lynch's Brook should intersect. And they do.

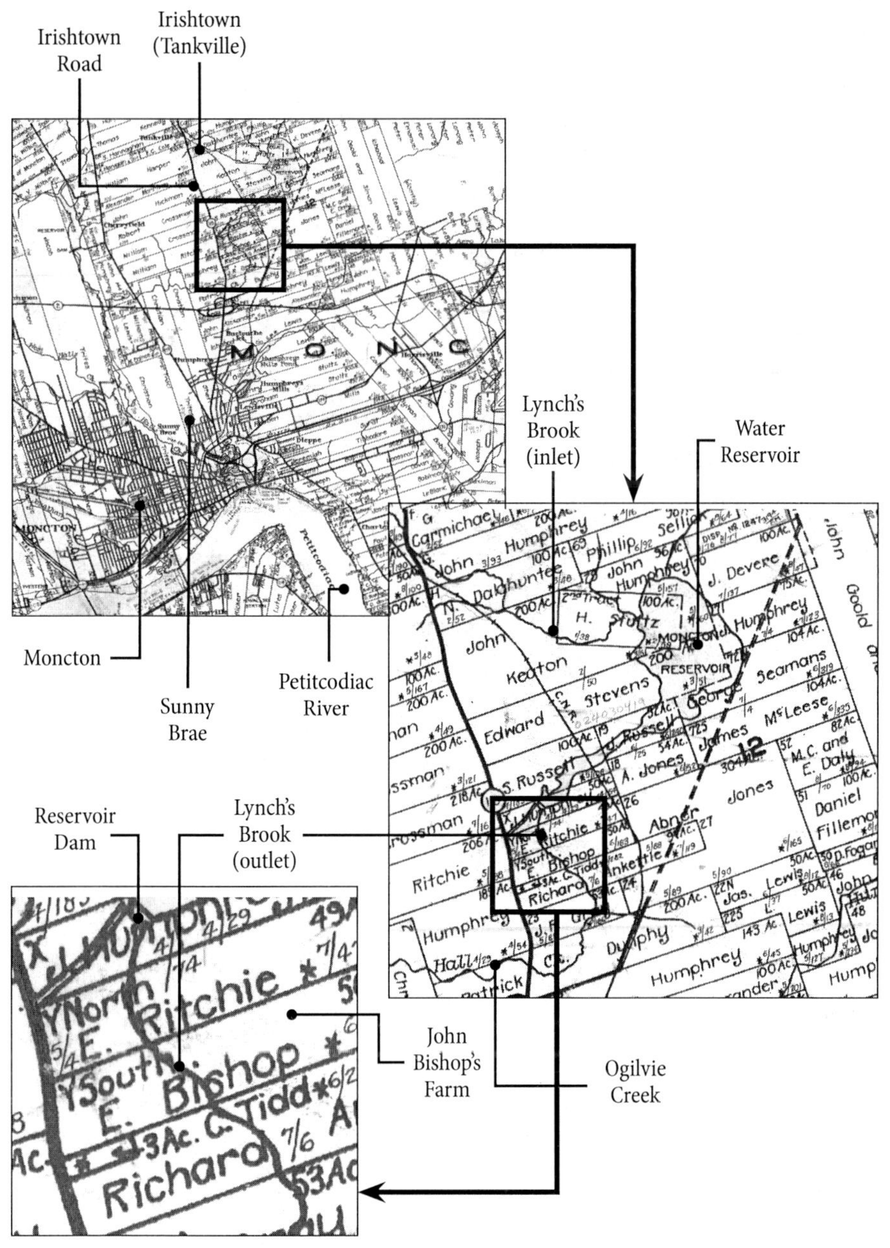

Simpson's dig site. Successive zooms on New Brunswick's cadastral map.
[PANB RS656-36-120]

The intersection of Bishop's property and Lynch's Brook marks the proverbial *X* on the ground.

When Blakeny invoked a "south running stream," he was not alluding to a random feature on Simpson's chart. Instead, he was narrowing down the location of the supposed treasure itself. Our rediscovery of Simpson's dig site is encouraging. But one riddle invites another. While we now know *where* Simpson looked, we have yet to understand *why* he chose that location—because searching on Bishop's land likely constituted plan B.

On the Ground

Today, the former Bishop farm exudes serene beauty. The vast, well-tended property can be disorienting for close-quartered urbanites. Forest borders its open fields on three sides. Lynch's Brook splits the land into two unequal portions.

Older buildings cluster near Irishtown Road. A newer residential development to the northwest appears to be the only concession to changing times. A dirt road cuts lengthwise across the plot's western half and adopts a slanted tack along the steep-sloped flanks of Lynch's Brook. Too boggy for crops, a wooded lot in the southeast corner remains unexploited.

So, what can we say about Simpson's dig site? Very little at first glance. Waist-high weeds, underbrush, and beach ball–sized boulders line the banks of Lynch's Brook, which never proved suitable for agriculture. Grazing cows kept them free of overgrowth. The area also seems devoid of anything that Blakeny's labourers might have forgotten or discarded. Few would ever guess that one of Canada's greatest treasure hunts took place in this very spot. To be fair, the quest entailed a surface operation on easily accessible premises. It is unclear what clues should survive today. On Oak Island, in contrast, boring drills probed the "Money Pit" and left lasting scars. Abandoned, now rusty gear serves as a testament to another shattered dream.[150] But while the Oak Island venture looked deep and narrow, Simpson searched shallow and wide. If traces of Blakeny's work linger, they are of the more subtle variety.

An unremarkable location at first sight, Simpson's dig site does exhibit a few oddities on second glance. For one, the banks of Lynch's Brook drop off steeply and paint a picture of adversity. Blakeny's labourers, rather than toil on flat land, slogged for months on sloped, rock-strewn terrain with grades between 16 and 40 percent.[151] Also, interesting features do appear in old aerial photographs. A high-altitude flight on October 17, 1944, imaged the property during a series of overhead shots.[152] The eighty-year jump back in time offers a peek at the more freshly excavated ground.

The 1944 overhead image (page 66) is puzzling. Tall trees, easily visible on the western bank because of their long shadows, are strangely absent on the eastern bank. A faint, egg-shaped feature on the eastern side defies explanation. But a high-contrast linear element on the western flank draws our attention. It took geographer Samuel Arseneault, retired emeritus professor of geography at the Université de Moncton, only half a second to identify

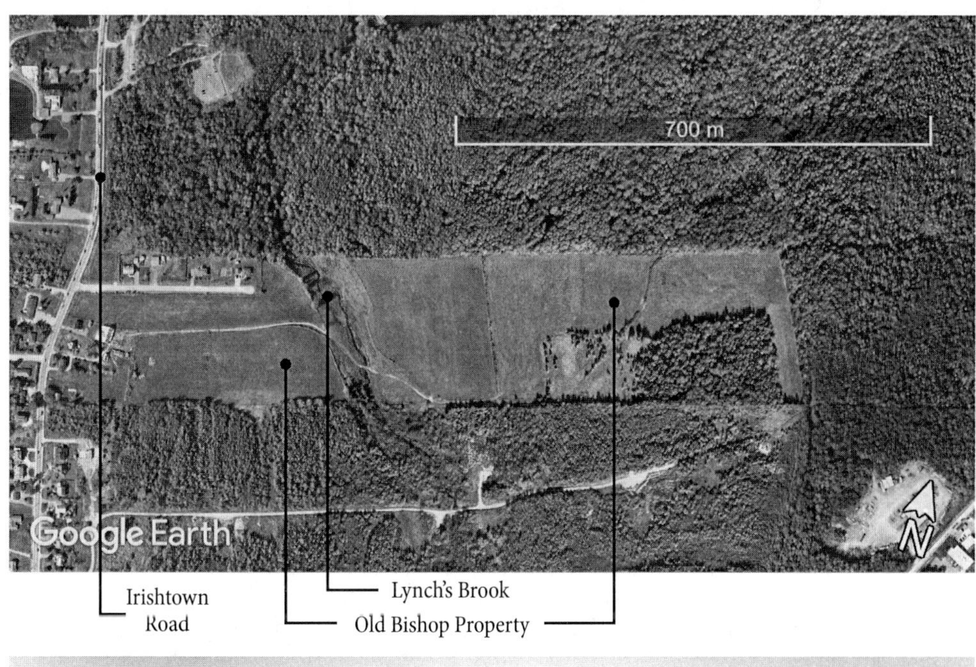

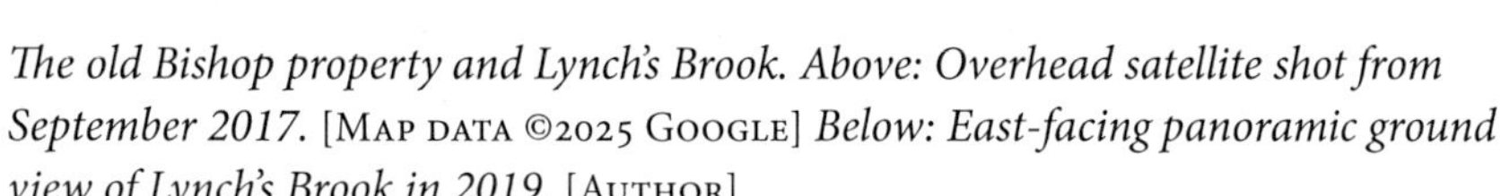

The old Bishop property and Lynch's Brook. Above: Overhead satellite shot from September 2017. [Map data ©2025 Google] *Below: East-facing panoramic ground view of Lynch's Brook in 2019.* [Author]

it. Obvious in retrospect, though enigmatic to the untrained eye, the linear element precedes Simpson's treasure hunt by twenty years. And it is as much a clue as to where Simpson dug as to where he did not.

Pipe Dreams

In the late 1870s, Moncton's water supply suffered both in quality and quantity. Small wells offered no protection against waterborne disease. Fire posed an ever-present risk. Insurance premiums were sky-high in a city without hydrants. In 1877, the municipality resolved to tap Lynch's Brook as a more reliable source.[153] The provincial legislature passed a bill incorporating the Moncton Gas, Light, and Water Company. The consortium, led by the Harris

An aerial photograph from October 17, 1944, shows Lynch's Brook on the old Bishop property. [National Air Photo Library, Natural Resources Canada]

brothers, set out to build the system. The project involved cutting down trees, excavating trenches, transporting pipes, erecting a dam, and burning fields. A slump in steel markets allowed the purchase of ducts at rock-bottom prices. Two schooners, the *Sam Ford* and the *Muskee*, sailed from Philadelphia up the Petitcodiac River and unloaded 750 tons of metal tubing at Moncton's public wharf.

Digging kilometres of ditches between Tankville and Moncton proved difficult. Workers staged a strike. High unemployment enabled management to replace them easily. City dwellers, unaccustomed to running water, celebrated the official turning on of the valves in October 1878.[154]

The Moncton reservoir will forever remain associated with Simpson's quest, and it is the proverbial elephant in the room. Its erection has profoundly altered the local landscape. Its location sits less than half a kilometre from the site of Simpson's operation. The reservoir was also too close for Blakeny's comfort; so much so, in fact, that the Sunny Brae excavator later believed Simpson's treasure lay under it. And details of the reservoir's construction add an important piece to our puzzle. There can be no mistaking the linear feature on the 1944 aerial shot: It is the reservoir's pipeline.

An 1878 easement paid John Bishop and his wife the sum of $40 (~$1,400), and in return, the Moncton Gas, Light, and Water Company built, used, and maintained the ductwork running across their property.[155] Crucially, then, the Bishop section of Lynch's Brook was far from pristine in 1899; as it turns out, it had already been the theatre of a large-scale exhumation two decades before. The steel pipeline lay on the western bank, a few metres from the brook. Simpson would have endangered Moncton's water supply had he dug anywhere near it.

The conclusion appears inescapable: Simpson searched only on the *eastern* side of Lynch's Brook.

Unlucky Seven

The reported scale of Simpson's treasure hunt—seven acres—is unexpectedly large. Without a doubt, dozens of men with horses, plows, and scrapers could move a fair bit of earth over a two-month period. But Blakeny's seven-acre figure does not add up.

Above: The Moncton Reservoir dam. Lynch's Brook cascades southward from the spillover. Below: The reservoir's gatehouse regulated the flow of water (1892). [MONCTON MUSEUM COLLECTION]

The old Bishop farm spans 200 metres from north to south. The Bishop section of Lynch's Brook, for its part, extends about 130 metres from east to west and therefore covers about 6.5 acres (200 m × 130 m = 26,000 m^2). Blakeny's statement of seven acres appears to capture the general area of Simpson's operation. But what about the size of the dig itself? The pipeline rules out the western bank, so the work could only encompass 3.5 acres at the very most. Perhaps Blakeny made an honest mistake. Or maybe the Sunny Brae excavator reasoned in volume (acre-feet) instead of area (acre). That is, seven acre-feet taken from a depth of five feet yields 1.4 acres, or roughly the extent of the egg-shaped feature in the 1944 aerial. For all we know, Blakeny inflated the scope of his undertaking for the same reason fishermen exaggerate the size of their catch. It matters little in the end. We must cut down Blakeny's seven-acre figure by at least half.

Plan B

Simpson's map necessarily dictated the search's location. The plan's "compass inscriptions" must therefore have pointed to the eastern bank of a brook as well. But Simpson, once he settled on Lynch's Brook, still had to decide which part of the stream he would target. Why, then, dig on John Bishop's land? A quirk in the pipeline's path suggests a possible answer.

On the old Bishop farm, the conduit runs half-buried along the western side of Lynch's Brook; however, it juts out of the ground near the property's very northern edge. From there, it jumps across Lynch's Brook over to the eastern side. The crossing resembles small rapids on overhead imagery. Causing the cascade is the blackish, half-submerged pipeline itself. The ductwork then continues northward to a now-vanished gatehouse.[156]

Simpson, who surrounded himself with "the best engineers we could get," was surely aware of the pipeline's peculiar route. Moreover, the conduit limited his options. Trench work twenty years earlier would have unearthed any gold buried along its path. If treasure still lay somewhere on the eastern side of Lynch's Brook, it could only be where the pipeline was not. In theory, Simpson could set his sights either north of the conduit itself or south of where it crosses the creek. In practice, though, digging north of the pipeline was simply out of the question.

The pipeline crossing Lynch's Brook on the northern edge of the old Bishop property (2019). [Author]

In 1878, water levels began rising north of the reservoir's dam. The original banks of Lynch's Brook dipped below the surface and have remained immersed ever since. The basin, though shallow by maritime standards, averages depths of about three metres.[157] If Simpson contemplated searching under it, he quickly realized his choices—draining, dredging, or diving—would be outright non-starters. Draining would deprive Moncton of its main water supply. Dredging the bottom would risk churning up sediments and introducing disease. Diving would require a bell or a hard-hat suit. Digging up the submerged flank of Lynch's Brook while toiling underwater would have been nearly impossible. Performing the same task on dry land proved difficult enough. Simpson, in short, had no alternative but to search south of the pipeline crossing.

South of the pipeline crossing, Lynch's Brook intersects three plots of land in turn—the former Bishop, Ankettle, and Grey farmsteads—before it merges with the westerly Ogilvie Creek.[158] Why, then, did Simpson set his sights on the northernmost property? The answer may have been under our noses all along. Blakeny mused about the treasure: "No, I don't think it will ever be found now. And the reason I don't think so is that I'm afraid Moncton's water reservoir at Irishtown—that's just a quarter mile from where we worked—is built right on top of it."

Blakeny's self-serving expedient appears to justify the search's failure. But we can now see that the remark carries another subtext. Blakeny is stating his belief that the gold lies *north* of where he looked. And because both the pipeline and the reservoir stood in its way, the operation simply began as far north as it could. In other words, the excavation started on John Bishop's property, as close to the pipeline crossing as possible. From there, it had no choice but to continue south.

The freshwater spring on Simpson's map has so far remained unaddressed. There are no springs on the old Bishop farm, but there is one immediately north of it on the eastern side of Lynch's Brook.[159] The rocky hillside is ideally suited for one.[160] The spring would have given Simpson one more reason to comb the area.

We still lack the telltale signs of a large-scale treasure hunt by Lynch's Brook. But, in the 1944 aerial shot, mature trees are notably absent on the eastern side. Perhaps the search involved felling on a large scale. Subsequent cow grazing would have kept regrowth at bay. The egg-shaped feature, for its part, could be a byproduct of Simpson's excavation. Depending on the season, its vegetation differs in colour from the rest of the bank, a likely indication of previous soil disturbance.

It would seem that Simpson, like Mr. Snoop, settled for plan B.

Blakeny's Backyard

Mr. Snoop's silly retort (page 61) is an opportunity to reflect on treasure hunting's uneasy marriage between geography and psychology. It should strike us as odd, for instance, that Blakeny recounted a legend that begins in his native Albert County. Odder still, his yarn ends in Irishtown, where he resettled as a young boy. The Sunny Brae excavator, like most of us, leaned toward the familiar. An outsider such as Simpson needed homegrown help to interpret his chart. Blakeny stepped in and influenced the quest with his mix of personal experience and local folklore. But Blakeny may have done more than introduce Simpson to the Irishtown area. In fact, he brought Simpson to the property of John Bishop, virtually next door to the virgin plot of land he and his parents had homesteaded during his youth.[161] In other words, Simpson literally exhumed Blakeny's own backyard.

Blakeny further justified the dig's location in these words: "Back 70 or 80 years ago the government itself had convincing enough evidence to finance a search. The government had men working in the area for two years, a couple of miles from where we searched later. I don't know how many thousands of dollars it spent."

In the eyes of potential investors, a state-led treasure hunt in the region decades earlier would have helped legitimize Simpson's map. The operation, though, may never have happened at all. Moncton's history books are silent on the subject, even though the public endeavour would have been an open secret by definition. Newspaper coverage was spotty at the time. Is a government-sponsored search even a viable proposition? Then, as now, such a project would constitute a misuse of tax revenue. A sampling of local administrative records shows it would have been beyond the pale even for that era.[162] Moncton's finances were also particularly dire at the time: The city declared bankruptcy in 1862 before it reincorporated itself in 1875.[163] Misallocation of the people's money would have irked citizens and entered collective consciousness accordingly. Moncton, it seems, was no place for official frivolity during the mid-to-late 1800s.

In Blakeny's defence, Irishtown had been a beehive of activity during the nineteenth century. A decades-long program of road development in the 1830s contributed to the parcelling of Crown land.[164] Subsequent surveying further divvied up large plots. The erection of the Moncton reservoir in 1878 brought in its own bevy of terrain-assessing experts, as did follow-up maintenance and expansion efforts.[165] The construction of the Moncton & Buctouche Railway, which began in 1883, introduced yet another round of reconnaissance and groundwork in the region.[166] The railway bridge that once spanned the Moncton reservoir represents one of many such examples of on-site planning and engineering. The young Blakeny could only have been awestruck by the pace at which modernity transformed his environment. But how reliable was his information that a government-led treasure hunt took place in the area "back 70 or 80 years ago"?

For all we know, cheeky surveyors in Irishtown told a little white lie to entertain the young Blakeny. Neither we nor he would be the wiser for it.

Simpson's dig site has reverted to a state of semi-natural splendour. But Moncton's ever-growing footprint threatens the locale. The old Bishop property itself, one of few remaining historical farms within city limits, is at risk of disappearing. It would take vision to annex it to the adjacent Irishtown Nature Park before predatory rezoning settles the issue.[167] Invoking New Brunswick's largest treasure hunt could help secure protections against such encroachment.

For those who would follow Simpson's lead, the course of action is clear. Had modern technology been available, our gold seeker would have sent scuba divers armed with underwater metal detectors into the Moncton reservoir to scan the now submerged former eastern bank of Lynch's Brook. But readers should consider the role mindset played in his quest before they embark on one of their own. Simpson attracted people prone to believing in improbable things. Legends of buried treasure filled the air. Everyday folk went to great lengths to find rumoured spoils. Print media were only too happy to fan the flames. Faith more than fact fuelled hopes of concealed booty. Blakeny was likely no exception. As the local expert, he had an outsized influence in steering the search toward Irishtown. But homegrown help was apparently not enough for our treasure hunter.

Because Simpson did not arrive in Moncton alone.

The Crossroads of Le Coude

HISTORICAL · CONTEXT ·

The late 1740s set the stage for what Blakeny described as "the battle that lost Acadia for France and gained it for England." The Sunny Brae excavator also claimed that the Petitcodiac River offered an escape route to French troops retreating from a superior British force. But where could such French troops flee to? And what path would they take?

By the early 1750s, French and British forces were eyeing each other on the Isthmus of Chignecto.[168] Britain had the upper hand at sea, whereas France had the advantage on land. Help from Indigenous Peoples and Acadians amplified the latter's edge on the ground.[169] Land portages allowed travel without fear of British naval patrols. Le Coude (present-day Moncton) was at the heart of it all. Then, as now, the Petitcodiac's elbow sat where north–south met east–west. Known today as the Hub of the Maritimes, Le Coude lay at a crossroads: the Bay of Fundy and Nova Scotia to the south, and the North Shore and Prince Edward Island to the east.[170] Le Coude's westerly reaches also connected Acadie to Quebec along the all-important Petitcodiac–Saint John River–Témiscouata portage.[171]

The strategic significance of Le Coude is evident on the 1751 map sketched by military engineer Gaspard-Joseph Chaussegros de Léry fils.[172] The chart, while crude, is notable for its period depiction of continental Acadie's interior. It illustrates the portage from the Petitcodiac to Beaubassin and the portage from Le Coude to Ejetdaik (Shediac, NB) on the North Shore, where a French outpost included "magazin" (storehouses). De Léry noted in his memoir: "The so-called road of Ejetdaik begins at the head of tide of the [Shediac] river and joins up with the Petkoutiak [Petitcodiac] seven leagues [~27 km] up from its mouth. It [the road] is five leagues [~19 km] long and fairly straight, but I have never seen such a detestable land. During great summer droughts, horses struggle to pull themselves out of bogs, and we were unable to use them this year. It would cost considerable sums to make it [the road] usable by wagons."[173]

The Shediac outpost served many purposes. The facility stood as one of only a handful of French seaports in continental Acadie. It handled supplies sent by ship from Quebec and Louisbourg. Its portage to Le Coude, while lengthy and difficult, proved no less vital. Critically, it opened a stealthy shortcut between the North Shore and the Bay of Fundy and provided a way to transport stores farther afield. Otherwise, French vessels had to dock in Baie Verte, part of which lay in British waters. Even less palatable was the voyage to the Bay of Fundy via a circuitous and perilous journey around peninsular Acadie.[174]

Despite their virtues, the Shediac outpost and its portage road soon outlived their usefulness. The French built the Shediac outpost in late 1749 but abandoned it in 1751. Once better defended by Fort Gaspareaux, the port of Baie Verte and its easier portage to the Bay of Fundy were the superior option. The Shediac portage has now faded from memories and questions remain as to its exact path.[175]

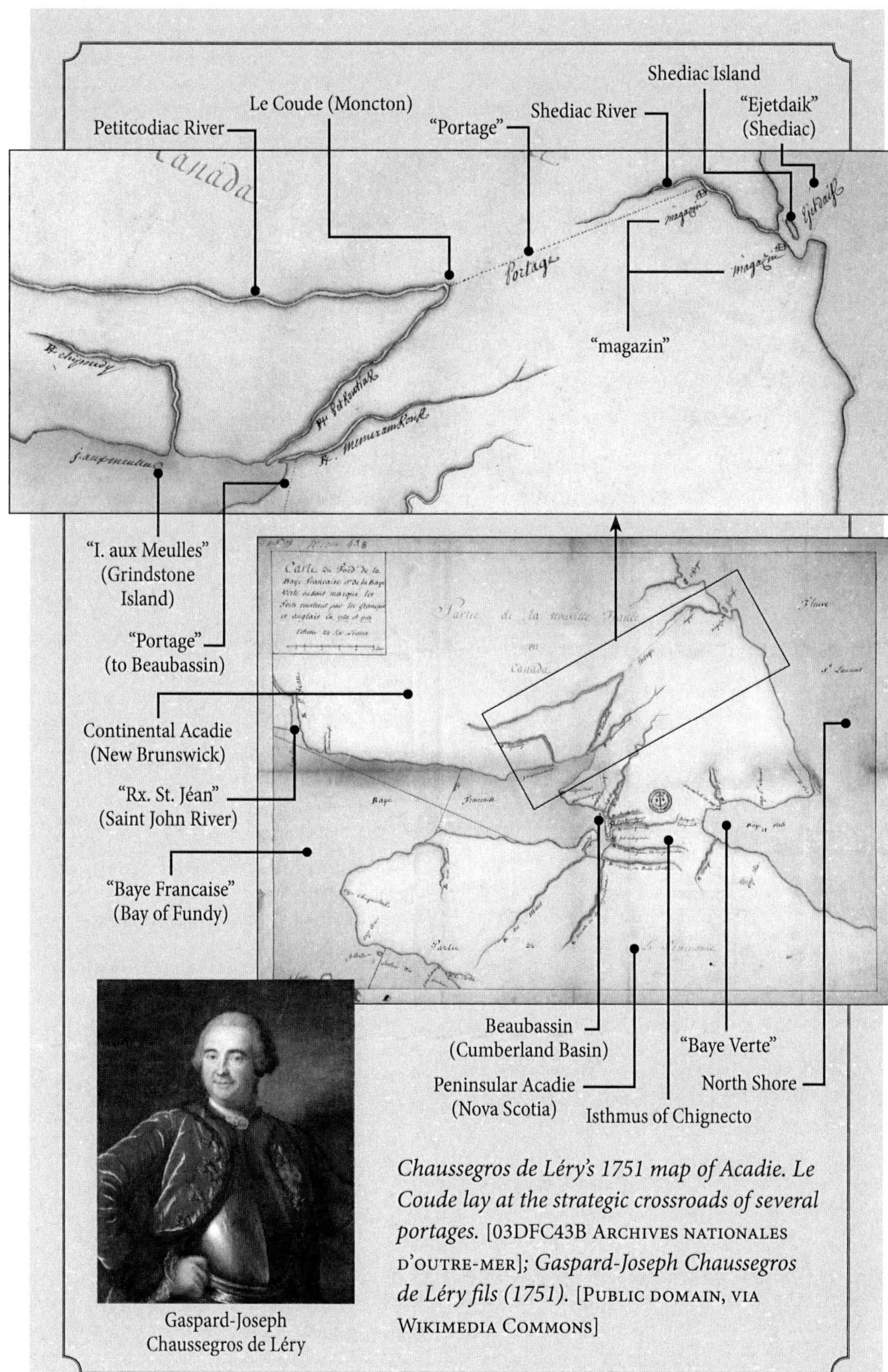

Chaussegros de Léry's 1751 map of Acadie. Le Coude lay at the strategic crossroads of several portages. [03DFC43B ARCHIVES NATIONALES D'OUTRE-MER]; *Gaspard-Joseph Chaussegros de Léry fils (1751).* [PUBLIC DOMAIN, VIA WIKIMEDIA COMMONS]

As for Blakeny's tale, the crossroads of Le Coude would offer a choice of escape to hypothetical French troops on the run—west toward Quebec or east toward the North Shore. But evidence is at odds with claims that French paymasters encountered a "large [British] force," sought refuge up the Petitcodiac River, reached the safety of a "French army," and joined a bloody retreat. No French army resided near Le Coude after the decommissioning of the Shediac outpost in 1751. Few British soldiers ventured into continental Acadie before the fall of Fort Beauséjour in 1755.[176] Blakeny's yarn implies French and British detachments simultaneously garrisoned near Le Coude. But the area, in fact, was more of a military no man's land at the time. The ground portion of Blakeny's legend, it seems, agrees no more with history than with common sense.

Chapter 8
Ontario: Yours to Discover

Not all who wander are lost.
– J. R. R. Tolkien

In 1906, the discovery of a dead body in a forested area of Cherryfield, near Irishtown, caused alarm. The remains were those of an elderly man approximately six feet tall. The badly decayed remnants were littered with several items, including a felt hat, leather boots, a jackknife, a pipe, a ring, a fishhook, eyeglasses, a pocketbook, and an unreadable piece of paper.[177] The clues, while numerous, did not allow the identification of the corpse. Suspicions pivoted to three locals who had disappeared some time previous: Abiel Edgett (a schooner captain), Paddy Donahue (a ninety-year-old Irish craftsperson), and a Sunny Brae resident variously cited as Joseph McNeil or John O'Neil.[178] Authorities ruled out the candidates, one by one, and buried the Cherryfield man anonymously.[179] But the mystery of the bones persisted.

News of the ghastly Cherryfield discovery circulated widely. It reached Philip Mohan, from London, Ontario. The woodworker and carriage-maker had not heard from his brother John Walton for the last seven years. Could the Cherryfield man be his long-lost sibling? He wrote to Moncton Mayor Edward O. Steeves, who relayed his message to the public via the Moncton *Transcript*.

The story of the Cherryfield skeleton would be of little interest were it not for a singular detail. Philip's letter made a passing but unmistakable reference: John Walton participated in a treasure hunt on John Bishop's farm near Moncton in 1899.

Philip Mohan's Letter

The *Transcript* published the letter a little over a week after Philip Mohan wrote it. The full transcription reads as follows:

London, Oct. 9, 1906

To the Mayor of Moncton:

Your Worship:

Dear Sir, – We read in a local London paper of the finding of a skeleton in a forest somewhere in the neighbourhood of Moncton, and the circumstances somewhat coincide with the mysterious disappearance of a brother of mine several years ago. I thought it advisable to correspond with you in the hope that we might hear all the particulars in connection with the case.

My brother, John Walton Mohan, left London in the Spring of 1899 (in search of treasure supposed to be hidden in the neighbourhood of Moncton) and after some surveying decided to search on the farm at that time owned by a man by the name of John Bishop, about four miles from Moncton. Having employed some parties not known to me to assist in the search, making an agreement with them that they should receive one-third of the treasure, if such could be found. I received several letters from him while there and corresponded with him until Nov. 14th of that year, when he asked me in the letter to not write to him again at Moncton as he was about to give up the search, and that he would let me know when he got settled in a situation. I also supposed that he might be low in finances as he spent considerable in further search. My brother might possibly be identified in such a condition, if it should be him, by an injury which he received on his left arm between the elbow and shoulder. Several pieces of bone were removed by an operation several years ago, and I think it could be traced in the bone of the arm. His weight when last seen was over 200 pounds, 5 feet 10 inches in height.

Hoping to hear from you as early as convenient, I remain, yours truly,

Philip Mohan,
London, Can.[180]

Absent from every source so far, John Walton Mohan makes his first appearance as our investigation's newest cast member. His brother Philip does not mention Simpson in his letter. Yet there is no room for coincidence: In 1899, John Walton took part in a treasure hunt on John Bishop's farm "about four miles from Moncton." How can we unravel the puzzle?

Philip claimed to know little about his sibling's activities in Moncton. His memo, however, is far from sterile. John Walton travelled from London for Moncton in the spring of 1899. He wrote a final note on November 14 when he "was about to give up the search." All told, then, John Walton looked for gold in Irishtown for at least half a year. The spring-to-fall pattern matches up well with Simpson's own 1899 timeline.

John Walton, it seems, selected Bishop's property only "after some surveying." The location appears to have been virgin ground for treasure hunting rather than the site of a previous and ongoing operation.

John Walton also recruited local assistance. Labourers would refuse to work for free. Philip testified to his brother's expenditures and precarious finances. The prospect of success—and the promise to share a third of the loot—further enticed hired help.

Philip explained that John Walton "left London in the spring of 1899 *in search of treasure*" (emphasis mine). The wording is subtle, but the implications are profound. Far from embarking on an aimless trip out east, John Walton *knowingly* set off from London to look for treasure.

Partners or Rivals?

Philip presumably passed on everything he knew to Mayor Steeves, lest he jeopardize chances of finding his sibling. But Philip's letter, rather than mention Simpson, reads as though John Walton led the charge. Could John Walton Mohan and Simpson have been rivals carrying out parallel quests? Either way, what brought the two men to dig in the same spot at the same time could only come from one source: Somehow, John Walton and Simpson share a link.

Simpson, we already saw, showed his map to prospective associates. John Walton might represent another case in point. John Walton could then have betrayed Simpson and rushed to Irishtown to beat him to the punch. Bitter rivalries are not unprecedented in the annals of treasure hunting.[181] But without Simpson's chart, it would be difficult for John Walton to convince anyone that buried riches lay waiting. The lower-budget operation would mean limited resources and diminished chances of success.

The implausible rivalry scenario reinforces the only other possible option: John Walton and Simpson teamed up. In all likelihood, John Walton did not mention our gold seeker in his correspondence with his brother. The reason could stem from casual disinterest or from fear that information, if leaked, could attract competition. Perhaps he also engaged in self-aggrandizing at Simpson's expense.

The partnership between John Walton and Simpson, while key, tells us little about either man. The former had family in London, Ontario. Blakeny, for his part, claimed that the latter's "home was in Quebec." The few clues we have on Simpson bar us from investigating him directly. But, with a name, a surname, a named sibling, and probable roots in Southwestern Ontario, his partner should be easier to pin down. Hints from John Walton's life story, in turn, may lead us to Simpson's all-important identity.

John Walton Mohan

Brothers John Walton and Philip grew up on the Mohan farm in McGillivray (Middlesex County, ON) some forty kilometres northwest of London.[182] The death of their father in 1879 precipitated the end of their rural ways, as did the advent of agricultural mechanization. Like many at the time, the family found refuge in the city.

By 1889, after a few years operating as a merchant in Centralia (Huron County, ON), John Walton moved to London, Ontario.[183] There, he shared accommodations with Philip, his widowed mother, and other siblings.[184] He worked as a waiter and bartender in London's Grand Trunk Railway (GTR) refreshment rooms. Six years his junior, Philip became an established London carriage-maker and patriarch. John Walton, meanwhile, remained unmarried and childless.[185]

During the same period, two more of John Walton's brothers—Francis (another carriage-maker) and Thomas (a carpenter)—emigrated to Detroit, a brief two-hundred-kilometre train ride from London.[186] There, in the late 1890s, a carriage-maker named Henry Ford pioneered a transportation revolution. Francis's and Thomas's relocations to the Motor City proved prescient: The booming town offered skilled young people—carriage-makers especially—promising employment opportunities. Many in the Mohan clan followed suit.

In 1890, the GTR appointed John Walton as manager of its refreshment room in Chatham, Ontario, about 120 km southwest of London.[187] Smaller than its London counterpart, the city's GTR station provided on-site living quarters for its employees. John Walton shared the apartment with his staff.[188] He appears in the 1892 Chatham directory's "Restaurants" and "Hotelkeepers" sections as the GTR's person in charge.[189] The GTR, unlike its competitor, the Canadian Pacific Railway (CPR), kept its main line farther out and did not bring its passengers directly to Chatham's core.[190] Accordingly, John Walton's stopover ran a modest but full-accommodation service—restaurant and hotel—for travellers unable to trek downtown during their layover.

John Walton, unlike his salaried roommates, did not earn a wage.[191] Instead, he had become a private restaurateur and hotelier who leased space on GTR premises.[192] The troubled railway company implemented such cost-cutting measures as it began restructuring.[193] Onboard conveniences, such as snack bars and dining cars, spelled the end of food amenities at second-tier stops. Hotels were similarly affected by sleeper cars that offered comfortable overnight travel. Several small stations ceased operations. Many vanished altogether.[194]

In 1895, John Walton married Mary "Minnie" Smith, also from Chatham.[195] Described as "one of Chatham's most popular young ladies," she worked for the Chatham *Planet* newspaper and printing house. The newlyweds rode the evening train to Toronto and "other Eastern cities."[196]

From that point on, John Walton's star seemed to be on the rise. D. J. McDonald "sold out" his C.P.R. Hotel to him in 1897.[197] The two-and-a-half-storey hotel, built in 1890 by William Baby, lay in the heart of Chatham, kitty-corner from the CPR station. It had no official connection with the Canadian Pacific Railroad. It is said that Baby profited from the CPR acronym but avoided legal action by claiming the name stood instead for "Chatham Pool and Recreation."[198]

The C.P.R. Hotel, like many guesthouses at the time, doubled as a saloon. A writ issued on May 27, 1898, enjoined John Walton to settle an account with a local liquor merchant.[199] At the age of thirty-eight, John Walton comes off as a secure, married hotelkeeper. A year later, in the spring of 1899, he travelled to Moncton and searched for gold in Irishtown over a six-month period.

The change in John Walton's behaviour is sudden and unexpected. Why trade an enviable position for a risky quest? If a far-flung treasure hunt was a luxury that a prosperous hotelkeeper could afford, then John Walton should have resumed his Chatham life soon after. That, we already know, is not what happened.

Not everything was as it seemed for John Walton. For one, he never owned the C.P.R. Hotel outright. The hotel's change of hands was, in fact, part of a chattel mortgage.[200] In other words, McDonald put up his hotel as collateral to secure a $1,500 advance (~$52,500) from John Walton. The amount, though substantial, fell well short of the property's value. McDonald regained control of his hotel as soon as he reimbursed his debt.

The loan to McDonald may have been John Walton's only way to stay in the hospitality business. The GTR's restructuring, by then in full swing, left John Walton without a fallback position. His Chatham GTR lunchroom was forced to close in 1897 due to modified train schedules. The revised tables gave passengers insufficient time to patronize the establishment.[201]

Things were seemingly no better at home for John Walton. His wife had returned to live with her mother and siblings by no later than 1901 and perhaps before.[202] Worse, the 1898 writ expected him to produce $389 (~$13,000)—a sum he may never have repaid. In John Walton's eyes, perhaps, treasure hunting out east literally offered a golden opportunity to escape a world of trouble.

John Walton apparently vanished after his 1899 treasure hunt in Irishtown. He does not appear in the 1901 Canadian census, the 1900 US census, the 1900-02, 1902-04, and 1904-06 Chatham directories, the London and Detroit directories, or other sources. The 1910 US census finds him living in Detroit with his older sibling, Anne Marie, who had followed her family to Michigan. She earned her "own income" and was head of the household. John Walton, for his part, reported no employment or revenue.[203]

That same year, in 1910, John Walton passed away in Detroit from cerebral hemorrhage at the age of fifty.[204] Nothing, including the occupation of gardener stated on his death certificate, hints at underlying illness. He may have crashed at his sister's place and taken odd jobs. Or he may have come to rely on relatives as he sensed his final days approaching. His remains were repatriated to London and interred in St. Peter's cemetery.[205] Tellingly, perhaps, none of his six pallbearers bore his last name.

The 1900–02 and 1902–04 Chatham directories do not list Mohan's wife, Minnie.[206] That alone does not prove that she followed her husband to New Brunswick or Michigan. She resurfaces in the 1904–06 edition and appears sporadically in subsequent releases.[207] She worked humble sales jobs and passed away in 1942.[208]

Left: Grand Trunk Railway Depot, London, Ontario (c. 1890). Window posters advertise the "Dining Room" tended by John Walton Mohan. [PG L10, Ivey Family London Room, London Public Library, London, ON]

Right: The Chatham GTR station (c. 1920). [SoftwareSimian via Wikimedia Commons]

It is difficult to paint a human picture from a few dry records. Yet elements from John Walton's character do emerge. Unhurried professionally. Slow to marry. Childless. Alienated from his spouse. Estranged from his relatives. Peripatetic. Missing from official documents. Even missing from family photo albums. John Walton may have been something of an outcast. More than a century after his death, he comes across as a drifter who made his mark more by absence than by presence.

We may never know whether Philip eventually reconnected with his long-lost sibling. Philip was on hand at his mother's funeral in 1901.[209] John Walton did not attend or send a note, or Philip would not have written his 1906 letter to Mayor Steeves. Any sign of life from John Walton after 1899 would have spared his brother worries about a dead body in Cherryfield.

John Walton's whereabouts in the years following the Irishtown treasure hunt remain shrouded in mystery. Maybe he took his quest to the northern wilderness. The Klondike gold rush had reached its end by late 1899, yet men continued to travel by the thousands in search of fortune during the less heralded 1899–1909 gold rush in Nome, Alaska. Census and directory canvassers struggled to keep up with itinerant adventurers heading to uncertain, remote destinations.[210]

Simpson: An Ontario Man?

John Walton's relationship with Simpson was unlike any other in this tale so far. Indeed, Simpson partnered with Blakeny, LeBlanc, Warman, and the two McSweeneys only *after* he arrived in Moncton. In contrast, Philip's 1906 letter leads us to a remarkable conclusion: Simpson joined with John Walton *before* he left for Moncton.

John Walton Mohan was only thirty-nine in 1899. Sources, meanwhile, describe Simpson as "old" and "elderly." Our treasure hunter may have needed the financial and physical assistance of an able-bodied associate. John Walton also had farming experience and management skills. These qualifications would make him a useful right-hand man for the digging operation. Simpson, freed from the daily nitty-gritty, could concentrate on the bigger picture.

John Walton's ties to Southwestern Ontario raise the all-important question of our gold seeker's own origins. Save for a honeymoon getaway in 1895, a small but steady stream of evidence pins John Walton in Chatham between 1890 and 1898. The limited reach of his wedding trip—Toronto and beyond—might reflect his idea of travel on a grand scale. And if John Walton did not move from Southwestern Ontario much, then maybe Simpson lived there as well.

Philip said in his letter that his brother left London for Moncton. Even if John Walton started his journey in Chatham, London served—and still serves—as an unavoidable waypoint between the two cities. Given his mounting Chatham troubles, John Walton could well have retreated to a familiar refuge in the weeks or months before his departure for Moncton.[211] Perhaps he even met Simpson in London.

John Walton and Simpson may have come to Moncton together. If Simpson resided in Southwestern Ontario, then Blakeny's "from Quebec" comment could refer to our treasure hunter's last pit stop rather than to his permanent domicile. This goes to show how little we know about our man's origins. John Walton's correspondence with Philip could prove invaluable in this regard. Unfortunately, Bill Mohan and Christine Stergar (née Mohan)—both descendants from John Walton's siblings—were unaware of their gold-seeking great-uncle, let alone of any letters from Moncton.

Below: Map of GTR-ICR (1888). [Bibliothèque nationale de France, Public domain, via Wikimedia Commons]

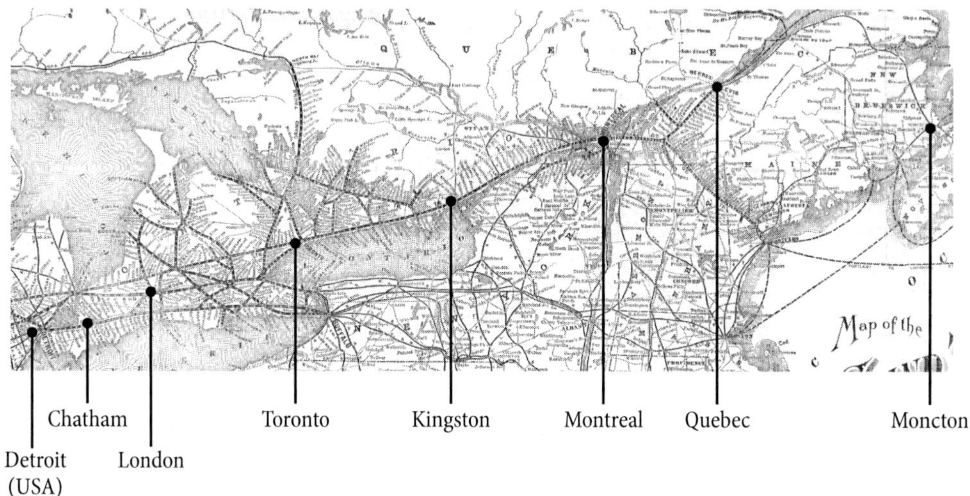

Philip's letter introduced us to John Walton Mohan—a waiter turned hotelkeeper turned treasure seeker from Southwestern Ontario. He came to Moncton in 1899 and searched John Bishop's farmland from the spring to the fall of that year. Simpson, meanwhile, was doing the same thing at the same time in the same place. The evidence linking the two remains circumstantial, but that would be pushing the coincidence angle too far. The men somehow connected with each other before travelling to Moncton together or separately. The most credible scenario by some margin is one of a partnership between them.

Blakeny failed to mention John Walton, as did Moncton's newspapers from 1899. The Ontarian may have made no strong impression. Or maybe working as Simpson's field manager in Irishtown kept him out of the limelight. Were it not for his brother Philip, he would have slipped under our radar and vanished without a trace. Still, how he crossed Simpson's path remains an open question.

And it may yet prove key in uncovering Simpson's all-important identity.

The Odyssey of *Le London*

HISTORICAL • CONTEXT •

In 1750, *Le London* raised its sails and left the port of Quebec. So began the seventy-ton sloop's clandestine mission to Acadie. Stored in *Le London*'s hold were foodstuffs, various necessities, and light weaponry. Jacques Jalain, an experienced mariner, captained the otherwise unarmed boat. His orders came from the very top, namely New France's powerful intendant François Bigot.[212]

Le London reached the coastal outpost of Shediac a month later. France had built the military settlement the year before to support its claims over the region. Officially, at least, *Le London*'s cargo would aid stationed troops, provide for Acadian exiles, and serve as trade goods for allied First Nations.[213] But *Le London*'s assignment was not all that it seemed.

In reality, Bigot had secretly instructed Jalain to assist Abbé Le Loutre's guerilla actions against British presence in peninsular Acadie.[214] Shediac, which lay far from British eyes and clear of the Chignecto hot zone, would act as a stealthy resupply base. The zealous priest and his fighters would strike in peninsular Acadie and rearm in Shediac before launching another offensive. British soldiers were fearful of the raids and rarely ventured outside their fortifications. So effective were the clergyman's tactics that historians refer to this period of Acadie as Father Le Loutre's War.[215] *Le London*, its Shediac delivery completed, spent the following months bringing mail and stockpiles to French settlements along the North Shore. Jalain stopped at Baie Verte, where Le Loutre handed him four English deserters. On August 18, the HMS *Trial*, a ten-gun warship of the Royal Navy led by Edward Le Cras, intercepted *Le London* off the coast of Remshec (near Wallace, NS). The discovery of the English defectors and the hold's remaining military supplies caused alarm.[216] Even more compromising were Jalain's papers, including receipts signed by Le Loutre, which exposed France's *sub rosa* actions in peninsular Acadie. All the more damning was that the records contravened the fragile 1748 Treaty of Aix-la-Chapelle. Upon hearing the news, Bigot lamented that Jalain did not have the presence of mind to throw his documents overboard before the boat's capture.[217]

An auction in Halifax put *Le London* up for sale. A trial began at the Vice Admiralty. British authorities imprisoned Jalain and his crew, who were soon freed in exchange for sailors held at Louisbourg. Jalain repurchased his boat. By June 1751, he had made his way back to Quebec with a cautionary tale to tell.[218]

The odyssey of *Le London* is a step removed from French troops burying nine leather bags of gold in Irishtown. But with a French supply vessel, a secretive payload, and the threat of British capture, it has commonalities with Blakeny's narrative. East Coast folklore rests in part on authentic historical accounts. And, as such, *Le London*'s story adds a patina of believability to later exaggerations.

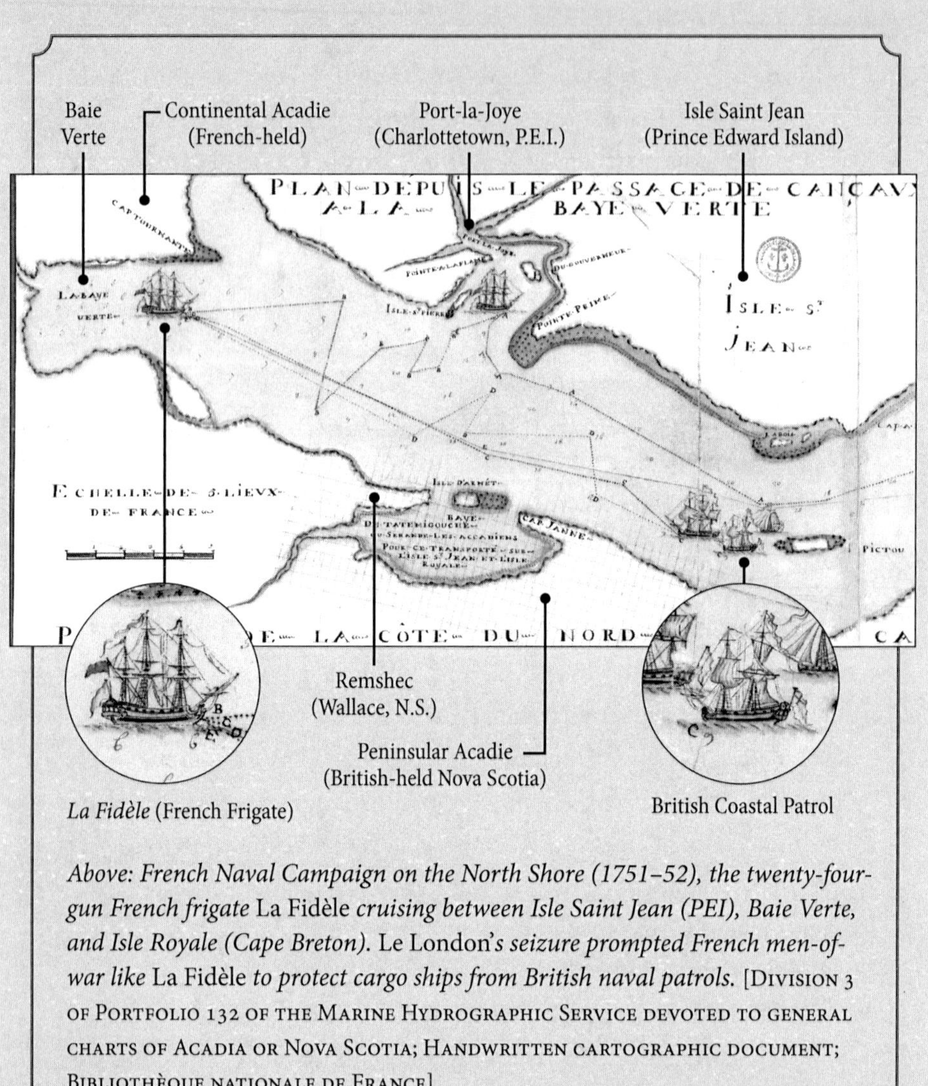

Above: French Naval Campaign on the North Shore (1751–52), the twenty-four-gun French frigate La Fidèle *cruising between Isle Saint Jean (PEI), Baie Verte, and Isle Royale (Cape Breton).* Le London*'s seizure prompted French men-of-war like* La Fidèle *to protect cargo ships from British naval patrols.* [Division 3 of Portfolio 132 of the Marine Hydrographic Service devoted to general charts of Acadia or Nova Scotia; Handwritten cartographic document; Bibliothèque nationale de France]

Chapter 9
Red Tape

If men were angels, no government would be necessary.
– James Madison

One day in 1908, George A. Stewart barged into New Brunswick's Crown Land Office in Fredericton. Agitated, he announced to the surveyor general and his deputy, "Don't think I am a fool or crazy, but I want a prospector's licence, and I must have it."[219] Afraid of being overheard, he insisted that he and the two officials retire to a quieter setting. There, he produced an empty leather pocketbook that had seen better days. On the inside flaps were marks written in a foreign language. How he came into its possession, no one knows. Stewart claimed that the inscriptions, once deciphered, referred to "six barrels of gold coins, and one barrel of precious stones and jewels, such as diamonds and rubies." The text, he believed, led to booty concealed by pirates in Charlotte County along the Bay of Fundy's coastline. He also maintained that the strange markings pinpointed the location of the cave guarding the hoard. There was just one problem: The cave lay on private land.

Stewart would be liable for trespass were he to step onto the property. According to the story reported in the Moncton *Daily Times*, an authorization from the surveyor general would confer access to—and ownership of—the riches. The deputy offered that "it was not customary for the department to issue prospecting licences for buried treasure," but he was "willing to give him the right to search for minerals." The surveyor general agreed that "the province could very well afford to make an exception in his case." Stewart obtained his permit on condition that he forfeit one barrel of gold should he ever find the loot.

Stewart's petition for a licence is more than a side anecdote. Quirky as it is, the account offers a window into government oversight—or lack of it—that applied to treasure hunting in New Brunswick around the turn of the twentieth century. Sorting out the red tape in Stewart's situation should provide a better understanding of regulations Simpson faced in his own quest. And that, in turn, should yield additional insight into our elusive seeker's thinking.

Surface, Subsurface, and Mineral Rights

Stewart's problem was that the treasure lay on private land. But under no circumstances would a prospecting licence grant him the authority to invade someone's property. On the face of it, Stewart's approach makes little sense. It becomes more intelligible, however, if we look at the advantages conferred by such a permit.

A common belief is that real estate includes everything on it, above it, and below it—the principle of *usque ad coelum et ad inferos* (to the sky and to the depths). But even at the time, land ownership applied only to the surface and objects on it (buildings, trees, etc.). Subsurface rights, by contrast, targeted underground strata, which belonged to the state.[220] Arguably, then, Stewart's licence could award him possession of subterranean gold.

Moreover, Stewart must have thought that he could keep any unclaimed gold and silver. Indeed, minerals are the preserve of government; in that light, Stewart's petition does not appear so outlandish. In the end, he likely assumed a permit could reward him with treasure lying not only under private property, but also on it.[221]

In the Archives

The surveyor general's reaction to Stewart's petition suggests that treasure-hunting licences were virtually unheard of in New Brunswick. One document that did turn up in the Provincial Archives of New Brunswick was a 1934 note written by Moncton's Sandford MacNeil to the Ministry of Land and Mines. MacNeil's memo sought permission to dig for booty in an unspecified

Left: Sanford MacNeil's handwritten petition for a treasure-hunt licence to the Minister of Lands & Mines. [PANB RS112]. *Below: The curt reply from the inspector of mines (1934).* [PANB RS112]

DEPARTMENT OF LANDS AND MINES
FREDERICTON, N.B.
RECEIVED
JUN 22 1934
A.M. 7,8,9,10,11,12,1,2,3,4,5,6 P.M.

65 Downing st
Moncton
N.B.
June 19/34

The Minister of Lands & Mines
Fredericton
N.B

Dear Sir:—
I recieved your letter as well as the literture on mining claims and as it dose not seem to be the thing I want would you please advise me how I would get permission to dig for burried treasures would I have to take out a claim in order to do so
Very truly yours
Sanford MacNeil.

June 23rd, 1934.

Mr. Sanford MacNeill,
65 Downing Street,
Moncton, N. B.

Dear Sir:-

Re yours of the 19th instant.

There is no provision under our Mining Law regarding searches for buried treasure.

Yours truly,

McM*AF

Inspector of Mines.

location. The one-line reply from the inspector of mines was curt, to say the least: "Dear Sir: – Re yours of the 19th instant. There is no provision under our Mining Law regarding searches for buried treasure."[222]

We may never know the information MacNeil thought he possessed. Nothing in MacNeil's note, other than Moncton's proximity to Irishtown, hints at a link with Simpson's earlier search. More revealing is the blunt reply by the inspector of mines. Whether for Stewart in 1908 or MacNeil in 1934, it appears New Brunswick officials had little treasure-hunting guidance on offer, which is the surprising part.

The Law of Treasure Trove

Europe abounds with buried riches. The phenomenon has its roots in the continent's tumultuous history and use of coinage for millennia. Known stashes of interred specie, be they Iron Age, Roman, Anglo-Saxon, Pictish, Viking, or Norman, number in the hundreds in Great Britain alone. Such finds are practically unheard of in Canada. It is perhaps for this reason that New Brunswick officials—the surveyor general, his deputy, and the inspector of mines—did not quote treasure-trove law, although it was already on the books at the time. Indeed, as a former British colony, New Brunswick inherited common law—and therefore treasure-trove law—from the UK. The neighbouring province of Nova Scotia enacted its own Treasure Trove Act in 1954. However, the British legal framework still applied to New Brunswick around the turn of the twentieth century.[223]

A treasure trove—or hoard—is a cache of money (gold, silver, plate, bullion, etc.) deliberately hidden for later retrieval. British common law stipulated that the depositor be long dead and without heir. Under this definition, barring a valid counterclaim, a hoard belonged to the Crown. Penalties for unreported finds ranged from fines to imprisonment. If a discovery did not qualify as treasure, the law of first finding would settle the question of ownership: possession would go to the claimant—either the discoverer or the landowner—with the better case.[224] At the time of Stewart's appeal, common law favoured landowners, but precedent was slim.[225]

Stewart was not wrong to fear that authorities could deny him his hoped-for booty. If he came across a deemed treasure trove, he might have to forfeit it to the Crown. If he unearthed something else, he risked losing the item to the landowner's potentially superior claim. However, his request for a prospecting licence, while creative, proved misguided. Subsurface and mineral rights apply only to *natural* deposits; other laws determine ownership of human-made objects—everything from treasure troves to worthless artifacts. Stewart's petition may have fooled the surveyor general and his deputy, but claiming buried gold by invoking subsurface or mineral rights would simply not have held up in court. What Stewart may not have understood, though, is that he could have seen his claim upheld on altogether different grounds.

During the second half of the nineteenth century, UK civil servants began rewarding finders—not landowners—who reported discoveries to authorities. They would confiscate important items and offer compensation at comparable antiquarian market value. Finders could either retain or sell the rest.[226] The state had not amended treasure-trove law per se. Still, British policy had become one of finders keepers, albeit one with a government first-dibs, buy-back twist. Law and practice, then, were at odds with each other. Never officially enshrined, the guidelines could be reversed at any time. It is uncertain whether British courts—let alone Canadian ones—would have interpreted the practice as a form of implicit precedent.[227]

The objective here is not to make pronouncements on historical legal matters. The point is simply that there was little clarity to be had about hoard ownership in New Brunswick around the turn of the twentieth century. Lawyers and notary publics of the era would probably have struggled to provide uniform advice on the issue.

Land Access

Stewart's prospecting licence, far from legitimizing trespass, reaffirmed the landowner's right to private property. It would be within the property owner's power to deny Stewart entry to the site. But that would not necessarily guard against the extraction of underground resources.[228] The 2007 period movie *There Will Be Blood*, which depicts Southern California's oil boom in the late-nineteenth and early-twentieth centuries, highlights potential complications. In one scene, the protagonist uses a metaphorical straw to explain directional drilling, or how he "drank" his rival's "milkshake" from his own concession by siphoning oil diagonally from under his neighbour's. In contrast, searching for treasure would usually require direct access to the premises. The landowner could ask for compensation in exchange, either a fee or a share of the spoils. Importantly, a contract detailing terms would take on outsized significance if finder and landowner were to dispute the ownership of a discovery. Seekers would risk charges of trespass and forfeiting their claims unless they obtained prior written permission.

Little else seemed to regulate digging on private grounds in New Brunswick at the time. The law lacked provisions for treasure-hunt licences; questions of ownership arose only once someone had made a find.[229] The situation is very different today. Only qualified archaeologists authorized to operate on-site can investigate locations of suspected historical consequence. A permit would be necessary under either New Brunswick's Historic Sites Protection Act or Canada's National Parks Act or Historic Sites and Monuments Act.

Restrictions, including zoning, environmental, health and safety, and cultural sensitivity, would also likely apply.[230]

Taxation

The surveyor general told Stewart he could keep his treasure provided that he hand over one of the six barrels of gold he expected to uncover. But what if Stewart unearthed only one barrel? Or ten? The conditions smack of improvisation. Perhaps the surveyor general and his deputy thought Stewart was just a deluded nuisance. Rather than get into an argument or look up uncertain laws, they may have issued him a licence in the hope of never hearing from him again. It probably worked.

Treatment of Stewart aside, the surveyor general's reflex to withhold a portion of loot raises the question of taxation. Treasure-trove law did not explicitly call for a levy. However, the British practice of compensating finders did impose an indirect toll. An 1886 Home Office brief instructed administrators to subtract between 10 and 20 percent from a hoard's worth on the antiquarian market.[231] Forced to sell their artifacts at a rebate, finders were also deprived of the potential to see their haul appreciate in value.

A treasure's discovery would be subject to taxation in today's world. But the rule did not exist in Canada during Stewart's time. Canada's tax-free National Policy incentivized immigrants to settle in the country. Federal receipts came from border fees and customs tariffs. Provinces profited from natural resources. Municipalities charged for real estate and services. Canada introduced personal and corporate income levies as a temporary expedient with the War Tax Act of 1917.[232] It never repealed the measure.

Simpson's Case

Using Stewart's case as a template, we have cleared much of the regulatory underbrush regarding treasure hunting in New Brunswick around the turn of the twentieth century. Simpson's 1899 quest preceded Stewart's by less than a decade and took place in the same jurisdiction. The legal parallels are obvious. So, what can we learn from them?

Simpson may have feared that any gold he unearthed would slip through his fingers. It seems unlikely he anticipated Stewart's creative strategy of reaching out to the New Brunswick surveyor general. Regardless, in the provincial Archives, I could locate no application for a licence or permit of any kind issued to Simpson or his group. Such an application, had it been made, would have been immensely helpful. We cannot know Simpson's legal approach without it. Still, the regulatory landscape at the time offers hints at Simpson's thinking.

Simpson may have fretted about treasure-trove law. New Brunswick officials may have been all too happy to rediscover it and confiscate the loot. A court challenge would have been Simpson's best hope of monetizing his prize. The British policy of compensating finders would have been an important argument in his favour. There is also not much Simpson could have done beforehand to secure the ownership of the gold for himself. Forfeiting the hoard to the Crown was a risk that, knowingly or not, he simply had to take.

The one thing Simpson could not afford to neglect was permission to dig on Bishop's land. We can infer from the *Daily Transcript* and the *Daily Times* articles from 1899 that he did obtain it, at least verbally. Other than consent, it appears that nothing at the time would have prevented him from searching on private property in Irishtown. Simpson only had a limited amount of money to offer Bishop. Shares in any future discovery were likely his best bargaining chip. Bishop had everything to gain and little to lose, save perhaps for the inconvenience of the operation itself. But even if he believed in finders keepers, Simpson may have feared that the farmer could mount a superior claim and keep the gold for himself. A written agreement would have resolved the twin issues of securing land access and distributing the spoils.

Taxation was probably not at the forefront of Simpson's mind. Government had yet to introduce personal income tax. But the worry that the Crown would withhold some—or all—of the loot may have gnawed at him. Could he have gotten away with hiding his treasure from the authorities? The answer appears to be an easy no.

We know that John Walton Mohan, Simpson's associate from Ontario, enticed local help with a third of the booty. Blakeny spoke of between twenty and thirty labourers. Even if a worker secretly hit paydirt, the newly minted man would soon be the talk of the town. Word would have spread. Blakeny, LeBlanc, Warman, and the two McSweeneys also had much to lose as prominent businessmen. Credibility was as good as gold for entrepreneurs attuned to the power of bad publicity. Anyone who clandestinely unearthed a massive hoard would face the unenviable prospect of monetizing their find without attracting government attention. Charges of conspiracy would round out the risk of fines and imprisonment. Plus, the yellow metal has little value in and of itself unless it can be traded for something else. Selling large amounts of it would flood any existing black market for the commodity in New Brunswick. Illegally exporting it would complicate matters and compound the crime.

It hardly seems worth it.

Stewart's odd story demonstrates that, around the turn of the twentieth century, treasure hunters in New Brunswick could not ignore government oversight, however lacking it may have been. Similar worries about red tape must have crossed the minds of Simpson and his associates. Our review of Simpson's regulatory hurdles has given us insight into his options, his actions, and even into his thinking. The dual requirements of securing land access and resolving competing claims between Simpson and Bishop magnify a would-be contract's importance. The document, if it ever existed, would make for a fascinating read. Sadly, Bishop's descendants were unaware of any such paper.

But, as we find out later, they did have a few intriguing tales to tell.

The Fall of Beauséjour

Profit, my dear Vergor, by your opportunity;
trim,—cut—you have the power.

– François Bigot (Intendant of New France)

HISTORICAL CONTEXT

One day in the spring of 1755, Louis Du Pont Duchambon de Vergor peered into the thick fog blanketing the Bay of Fundy. He could not see what reports had told him about moments before: Thirty British ships lay at anchor near the mouth of the Beaubassin channel (Cumberland Basin, NS). The battle of Fort Beauséjour had begun. Vergor, the fort commander, could be under no illusions. Without reinforcements, he would lose the fight. Time worked against him: It would take three days to contact Louisbourg and more than a week for word to reach Quebec. Fort Menagouèche, at the mouth of the Saint John River, could spare no one guarding the route to Quebec.[233]

Vergor was much to blame for the disastrous situation. A formal note stated he was "mediocre in every respect."[234] Yet he prospered under Bigot, the intendant of New France. Appointed Fort Beauséjour's leader through his protector's patronage, he had had a full year to upgrade defences. In the face of escalating tensions, he instead opted to embezzle funds and disregard advice from Louis-Thomas Jacau de Fiedmont and other, more capable officers.[235] Only *after* the British appeared in Beaubassin did he consent to makeshift improvements.[236]

Meanwhile, Abbé Le Loutre, the controversial French priest, had not made matters any simpler. He diverted Acadian personnel from arguably more pressing defensive tasks with the 50,000 livres (~$835,000) he obtained from France to build new dikes and aboiteaux. The British also had a spy on the inside. Thomas Pichon, Fort Beauséjour's clerk to the illiterate Vergor, passed on plans to facilitate the stronghold's capture. He also undermined French morale at every turn.[237] The British were now at Fort Beauséjour's doorstep. It was, by then, already much too late.

Vergor had only 160 soldiers from the compagnies franches de la Marine to oppose the Anglo-American force of 2,300 troops. Approximately 100 Mi'kmaw and Wolastoqiyik warriors shored up French ranks. Cornered, Le Loutre appealed to the same Acadians whose village of Beaubassin he had set ablaze five years earlier. The Acadians, both resentful and fearful of French and British retribution alike, were understandably lukewarm when summoned to the fort's defence. Around 300 Acadian militiamen—half the available total—answered the call. Acadian families fled to the woods after Vergor destroyed their homes in a futile attempt to slow the enemy's advance.[238]

The British, led by Robert Monckton, John Winslow, and George Scott, laid siege to Beauséjour.[239] Units crossed the Missaguash River, took a small redoubt, replaced a burned bridge, and consolidated positions with trenches, cannons, and mortars. Meanwhile, a British squadron cruised the Gulf of Saint Lawrence and blockaded the port of Louisbourg. Vergor, after having mollified his forces with promises of relief, learned that none was forthcoming. The bad news leaked. French resolve sank.

After a few days of British shelling, a bomb fell on Beauséjour's officer's mess. Vergor relented, to Monckton's surprise and to Le Loutre's dismay. Beauséjour had capitulated only two weeks after the enemy fleet first appeared. Fort Gaspareaux, the fortlet near Baie Verte, on the other side of Chignecto, surrendered the next day. French troops were rounded up and sent to Louisbourg. Le Loutre vanished under the cloak of disguise. The isthmus's portage roads, which once provided a vital link between Louisbourg and Quebec, could no longer serve the French cause. The Acadians, henceforth undesirables on their own lands, would soon find that mercy was far from what the British had in mind.[240]

As for Blakeny's legend, could Vergor or Le Loutre have anticipated Fort Beauséjour's demise and put its gold reserves onboard a ship bound for Quebec?[241] The scenario is problematic. The British coast guard patrolled the Bay of Fundy, including the narrow Beaubassin channel. Quebec never resupplied Beauséjour directly by sea for that very reason. Instead, men and material sailed to Baie Verte on the North Shore and travelled overland to Beauséjour along a serviceable path. Britain left nothing to chance and cut off the Baie Verte portage during the 1755 siege.[242] In the end, any gold held at Fort Beauséjour would have had few, if any, means of escape.

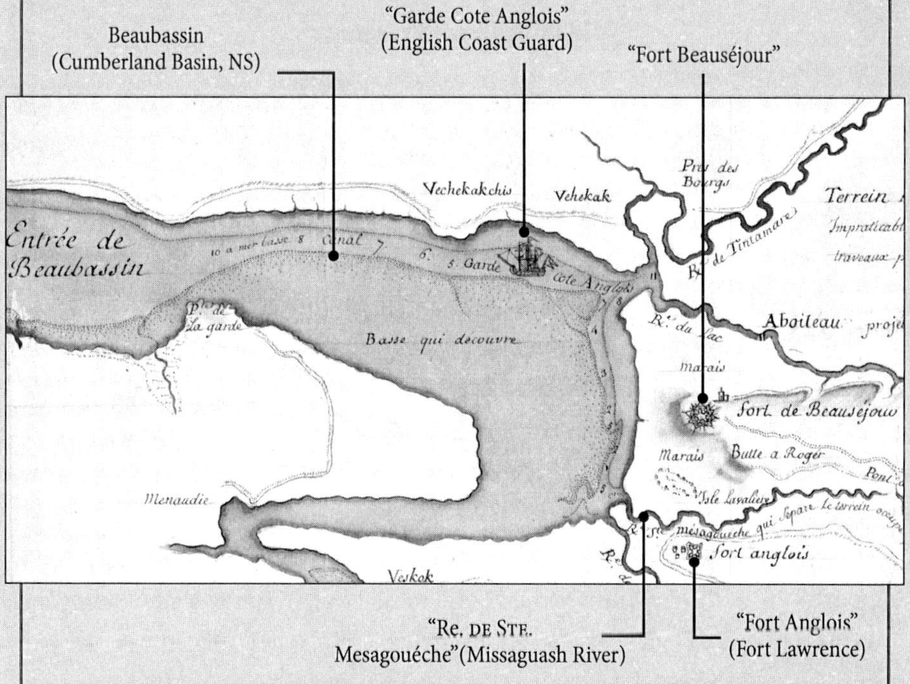

Above: Franquet's map of Beaubassin shows the narrow channel along with Fort Beauséjour and Fort Lawrence ("Fort Anglois") on either side of the Missaguash River. The British coast guard ("Garde Côte Anglois") was an ever-present threat.
[Division 3 of Portfolio 132 of the Marine Hydrographic Service devoted to general charts of Acadia or Nova Scotia; handwritten cartographic document; Bibliothèque nationale de France]

Chapter 10
Winters of Discontent

Now is the winter of our discontent
Made glorious summer by this sun of York.
– William Shakespeare, *Richard III*

Seeking inspiration in Shakespeare is perhaps not the soundest advice for moving an investigation forward. But the Bard of Avon did understand human psychology better than most. In the opening line of his soliloquy, the future King Richard III laments the hardships he and his family endured during the Wars of the Roses. His winter of discontent is not without parallels to Simpson's own situation in November 1899. The latter had failed to unearth any gold. Funds had dried up. His partners had quit. The ground had frozen over. Winter indeed.

But, in the second line of *Richard III*, hope. Undaunted, Richard sees opportunity in the crowning of his brother and rival, a "sun of York." Simpson, for his part, faced external forces—money, people, and climate—that reveal little about his internal resolve. Did the belief that drove him to seek treasure in Irishtown run deeper? If he could enlist another "sun of York" to finance another quest, he could still aspire to turn his winter of discontent into a summer of glory. Maybe Shakespeare is telling us that, despite a first setback, Simpson would have wanted to return.

The question is, did he?

In the Press

Leafing through Moncton's newspapers for the whole of 1900 is a project unto itself. The infamous Zeppelin airship recorded its maiden flight. A devastating fire jumped across the Outaouais River to Ottawa from neighbouring Hull.[243] The world mourned the death of Oscar Wilde.[244] But, without any sign of Simpson for 1900, my quest began taking on its own air of wintry despair. Due diligence demanded I repeat the exercise for the following year.

In 1901, Britain ceded the Panama Canal to the United States. Sweden held the inaugural Nobel Prize ceremony. Guglielmo Marconi, later an avowed Mussolini fascist, received the first wireless transatlantic signal at the aptly named Signal Hill in Newfoundland. But, amid the twentieth century's busy first year, this appeared in the *Daily Transcript* on September 25, 1901:

A Search for a Buried Treasure

Being Conducted on the Bishop Farm, Irishtown Road

> It will be remembered that some two years ago the Transcript published a report about a search for a hidden treasure supposed to be located on the John A. Bishop farm, on the Irishtown road, about a quarter of a mile this side of the waterworks reservoir. A Mr. Simpson, who for the past three or four years has been carrying on the search, has again arrived and this year he is accompanied by three other gentlemen, named Wheld, Lewis and Cobb, all belonging to London, Ontario, and stopping at Mr. T. B. LeBlanc's hotel on Duke street. Mr. Simpson and party represent a company, and it is the intention to continue the search for the millions of gold which Simpson alleges is buried in this vicinity. Last year operations were carried on along a small creek just below the city reservoir. This creek passes through John Bishop's farm. About an acre of ground was plowed over, harrowed and nug [*sic*] into to the depth of about four or five feet. A diligent search was made by Simpson and his fellow workmen on the previous visit, but their search proved futile. The treasure is supposed to amount to between two and four millions of dollars, and is supoosed [*sic*] to have been buried by French soldiers who were taking it to Quebec. The French were all captured but one escaped and returned to France, leaving a plan of the country

> where the money was buried as a legacy to his son. Simpson says the money is on the Bishop property or it is nowhere. Two spans of horses and scoops are at work, and Mr. Simpson has purchased scrapers from the R. F. & M. Co., and will commence operations tomorrow. Mr. John A. Bishop and his Uncle George Bishop are in charge of the work.[245]

This is a lot to take in. An easy skim for casual readers, the *Daily Transcript* column is complex from an investigative standpoint. As we always do, let us break it down and explore its ramifications. But first, a reassuring note. The text refers to an article printed "some two years ago." This can only be an allusion to the *Daily Transcript* piece published two years before to the day. If nothing appeared in the interim, it would seem we did not miss anything.

Timeline

We have assumed until now that Simpson's treasure hunt limited itself to 1899. But the article makes plain that the operation was no mere one-year affair. In fact, it involved at least two other efforts: one in 1900 and one in 1901. Moreover, the journalist claims that our gold seeker had been scouring John Bishop's property "for the past three or four years." The reporter's statement could be interpreted as a hint that Simpson mounted a search in 1898 as well. If the columnist omitted the upcoming 1901 bid in his calculation, he could have been hinting at an even earlier campaign in 1897. His hesitating words, though, invite caution about taking pre-1899 attempts for granted.

But in which edition of Simpson's quest did Blakeny participate?

The 1901 text gives us grounds to rule out 1900 and 1901. Simpson excavated only a single acre in 1900, or less than even a conservative read of Blakeny's seven-acre figure. The presence of three Ontario men in 1901 also appears to preclude local partners. The arguments are not bulletproof. Taking on renewed significance is our own independent dating that puts Blakeny's operation between 1896 and 1899. All told, then, evidence still points to 1899 as Blakeny's year.

The London Connection

We still lack sufficient clues about Simpson's identity. The article even refers to "*A* Mr. Simpson" (emphasis added). It is as if our gold seeker dared the reporter to suss him out. Otherwise, the text reveals that three men from London, Ontario—Wheld, Lewis, and Cobb—participated in the 1901 search. It does not provide their full names.

John Walton Mohan, who accompanied Simpson in 1899, hailed from Southwestern Ontario. Was our treasure hunter from there as well? The fact that Simpson's 1901 associates came from London, in the same locale, ratchets up our suspicions. So why did the columnist not divulge Simpson's own origins? In all likelihood, our elusive protagonist kept his guard up around journalists. But it would be remarkable if he called Quebec home, as Blakeny claimed, yet brought Southwestern Ontarians to Irishtown on two separate occasions some two years apart. It appears Simpson either resided in Southwestern Ontario, like his comrades, or at least entertained strong ties to it.

The article writes that "Mr. Simpson and party represent a company," which seems to lump Simpson together with Wheld, Lewis, and Cobb as would-be corporate delegates. Did the organization mirror his legal arrangement with the Moncton backers from 1899? Or does the phrase mean that Simpson was a member of a four-man search team dispatched to Irishtown by unnamed Ontario stakeholders ("a company") as their representatives? A commercial group with another raison d'être—perhaps one with prior links to him and his Ontario partners—could have sponsored the quest. Either way, evidence of geographical and professional proximity may yet help reveal our man's identity.

A Missing Stone

We have a direct quote from Simpson himself: "The money is on the Bishop property or it is nowhere." Brave words for someone with nothing to show for at least two years' worth of effort. How did our treasure seeker convince new sponsors to disregard previous failures and fund another search? His return in 1901 is surprising given that the 1900 excavation plowed "about an acre of ground" on top of whatever area Blakeny had covered the year before. The combined extent of the 1899 and 1900 efforts was already improbably vast. It would remind potential backers that, at best, Simpson only had a vague idea of where to look. What reason could warrant faith in yet another round of exploration?

In 1899, the operation unfolded "on the bank of the brook." In 1900, we now know, it proceeded "along a small creek just below the city reservoir." The repeated targeting of Lynch's Brook suggests that Simpson followed the riverbed. The key here is that the bank of a stream is necessarily long and narrow. If our gold seeker believed treasure lay on the brook's eastern bank, then even a budget of one acre would span much of the brook's running length. This follow-the-bank approach would be all the more encouraging given that the creek does not carry on forever. Simpson would not only be breaking new ground, he would also be rapidly shrinking whatever area remained. Chances of a find would skyrocket. And *that* could get sponsors excited.

Simpson's follow-the-bank strategy puts the disagreement between Blakeny's engineers in a different light. Blakeny remarked: "One fellow would say, 'There is the spot,' and another would indicate a place half a mile away and say the same thing. We had the best engineers we could get, too."

The dispute becomes more intelligible if, rather than radiate in every direction, Blakeny's "half-a-mile" extended only lengthwise along Lynch's Brook. To give a sense of scale, the creek meanders through Bishop's land for about one-quarter of a mile. Simpson's search could well have spilled onto neighbouring properties on this basis alone. From the pipeline crossing, Lynch's Brook tacks south for about one mile before it links with the westerly Ogilvie Creek. The engineers' half-a-mile wrangle easily fits within that section. A half-mile upstream and downstream—a full mile, if that is what Blakeny meant—covers the section entirely.

Simpson's follow-the-bank strategy is coming into focus. But why was Simpson unable to home in directly on the supposed gold? With a bona fide treasure map in hand, he could presumably have dug in more or less the right spot to begin with. Part of the answer may lie in Blakeny's words: "We did find landmarks shown on the chart—a south running stream and a spring. It showed the treasure as being buried behind a big rock but a lot of building stone had been taken out of the place and the rock was gone, so that wasn't any help."

Blakeny never doubted he had identified the south-running stream. But the large boulder guarding the loot was nowhere in sight. Pinpointing the correct location would be difficult without it. Brute force—an expansive search along the eastern bank of the creek—would have to compensate for the missing landmark. Here again, we can perhaps make out the faint outlines of two separate efforts in 1899: an exploratory one in the spring and a comprehensive one in the fall.

According to Hanford, Blakeny's son, the stone guarding the gold had "a picture of a frog carved on the bottom." The meaning of "bottom" is ambiguous in this context. One interpretation is that the frog marking was on the underside of the rock and therefore shielded from view, but the idea is problematic. Thanks to Blakeny himself, we know that several large rocks dotted the banks of Lynch's Brook. Even with the help of Simpson's map, any attempt at recovering the treasure would require toppling and inspecting a considerable number of large stones to find the correct one. The other possibility is that the frog carving was in plain sight, etched at the foot—or "bottom"—of the big rock in question. Still, the use of a visible landmark to flag a cache is a risky proposition, as it could draw unwanted attention to the location's importance.

The large missing stone reportedly hampered Blakeny's efforts. But that in itself fails to fully account for Simpson's follow-the-bank strategy. Had the chart traced out the brook's contours to scale, Simpson could still have pinpointed the key spot without the help of any human-made clues on the ground. The need for an unequivocal landmark constitutes additional evidence that Simpson's document was of the crudest variety. Further proof of its rudimentary layout is that Simpson searched over several hectares rather than mere square metres. Its alleged origins—a rough parchment drafted by French troops unfamiliar with local terrain—also align with the notion of a primitive plan.

Digging Operations

The article dated September 25, 1901, reveals that Simpson "will commence operations tomorrow." It offers no explanation as to why the excavation should start so late in the year. Digging in peak summer heat would be hard work.

Perhaps Simpson could recruit help more easily with the end of the harvest in sight. Whatever the reason, the effort could not have lasted more than a month or two. In Irishtown, shortening days and dropping temperatures arrive well before the official onset of winter. As for the 1900 attempt, we have few details. Still, the use of plowing and harrowing is consistent with Blakeny's strategy from 1899, as is reaching a depth not in excess of five feet.

The article adds two remarkable observations. First, the landowner himself, John A. Bishop, and his uncle George led the 1901 operation. Relying on local labour fits Simpson's approach. Offering a stake in the outcome may have been his go-to trading currency. The involvement of John A. and George further raises the storytelling potential of the Bishop family.

Second, the article reveals that Simpson purchased scrapers from the R. F. & M. Co., the Record Foundry and Machine Company established in Moncton in 1855 by Charles B. Record.[246] The manufacturer of plows and other farming equipment would have been a natural supplier for a large treasure hunt. The patented 1883 Fresno scraper, the late-nineteenth-century equivalent of today's motorized bulldozer, revolutionized earth moving. Earlier systems pushed soil aside or shuffled it forward. Scrapers, on the other hand, sliced the earth with a horizontal blade and rolled it within a vertical C-shaped bowl. Advantages included reduced friction, controlled depth, and directed dumping. The use of scrapers—which Blakeny also attested to—implies that the enterprise was thoughtful and delicate. Some sales receipts for the R. F. & M. Co. do survive at the Moncton Museum. Unfortunately, a lack of records for the years in play prevents us from unmasking Simpson that way.[247]

Hotel LeBlanc

A good example of newspapers emphasizing local connections is the mention of Simpson stopping "at Mr. T. B. LeBlanc's hotel on Duke street." The 1901 search had not yet begun in earnest. Perhaps the reporter struck a conversation with Simpson's group in LeBlanc's saloon. It is odd, however, that he makes no reference whatsoever to LeBlanc's participation in Simpson's 1899 quest. Why?

In all likelihood, the journalist was simply unaware of the hotelkeeper's prior involvement. That would be no surprise; the article from September 1899 also fails to identify any of the "two or three Moncton men" who sponsored Simpson's bid. Presumably, a columnist would have identified homegrown collaborators had he had the chance. To our knowledge, the implication of LeBlanc, Warman, and the two McSweeneys only became public in 1937 as part of Blakeny's interview.

Simpson's presence at Hotel LeBlanc in 1901 is still worth pondering. Was our gold seeker paying a visit to his one-time associate? If so, why did he not extend the same courtesy to Blakeny? Indeed, the Sunny Brae excavator seemed uninformed that the Irishtown treasure hunt had been a recurrent, yearly affair. In fact, had he participated in the later 1900 or 1901 attempts, Blakeny would necessarily have learned about any earlier effort from Simpson himself. There can be no more doubt: Blakeny's operation took place in 1899.

Rather than pursue his former partner to reminisce, Simpson likely stayed at LeBlanc's establishment each year out of habit. The mid-tier guesthouse would be in line with his reportedly limited budget, and its saloon would act as a natural venue for meeting sponsors. The innkeeper's personal network is perhaps how our gold seeker hooked up with Blakeny and the other three Moncton financiers. Otherwise, Simpson probably boarded in Irishtown for most of the dig's duration; a round-trip commute between Hotel LeBlanc and Irishtown would deprive him of about two hours each day. Blakeny, recalling he had "slept out there at Irishtown one night," hinted that living on-site was the standard arrangement. We might even have spotted Simpson and his companions in the 1901 Canadian census had canvassing taken place in the fall. The tally, as it turns out, occurred in the spring.

LeBlanc's hotel seldom attracted lodgers deemed worthy of public interest. Accordingly, newspaper gossip sections did not monitor its comings and goings. The establishment's guestbooks, if they survived at all, are presumed lost. Hopes of uncovering Simpson's identity that way seem to have reached an impasse.

Simpson and his partners no doubt journeyed to Moncton by train. Travel agents usually issued anonymous passes containing only information such as ticket number, fare, class, and destination. In the world of seafaring, ships could not leave a harbour before handing over passenger manifests to port authorities. Railways had no need for such records and did not keep any. Documents ranging from receipts to reservations were discarded soon after use.[248] Mass data collection and the tracking of an individual's movements are decidedly modern-day phenomena. And that is why Simpson is once again able to give us the slip.

Legend

The 1901 article includes a legend that largely mirrors Blakeny's account of French troops burying treasure in Irishtown. What the *Daily Transcript*'s version lacks, however, is the naval portion of Blakeny's tale—a pay ship docking at Grindstone Island and dories heading up the Petitcodiac River. The newspaper's variant, for its part, adds a wrinkle to the story of Simpson's map: One of the French soldiers escaped British capture and returned to France. Only afterward did he give the chart to his son as a legacy. So far as the myth goes, the document could have been hastily scribbled on-site, as in Blakeny's yarn. Or it could have been sketched from memory some time later.

Last but not least, we learn that Simpson expected the gold to be worth between $2M and $4M, or between $70M and $140M today. According to his valuation, the Irishtown treasure would comprise anywhere between 400,000 and 800,000 louis d'or gold coins. The booty would weigh on the order of three to six metric tonnes, and each of the legend's putative nine leather bags would tilt the scale at between a third and two-thirds of a tonne.[249] The staggering sum is at odds with the minimal currency that circulated in Acadie during that period.[250] The numbers are difficult to reconcile with Blakeny's yarn. Still, in Simpson's mind, at least, there would have been more than enough treasure to share and too much leftover to spend.

The *Daily Transcript* edition of September 25, 1901, adds several dimensions to Simpson's treasure hunt. The search, we now know, unfolded over at least three years: 1899, 1900, and 1901. Our gold seeker's identity still eludes us, but new evidence reinforces our suspicions that he hailed from Southwestern Ontario. We have learned that he concentrated his operation on the bank of Lynch's Brook. And we have seen how a missing stone marker and a map's crude design undermined his efforts. Details about Simpson's methods, habits, and mindset also paint a richer picture of his quest.

Simpson experienced no fewer than two disappointments by the time he returned to Irishtown in 1901. That, in itself, is a testament to his resilience. The elderly treasure hunter was surely aware of his own lengthening shadow, as each day grew shorter on John Bishop's farmland. He must have wondered how much longer he could carry on. In the end, would he have his summer of glory? Or would he face yet another winter of discontent?

Fort Menagouèche

HISTORICAL · CONTEXT ·

In 1755, after the capture of Fort Beauséjour, the task of seizing Fort Menagouèche (Saint John, NB) fell to naval captain John Rous.[251] Lieutenant Charles Deschamps de Boishébert, the fort's young and capable commander, anticipated the attack.[252] The two men had come to know each other well.

Six years earlier, in 1749, Quebec had sent Boishébert to the Saint John River, where he reaffirmed French presence in the area, guarded a major link to Quebec, and supported Acadian exiles.[253] Rous, for his part, made his quarters at Annapolis Royal (formerly Port Royal) from where he patrolled the Bay of Fundy.[254] France and Britain, while still nominally at peace, each considered continental Acadie as theirs to defend. Rous and Boishébert, it seems, were foreordained enemies.[255]

That same year, Rous sailed his fourteen-gun *Albany* into what is now Saint John Harbour. He called on Boishébert with typical gallantry for the times: "It would afford me much pleasure...," "Until I shall have the honour, as I hope, of seeing you...," "I am very truly, Your Humble Servant...," etc. Invited onboard the *Albany*, Boishébert promised not to shoot first but to stand his ground while diplomats in

Europe haggled over borders. Cordial chivalries aside, both men knew their fight had just begun.

In 1750, the *Aimable Jeanne* left Quebec for Saint John. French authorities, stung by *Le London*'s recent capture, dispatched the armed *Saint-François* to escort it. Vergor, the same ham-fisted officer who would later preside over Fort Beauséjour's defeat, commanded the ten-gun vessel. Rous spotted the French convoy near Cape Sable and gave chase. The outmatched *Saint-François* turned about to confront Rous and enabled the *Aimable Jeanne* to escape.[256]

In 1751, Rous's second, Sylvanus Cobb, seized the supply ship *Aimable* and taunted Boishébert, "If he [Boishébert] maintained the land, I [Cobb] would the sea."[257] In what would constitute a daring *fait d'armes*, Boishébert claims to have led canoes toward the *Aimable* under the cover of his own musketry. He reportedly retook the boat from one side while Cobb and his men abandoned it from the other.[258]

By 1753, Boishébert had erected Fort Menagouèche at the mouth of the Saint John River. In 1755, a month before the siege of Fort Beauséjour, Cobb spotted the *Marguerite* berthing nearby. He alerted the gunboat *Vulture*, which then seized the French vessel.[259]

After Beauséjour's fall, Rous confronted Boishébert one last time. Overmatched, the French officer blew up Fort Menagouèche and retreated up the Saint John River. Rous feared an ambush and refrained from chasing him inland.[260] Henceforth, Boishébert worked at protecting Acadian refugees and at pre-empting Anglo-American raids into continental Acadie.

Blakeny's legend, while uncorroborated, correctly evokes British threats against French supply ships in the Bay of Fundy. Some events even bear superficial similarities to Blakeny's tale. For instance, in November 1750, a French cargo ship bound for Saint John encountered a British cruiser in the waters between continental and peninsular Acadie. It sought shelter ashore near Chipoudie (Hopewell, NB), an Acadian village within view of Grindstone Island. Two of the cruiser's whaleboats pursued it landward and ransacked it. The British would have seized the vessel itself had it not been for a nighttime intervention by Chipoudie's inhabitants.[261]

Naval conflict was inevitable in the Bay of Fundy. Fort Beauséjour could get deliveries via Baie Verte, but Fort Menagouèche was more isolated. Only small quantities of goods could travel there by portage. France therefore had no choice but to send food and materiel on a long and difficult journey around peninsular Acadie.[262]

Conceivably, Blakeny's legend could be rooted in the French imperative to resupply Fort Menagouèche. The scenario, though, suffers from plot holes of its own. Boishébert only had a few men under his command and only a few Acadian families to protect. His encampment, like Fort Gaspareaux, was little more than a fortified warehouse.[263] Boishébert also received instructions to build and operate the place at very low cost.[264] He was always in need of provisions. What he did not require, though, was vast sums of money. Moreover, the introduction of gold coins in Acadie would immediately face an insurmountable problem unless it were accompanied by a corresponding influx—and wide circulation—of smaller silver, copper, and token denominations. A single louis d'or had a nominal value of 24 livres at the time, or about $680 in today's currency.[265] Most transactions could not take place without the ability to give back change. Chances that a French ship risked carrying nine leather bags filled with gold into the well-guarded Bay of Fundy appear less than slim.

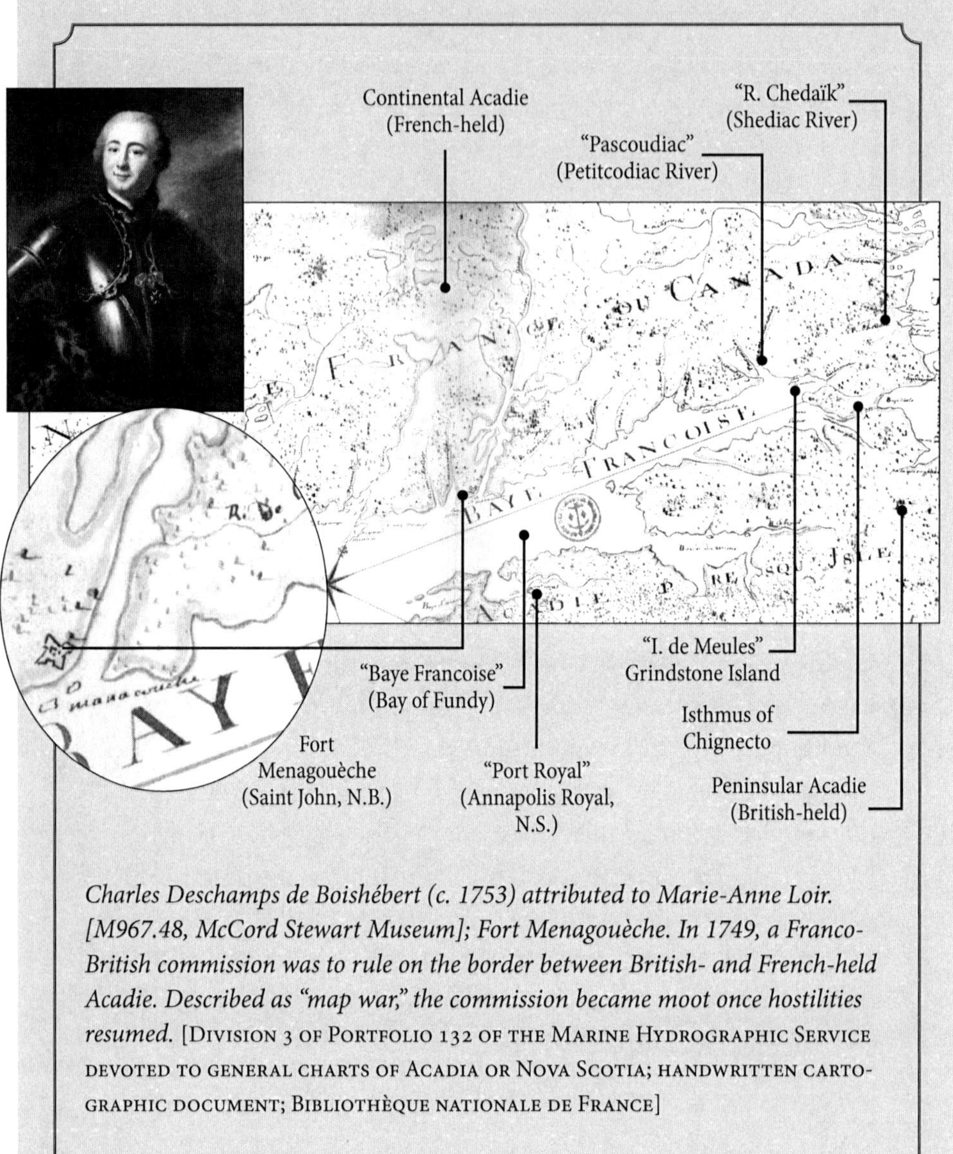

Charles Deschamps de Boishébert (c. 1753) attributed to Marie-Anne Loir. [M967.48, McCord Stewart Museum]; Fort Menagouèche. In 1749, a Franco-British commission was to rule on the border between British- and French-held Acadie. Described as "map war," the commission became moot once hostilities resumed. [Division 3 of Portfolio 132 of the Marine Hydrographic Service devoted to general charts of Acadia or Nova Scotia; handwritten cartographic document; Bibliothèque nationale de France]

Chapter 11
The Trilogy of the Times

One time is happenstance, two times is coincidence, three times is intentional.
– old adage

On December 2, 1876, the Chicago *Daily News* posted the headline "Er us siht la Etsll iws nel lum cmeht" for an article warning of famine in Serbia. Its rival, the *Evening Post*, belonged to the McMullen brothers, who reprinted the dispatch verbatim the next day. Only, when not spelled backwards, the headline reads, "The McMullens will steal this sure." The McMullens had indeed lifted their competitor's material, as they had often done before. Their newspaper, exposed by the stunt for its fraudulent ways, saw its subscriber numbers nosedive. In a karmic twist, the *Daily News* repurchased the diminished *Evening Post* two years later.[266]

While the *Daily News*'s ruse revealed blatant plagiarism, thieving was usually not to blame if different publishers put out identical columns. Rather, matching local content was more likely the work of freelancers who sold their pieces' non-exclusive rights to more than one outlet. Nothing prevented the authors from reworking their submissions. Separate versions could contain repurposed bits mixed in with novel elements.

It is with freelancing in mind that we approach the account of Simpson's return to Irishtown in 1901. Not to be outdone by its *Daily Transcript* rival, the *Daily Times* posted a similar story to theirs on the same day. The two reports are undeniable siblings, yet each includes information that does not appear in the other. We can therefore rule out wholesale plagiarism and treat the two pieces as adaptations written by a common author, especially since they appeared in print on the same day. We will skim over redundant portions and concentrate on new details. To its credit, though, the *Daily Times* also did something the *Daily Transcript* never did: It followed up.

Two additional articles, printed on October 17 and 30 respectively, updated readers on Simpson's progress. Let us tackle each column from the *Daily Times* trilogy in turn. Each of them is reproduced in full under the date on which it appeared.

September 25, 1901

Persistent Treasure Seekers

An Ontario Man's Search for Hidden Millions.

Supposed to Have Been Buried Near Moncton
by the Early French Settlers.

> Two years ago THE TIMES contained an account of a search being made for hidden treasure a few miles out the Irishtown road by a man named Simpson, hailing from Ontario. On Thursday last the same gentleman, who is a man of about sixty years of age, arrived in Moncton in company with three other gentlemen named Wheld, Lewis and Cobb, all belonging to London, Ontario, and stopping at Mr. T. B. LeBlanc's hotel on Duke street. Mr. Simpson and party represent a company and it is the intention to continue the search for the millions of gold which Simpson alleges is buried in this vicinity. Last year operations were carried along the small creek just below the city reservoir. This creek passes through John Bishop's farm. About an acre of ground was plowed over, harrowed and dug into to the depth of about four or five feet. A diligent search was made by Simpson and his fellow workmen on the previous visit. Huge stones were quarried from the ground, trees were uprooted and the most minute search possible was made upon the plot of ground fixed upon as the probable location of the much sought for treasure. So far as known, however, the relentless search of Simpson and his friends has been fruitless. This conclusion is borne out by the fact that the Ontario man has returned again this year with reinforcements to continue the search.

The party are equipped with charts and engineers have been engaged at different times to aid the seekers in locating the plot of earth which is expected to yield up its treasure.

Mr. Simpson is accompanied each year by new men, showing that he is able to convince more than one individual of the likelihood of the labors eventually being rewarded. This year, however, the number of searchers has been increased from two to four. Since arriving here Mr. Simpson and party have been looking over the ground and Mr. Geo. W. McCready has also been taken along to do some engineering before the work of digging is commenced. Messrs. Simpson and Lewis are men well up in years, the former being sixty or over and the latter probably seventy, while Wheld and Cobb are younger men. Wheld appears to be the financier of the party and leaves the impression that he has sufficient of this world's goods already to keep him being classed with the ordinary mortals who have to toil for the daily bread.

Simpson is the main man in the search. He is supposed to hold all the secrets relating to its location, how it came to be consigned to the earth for safe keeping and the amount that will be found in the pot when it is unearthed. But he is very reticent about the matter and is a man of action rather than talk, at least while he is in Moncton.

The treasure the Ontario men are in search of is supposed to amount to from two and a half to four million dollars in gold, and it is alleged was buried in the neighbourhood where the search has been carried on, by the early French settlers at the time the English took possession of the country. The story runs that the men who buried it were all captured by the English, but one of the party who afterwards escaped and made his way back to France, left as a legacy to his son a description of the hidden gold and a chart showing its location. This information left to the descendants of one of the early French settlers of this part of the country, finally passed into other hands, and, it is said, that it is this information upon which Simpson and his friends are now working. Whether the brittle thread of life will hold out long enough for the man who began the search, to induce the soil along the Irishtown road to give up the fabulous sum it is thought to have entrusted to its keeping, time alone will tell.[267]

The *Daily Times* column differs from its *Daily Transcript* counterpart in several important respects. Crucially, it provides fresh details about the treasure hunters. The subheading—"An Ontario Man's Search for Hidden Millions"—confirms our suspicions that Simpson called Ontario home. The text alludes to his origins twice more, but it does not offer much else. "Ontario" appears to be good enough for our gold seeker. Wheld, Lewis, and Cobb, however, benefit from the much more specific "London." Clearly, Simpson—a "very reticent" individual who was "a man of action rather than talk"—remained coy around reporters. For all we know, he resided in London as well and simply declined to say so.

The article also paints a more fleshed-out picture of Simpson and his companions—"new men" who had not accompanied him before. Simpson and Lewis were both "well up in years." Simpson was "about sixty" and/or "sixty or over." Lewis was "probably seventy." Wheld and Cobb were "younger men." Wheld seemed to be one of the expedition's sponsors. Perhaps he represented the "company" that held a stake in the hunt.

We still lack first names, but Wheld, Lewis, and Cobb may yet help us crack Simpson's identity. Any grouping of the surnames—a shared London employer, for example—would constitute an encouraging lead. Wheld, a younger, wealthy London individual with an uncommon patronym, is especially promising in that regard. We will tackle his case in a later chapter.

The article offers new details about Simpson's search the year before. Only one man accompanied Simpson in 1900. Also, far from being plow-ready, the site was scattered with stones and vegetation the operation had to remove. The absence of trees on the eastern bank of Lynch's Brook in the 1944 aerial shot ties in well with this information.

The text specifies that Geo. W. McCready did some engineering before the start of the 1901 dig. George Wellsley McCready, Moncton's go-to scientist at the time, was a gifted mathematician and inventor. He earned a US patent in 1874 for a small boring machine.[268] The British Chronological Association elected him in 1892 and named him premier chronologist of Canada. His 1887 work on a perpetual time reckoner enabled "a person to fix any date, no matter how remote, past or future, (limited to the Christian era)."[269] He also kept temperature records, observed astronomical phenomena, and calculated timetables for Moncton's tidal bore—the single breaking wavefront that fills the Petitcodiac River in one fell swoop as the Bay of Fundy's waters rise.[270] As it happens, his brother Samuel searched for Captain Kidd's treasure on the Bay of Fundy's foreboding Isle Haute in 1879.[271] He and his companions were feared lost when their empty boat washed ashore. Only later did George McCready learn that the men were unharmed.[272]

McCready was a key developer of Moncton's infrastructure. He worked closely with the Harris brothers, who helped introduce gas and light to the city in 1878, erect its sugar refinery in 1880, and launch its street car in 1894.[273] The Harrises also oversaw the Moncton Gas and Water Company that built the Moncton reservoir and brought running water to the city.[274] McCready's familiarity with the pre- and post-reservoir hydrography was instrumental to the project.[275]

George Wellsley McCready, gifted mathematician, inventor, first city engineer of Moncton, and Simpson advisor. [PANB P304-1-10]

Clearly, the experts Simpson relied on were no amateurs. McCready, it turns out, was also Blakeny's first cousin. He may well have led the quest's engineering team in 1899. Living descendants of McCready were unaware of his involvement.[276]

As for buried treasure, the *Daily Times* and *Daily Transcript* offer similar backstories, but they diverge on one important point. The first claims that "early French settlers" interred the gold, whereas the second attributes the deed to "French soldiers." To be sure, the fall of Fort Beauséjour and the ensuing Acadian expulsion are the military and civilian sides of the same coin. Either way, people hide valuables during upheavals. It is little surprise, then, that local legends should revolve around either French troops or Acadian colonists. The discrepancy may come down to command of the region's history. At the time, English-speaking newspaper editors perhaps thought of "early French settlers" and "French soldiers" as vaguely interchangeable. More noteworthy for us, though, is that the naval component of Blakeny's tale is again missing.

October 17, 1901

The Treasure Seeker's Dream

To those who are familiar with the history of the search being made by an Ontario man named Simpson for treasure supposed to be buried near Moncton, there is something interesting in the excavating operations now being carried on out the Irishtown Road. For the last four or five weeks Simpson and party have been hard at work with a gang of men and teams plowing and digging into the earth with the quiet determination of men who seemingly know what they are about. Search for the several millions of dollars in gold, supposed to have been consigned to the earth by the French at the time the English took possession of the country, is confined to the east bank of the small stream leading from the city reservoir, on the farms of John Bishop and Richard Anketell. Last year Simpson directed operations in that locality, and this year the work of plowing and scraping the earth out of the hill has been continued along down the stream. The work is carried on systematically and a stretch of territory about two or three hundred yards in length has been gone over. The men dig to the depth of three and four feet and in some places find the ground at that distance very hard to work with the plow. At the present time the four men interested in the search stand guard over eight labourers and four teams. Two men and a team are kept busy and three teams follow in the wake with scrapers. And thus the work has gone on for the past month.

A TIMES representative, who visited the scene of operations yesterday at the rear of Mr. Richard Anketell's farm, was told by one of the promoters that the search would be continued for two weeks longer. If nothing was discovered at the end of that time, the

> searchers fear that the buried treasure will never be unearthed. The men promoting the work represent a company in Ontario and are prosecuting the search according to a chart alleged to have been handed down by some of the old French settlers and which is now in the possession of Simpson. As near as can be figured out from this chart the gold is supposed to have been buried on the bank of the creek where the Ontario men are now at work. The chart designates a starting point on the old French road leading in the direction of Shediac, and states that the treasure was buried on the east bank of a south running stream; and, according to the best interpretations of the plan, the small creek where operations are now being carried on, is the stream referred to.
>
> The searchers are not very sanguine about finding the millions which the chart alleges are buried there, but are working on the principal that if nothing is invested nothing will be found.
>
> The man who began the search years ago still has dreams, however, of unearthing the pot of gold, and followed the plow listening for the expected clink of the steel against the metal vessel supposed to contain the gold, with almost as much eagerness as when he began his search.[277]

Simpson's group kept a watchful eye on hired labour. The worry, no doubt, was that a worker would fail to report the treasure and later retrieve it for himself. A plow first opened the soil, like before; a trailing queue of scrapers then exposed thin layers of dirt. The operation carried on in this way "along down the stream"—a confirmation of its southward progress. Had the journalist used "up along the stream" instead, a northerly march would come to mind. The southerly advance is also evident from its evolution on the ground: Between September 25 and October 17, the enterprise invaded the property of Richard Anketell, John Bishop's immediate neighbour to the south. During that interval, Simpson presumably exhumed whatever stretch remained of the Bishop section.

The column specifies that the search has scoured a stretch of territory "about two or three hundred yards in length." The statistic could refer to headway made either in 1901 alone or since 1899. Regardless, the figure fully covers the Bishop portion of Lynch's Brook. But why does Blakeny speak of acres, whereas the article mentions yards? The switch in units is sensible given

Simpson's follow-the-bank strategy: By 1901, length—not area—had become a better descriptor of the excavation's growing, snake-like shape.

The text also offers fresh details about Simpson's map: "The chart…states that the treasure was buried on the east bank of a south running stream." The dig site, as we might expect, had no choice but to agree with the document. We now have black-on-white confirmation that Simpson searched only on the eastern side of Lynch's Brook.

A new feature on Simpson's map is also the most identifiable: "the old French road leading in the direction of Shediac." Historical sources tell us the old French road to Shediac was a portage route used by France's military between 1749 and 1751. A rough trail through marshes, forests, and rivers, it fell into disrepair after Britain's conquest of Acadie. Visible signs of it vanished soon thereafter. But, when put in proper context, the parchment's reference to the ancient path is nothing short of extraordinary.

Memories of the old French road to Shediac—let alone of its location—evaporated within a few generations.[278] Today, we are aware of its existence only because twentieth-century archivists catalogued overseas papers pertaining to Acadie's past.[279] How, then, could the maker of Simpson's chart incorporate the forgotten trackway unless he himself was a contemporary of it? The implications are profound. We cannot ascertain, at this stage, whether the document was a bona fide treasure map. The text, though, could well constitute an original French manuscript from the mid 1700s.

The mention of the "clink of the steel" against the "metal vessel" runs counter to the nine leather bags referenced in Blakeny's story. And again, the naval portion of Blakeny's legend is missing.

Lastly, Simpson's group was losing faith. Should the next two weeks not yield anything, the article writes, "searchers fear that the buried treasure will never be unearthed." Members of the expedition were also "not very sanguine" about their chances—a lowering of expectations that prepares the mind for failure. Aphorisms such as "if nothing is invested nothing will be found" propped up hopes. But these are the words of men who entertain thoughts of defeat as much as victory. Simpson, for his part, remained upbeat and dreamed of gold "with almost as much eagerness as when he began his search." His irreducible belief in an Irishtown hoard, like Blakeny's, appeared to sooth his anxieties. Any number of excuses—a crude map, altered terrain, a missing stone, insufficient money, engineering errors, or too little time—could explain away his inability to locate the loot. Blaming fate would spare him the torment of re-evaluating his quest's legitimacy.

October 30, 1901

The final article in the *Daily Times* trilogy appeared under the headline "The Treasure Seekers" and said, in full:

> The Ontario treasure seekers, who have been carrying on operations on the farms of John Bishop and Richard Anketell, Irishtown road, in search of buried millions, have quit work for the season and returned home. So far as those engaged at the work are aware, Simpson and party did not succeed in unearthing the treasure but returned to Ontario with nothing more than photographs of the field of operations to show the other parties financially interested in the search.[280]

This last article is the shortest of the *Daily Times* trilogy. It may also be the anticlimactic finale of the saga. Pictures of field operations, if they still exist, would be a fitting coda. Simpson and his partners "quit work for the season." But it would be reading too much into the statement to suggest that they came back in 1902. Hopes were already dwindling. After having claimed that "the money is on the Bishop property or it is nowhere," our gold seeker would find it difficult to convince new sponsors to look elsewhere.

Previous accounts of Simpson's quest are akin to snapshots. The *Daily Times* trilogy, in contrast, is more like a movie. The period between September 25 and October 30 captures the search in unprecedented detail. We can monitor progress on the ground. We can sense how hope turned to despondency. The article from October 30 is also the final contemporaneous depiction of Simpson's dig my research has uncovered. Unfortunately, issues of the Moncton *Daily Times* for the whole of 1902 and much of 1903 are missing, and I could locate no further mention of Simpson's adventure in the *Daily Transcript*. I was lucky to find as much as I did. If other articles have not survived, they are our collective loss.

We have reached something of a natural conclusion to Simpson's day-to-day operations in Irishtown. Perhaps it is just as well. The last two chapters have railroaded clues to later parts of the book. We are now free to retake control of the investigative narrative. Simpson's map remains its most intriguing element. But, unless we crack our elusive treasure seeker's identity, there can be little hope of progress. Our own quest has now become a manhunt.

Simply put, who was Simpson?

The Great Acadian Expulsion

We are now upon a great and noble scheme of sending the neutral French out of this province.

– *Pennsylvania Gazette*, September 4, 1755

HISTORICAL · CONTEXT ·

The fall of Fort Beauséjour in 1755 spelled the end of an Acadian golden age.[281] Britain immediately began removing thousands of Acadians from the only land they and generations of their ancestors had ever known. Some fled across forests and rivers. Untold numbers perished from starvation and disease while hiding in refugee camps.[282] Those who sheltered in Quebec were arguably the luckier ones. Yet many who survived the difficult trip died soon thereafter.[283] Only a minority of Acadians eluded the dragnet. All suffered its consequences.

In the end, the British deported upward of eleven thousand people—more than three-quarters of the Acadian population at the time—to faraway destinations. The New England colonial press extolled the mass eviction as "A Great and Noble Scheme."[284] Hundreds drowned at sea. Families were separated. Those sent to New England, Great Britain, or the Caribbean found their surroundings foreign and unwelcoming.[285] Those who eventually reached France received only mixed sympathy. The Acadians' desire to band together vexed the French government's efforts at taking them in or at resettling them elsewhere. Some did establish a permanent home in France. Others left for Louisiana, where they and their descendants became known as Cajuns.[286]

Britain's policy of forced removal lasted until 1763. Small groups of Acadians began returning the following year after swearing allegiance to the British crown. Destitute and stripped of their old lands, they had no choice but to begin anew in less fertile areas of their former colony. Most had been farmers steeped in pastoral traditions. Many had to reinvent themselves and earn a living from fishing or logging.[287]

The Great Acadian Expulsion—or *Grand Dérangement*, as the Acadians call it—constitutes a dark chapter in Canada's history.[288] In 1847, American writer Henry Wadsworth Longfellow brought the plight to public attention with his widely read epic poem *Evangeline, A Tale of Acadie.* Repercussions of the deportation still reverberate to this day. Yet there is perhaps no better tribute to the resilience of the Acadian people than their own modern-day successes. Acadian author Antonine Maillet, for instance, won France's prestigious Prix Goncourt in 1979 for her novel *Pélagie-la-Charette*. Nowadays, Acadians are active in every sphere of society, and they are thriving while keeping their heritage alive.[289]

Great upheavals prompt the vulnerable to hide their valuables. In the English-speaking world, East Coast legends tell of treasure buried by Acadians as the British menace neared.[290] The stories are not without foundation. A trickle of small finds on old Acadian lands has sustained the romance.[291] Acadian folklore itself is also not without tales of long-lost riches. One rumour tells of gold and silver found near Moncton by Eustache Babin in Leger Corner (now Dieppe) in the mid-to-late nineteenth century. Understandably, though, Acadian folklore makes virtually no references to the wealth of its own people.[292] In truth, the Acadians lived modestly and had few assets to conceal before the *Grand Dérangement* forever upended their existence.[293]

A 1758 watercolour by British army officer Thomas Davies depicts the British attack on the Acadian village of Grimross. It is the only contemporaneous illustration of the Great Acadian Expulsion. [Thomas Davies, Public domain, via Wikimedia Commons]

Chapter 12
The House of Weld

We few, we happy few, we band of brothers.
– William Shakespeare, *Henry V*

In 1891, William Weld tried to repair a water leak at his residence in London, Ontario. A tank lay suspended from the ceiling. A small swing window below the roof's overhang provided the only means of access. Weld climbed through the opening and slipped headfirst into the reservoir. Unable to extricate himself, he may have cried out for help. If he did, his calls went unanswered. Weld drowned.

Weld's passing sent shockwaves throughout the country. Born in England in 1824, he emigrated to Canada and settled near London, Ontario. There, he studied the breeding of plants and animals. He founded the *Farmer's Advocate* newspaper to keep readers abreast of developments in the field. He distributed improved grains across the land from his Weldwood estate, the first experimental farm in Canada. He also owned the William Weld Company and the London Printing and Lithographing Company. Original, passionate, and high-minded, he laid the groundwork for scientific agriculture in the nation.[294]

Could Weld have anything to do with Wheld, the London man who reportedly bankrolled Simpson's quest in 1901? It would take more than a shared city and similar surnames to intuit a link; however, when he emigrated to Canada, Weld introduced a new family name into the country.

And *that* may bring us a step closer to Simpson.

Soundex Magic

An online query in the digitized 1901 Canadian census for the name "Wheld" returns exactly…nothing. But twenty-first-century technology has a few tricks up its sleeve. Any number of reasons could account for corrupted census text: illiteracy, poor handwriting, misspellings, transcription errors, etc. One way around this problem is the Soundex algorithm, which indexes words based on sound rather than spelling. This way, patronyms with similar pronunciations (e.g., Sherman, Sharman, Shireman, and Sirman) fall under the same Soundex code.

The Canadian tally for 1901 includes millions of entries. It is no surprise, then, that a Soundex query for Wheld yields nearly one thousand results with over sixty spelling variations. But we also know that Wheld was "younger" than Simpson's "sixty or over" and that he was from London. If we filter for males between twenty and sixty for that city and its encompassing county of Middlesex, the list dwindles to only sixteen men and five patronyms: Walt (2), Weld (8), Wild (4), Woollatt (1), and Wyld (1).

Further querying reveals that the name Weld was a rarity outside the London region. Of the fifty-eight people in Canada called Weld, fifty-three (91 percent) resided in Ontario, and forty (69 percent) made their homes in London or Middlesex County. By comparison, Ontario accounted for only 40 percent of Canada's population. London/Middlesex, for its part, constituted only 2 percent. The overrepresentation of the Weld patronym in and around the city is attributable to one thing: William Weld had nine sons.

It would be remarkable if, despite its dense clustering around London, the Weld surname were unrelated to Simpson's treasure hunt. Still, statistics can mean little in the search for a single individual.

It is now apparent that the Moncton journalist committed a typographical error. No one in Canada—let alone London—went by the name Wheld. But even if the Soundex algorithm detects a similarity between Wheld and Woollatt, for instance, the human ear does not. Readers can also judge for themselves that Weld has the same pronunciation as Wheld, whereas Walt, Wild, or Wyld do not.

Money is the other clue to Wheld's identity. He appeared "to be the financier of the party" and he seemed to have "sufficient of this world's goods already to keep him being classed with the ordinary mortals who have to toil for the daily bread." His affluence rules out the two Walts (dry-goods clerk; farmer), the four Wilds (GTR worker; carpenter; labourer; farmer), Woollatt (foreman), and Wyld (labourer). No matter how we tackle the problem, the Weld patronym rises to the top. William Weld, dead since 1891, could not have taken part in Simpson's treasure hunt himself. But someone in his immediate family most assuredly did.

The House of Weld

The Weld surname had become a prominent one in London by the turn of the twentieth century. The House of Weld—a term *Maclean's* magazine coined in 1931—also applied to William Weld's nine sons, one of whom was Simpson's likely search partner and potential financier.[295]

Name	Home (1901)	Profession (1901)
William Stephen	Delaware, Middlesex, Ontario	Farmer, Weldwood Experimental Farm Corporate holder, former president, William Weld Co. Ltd.
Joseph	London, Ontario	Secretary, Assistant Manager, William Weld Co. Ltd., Farmer's Advocate
Henry	—	—
John	London, Ontario	General Manager, William Weld Co. Ltd., Farmer's Advocate Vice President, London Printing and Lithographic Co.
Edmund	London, Ontario	Barrister, Solicitor
Octavius	Burrard, British Columbia	Medical Physician
Thomas Saxon	London, Ontario	President, London Printing and Lithographic Co.
Charles George	Essex, Ontario	Farmer
Corbin	London, Ontario	Commercial Traveller (salesperson), London Printing and Lithographing Co.

From the table on page 127, we can immediately rule out Henry, who passed away in 1887.[296] Weld's eight remaining sons were between thirty-three and fifty-five years old in 1901—well within the *Daily Times*'s description of Wheld as "younger" than Simpson's "about sixty" and "sixty or over." Five sons worked at their father's businesses and lived in or around London. Three others had struck out on their own.

We now have eight Weld brothers under scrutiny. Our task is not unlike the one in which we whittled six McSweeney siblings down to two. But while events in Hanford Blakeny's biography were key in identifying the two McSweeneys, we have no such luxury in Wheld's case. Another approach is to proceed by alibi. That is, by necessity, a Weld brother could not be in two locations at once. Any evidence putting him far from Moncton during the 1901 dig would rule him out. First, though, let us refresh the time frame of Simpson's visit that year.

The Moncton *Daily Times* wrote on Wednesday, September 25, that Simpson and his group arrived in Moncton "on Thursday last," or September 19. It also reported on October 17 that "the search would be continued for two weeks longer." The update from October 30 bears this out. Proof of a Weld brother not in Moncton during that time frame constitutes a valid alibi.

William Stephen managed the family's Weldwood farm in Delaware (Middlesex County, ON). The Delaware Agricultural Society's fall show attracted a large crowd on October 9. We do not know whether William Stephen attended the event. Still, he was most likely on hand at some point during the twenty-day lead-up in his capacity as fair director.[297] By alibi logic, William Stephen is at best an improbable candidate to fill Wheld's shoes.

Four Weld brothers—Joseph, John, Edmund, and Corbin—played lawn bowling at the London Rowing Club. Local newspapers published competition results along with participant names. Joseph Weld took part in a game on September 25, 1901—six days after Wheld arrived in Moncton.[298] John Weld presented medals and prizes as club president on October 9, 1901, or fourteen days into the Irishtown search.[299] Edmund recorded his last match on September 21, two days after Wheld set foot in Moncton.[300] These three brothers have valid alibis.

Octavius, a medical doctor, settled near Vancouver. He was anything but a Londoner by 1901, given his six-year practice in Vancouver and prior stints elsewhere in the world. His first child was born in 1900. His wife expected another one in early 1902. For professional, geographical, and personal reasons, he would have been hard-pressed to prepare an expedition to Moncton with Londoners Cobb and Lewis, let alone take part in one.

Thomas Saxon did not play lawn bowling, unlike the other London-based brothers. The reason, perhaps, is that he was in ill health.[301] He left for southern France to care for his fragile state on November 16, 1901, only two weeks after Simpson's group had quit Moncton.[302] He continued shunning Ontario winters before eventually settling in England, where he died at forty-five. His undocumented ailment caused him to abandon his breeding of racehorses.[303] He was evidently prosperous and fit enough to travel. Yet it is debatable whether his medical condition would have allowed him to keep up with Irishtown labourers for long hours, on rough terrain, and in variable autumn weather. At best, he is a potential but uncertain candidate for Wheld.

Early fall was harvest season. Everyone's presence in the field was mandatory. A farmer such as Charles George could ill afford to leave home for a month around mid-September. He should be all but ruled out on that basis. For that matter, so should William Stephen, the Delaware farmer and fair director who inherited his father's Weldwood estate. For good measure, Charles George settled near Windsor and was no longer a Londoner himself in 1901.[304]

Corbin recorded his last bowling game on September 7, well before Simpson's late-September expedition.[305] He married in 1900 but remained childless until 1910.[306] He worked as a travelling salesperson for the *Farmer's Advocate*.[307] He was likely more at liberty than his other siblings to journey elsewhere for long periods. A London urbanite who cycled in full gentleman regalia, he could have struck a Moncton reporter as someone from the upper class. He easily tops our list of Weld candidates.[308]

But can clues from Corbin's life move our investigation a step further?

Corbin Weld

Corbin, the youngest of William Weld's nine sons, had his pick of models to emulate. He joined sports clubs and was fond of hunting, cycling, lawn bowling, and lacrosse.[309] He attended celebratory banquets of the St. George's

Lawn bowling in London, Ontario (c. 1905). The sport was popular near the turn of the twentieth century. Newspapers printed scores of local tournaments almost daily. [Archives of Ontario via Wikimedia Commons]

Society and Saint Andrew's Society.[310] His profession of salesman no doubt involved networking and would require an affable disposition. And his birthright to the House of Weld perhaps provided him additional means and notoriety. All told, he had the early makings of a socialite.

Corbin wed Ida English in 1900 at the age of thirty-two.[311] The Weld family dispatched him to Manitoba a few years later to manage the Winnipeg arm of its *Farmer's Advocate* newspaper.[312] His only child, Florence Muriel, was born there.[313] He recycled himself as a produce inspector by 1916.[314] He then moved to Kelowna (BC) and worked in insurance.[315] His marriage did not last. The couple eventually separated but never divorced.[316] He returned to Manitoba and retired in 1932 as a fruit importer. He passed away in St. Boniface, near Winnipeg, in 1942.[317]

An interview with Corbin's only surviving grandchild, Elizabeth Muriel Anderson, did not teach us much else. She never met her grandfather and learned nothing about him from her mother. Ultimately, we know little about Corbin's life. No hard evidence confirms his potential association with Simpson.

His love of lawn bowling, however, may yet shed some light.

The Cobb "Coincidence"

In 1911, Corbin travelled back to his native London to participate in a competition of the Western Ontario Bowling Association. He skippered Winnipeg's London Old Boys and brought along three teammates.[318] His registration on the tournament roster, interestingly, is under the name Cobb Weld. Indeed, the local press made much of "the inimitable" Cobb Weld's return to the city.[319] The London *Advertiser* switches seamlessly between Corbin and its Cobb diminutive.[320] Corbin, it seems, carried the moniker Cobb during his youth and kept using it into adulthood.

Simpson's four-man party from 1901 included Wheld, Cobb, and Lewis. The revelation that Corbin went by "Cobb" is therefore troubling. What are the odds, in a group of four, that an uncommon name constitutes one person's first and another's last? The apparent coincidence deserves a shot at a better explanation.

Perhaps the Moncton reporter mistook Corbin's first name for another searcher's last name. If he did, then he unwittingly confirmed Wheld's identity. Still, the interpretation remains unsatisfying. We should seek a scenario in which the confusion between Wheld and Cobb comes about more naturally. One possibility stands out: What if there had been not one Weld brother in Irishtown but *two*?

Thomas Saxon, the frail president of the family's London printing business, is worth reconsidering. His status and demeanour could have overshadowed his younger sibling as the expedition's likely financier. But if he joined Corbin in Irishtown, how could the newspaper have ended up with "Wheld" and "Cobb"?

The journalist would only need to introduce himself.

Maybe Thomas Saxon replied with his last name: Weld. Corbin, meanwhile, could have answered with his first name: Cobb. Another possibility is that, instead of soliciting information directly, the reporter inferred surnames from casual observation. It would be easy to assume, for instance, that someone addressing Corbin as "Cobb" made a reference to his last name rather than his first. Either way, we already know the correspondent erred on spelling. He could have settled on "Wheld" and "Cobb" when, perhaps, he should have noted "Weld" and "Weld."

Speculation about two Weld brothers in Irishtown is by no means proof of it. Coincidences do happen occasionally. Under the happenstance scenario, Simpson's companion could have been James Cobb, a twenty-four-year-old labourer who lived in Delaware (Middlesex County, ON).[321] Nothing seems to link him to the Weld family; the Weldwood farm, also in Delaware, lay some distance away. No one else between the ages of twenty and sixty and with the Cobb surname (including Soundex variations) resided in or around London. With Cobb's very surname in doubt, further deductive progress is difficult.

We can conclude much the same about Lewis, the other member of Simpson's search party. He appeared promising initially because he was "probably seventy" and made his home in London. But his surname was a common one. The city and its surrounding county were populous even at the time. In all, there were twelve Lewis men between sixty and eighty in and around London (including Soundex variations). None had any discernable ties to the Weld clan. The appellation is also valid both as a last name and a first. Who is to say the reporter did not confuse the two? The Lewis lead may well have run its course.

Whether Thomas Saxon—or another Weld brother—travelled with Corbin to Irishtown remains speculative. The idea, though, is still very much worth pursuing, albeit by using another approach.

Follow the Money

Let us set aside geographical alibis and follow the money trail instead. Blakeny's figure of $1,000, the amount raised in 1899, is a good indication of cost for searching for treasure on Bishop's farmstead. The 1901 effort was shorter (one month vs. two), involved fewer labourers (eight vs. twenty to thirty men), and used fewer teams of horses (four vs. six or seven). Even then, if we include Simpson's purchase of scrapers, the 1901 operation would add up to a substantional portion of the funds spent in 1899. Simpson needed no fewer than four of Moncton's wealthiest elites in 1899 to tackle the project. So how could Corbin—a travelling salesperson—have singlehandedly sponsored a comparable attempt in 1901? The answer is simple: He could not.

The 1901 Canadian census recorded income from wages. Corbin likely worked on commission, and so the tally reports no salary in his case.[322] But he could not have taken home more than his boss and brother, Thomas Saxon, who received $600 a year as president of the London Printing and Lithographic Co.[323] John, the general manager of the William Weld Co., pocketed $1,200.[324] Joseph, the secretary and assistant manager, collected $600.[325] If his peers are any indication, Edmund made about $2,000 as a London barrister and solicitor. Octavius, the Vancouver physician, netted $3,000.[326]

The cost of Simpson's expedition would represent more than a full year of Corbin's earnings. To be sure, he and his brothers may have been better off than what the census reflects, given their shares in the family corporations and perhaps some inheritance money. Still, they were by no means wealthy.[327] William Weld, the clan's founder, started his commercial ventures out of belief in his cause. He sustained his projects by selling two farms, mortgaging his homestead, and taking a chattel mortgage on his stocks. The *Farmer's Advocate* was never very profitable. It first peddled its subscriptions on foot.[328] In the end, the patriarch left behind neither an empire nor vast cash reserves but modest, well-run operations that paid senior management upper-middle-class wages.[329] Weld and his descendants had to work for a living.

In short, no Weld brother could have financed Simpson's search effort on his own. Collectively, though, the Weld family easily had the means to do so. And it could have done so in one of two ways. Chipping in personal funds would be the more straightforward option. Alternatively, perhaps one of the Weld businesses justified underwriting the 1901 venture as a high-risk, high-reward investment. The Moncton reporter did relay that Simpson and his party "represent a company." There is little evidence to go on. On balance, however, commercial interests may well have sponsored Simpson's 1901 expedition. If they did, then traces could persist in the Welds' firm records. Sadly, account books for the period, if they have survived at all, have seemingly vanished.

If the Welds joined forces with other London backers, they must have done so privately. The Archives of Ontario lists no full or limited partnership involving any of the Weld brothers or any individuals named Simpson, Cobb, Weld/Wheld, or Lewis in the whole of Ontario for the years in play. Incorporation documents and letters patent, for their part, suffer from poor indexing. But, as

The brick building at 122 Carling Street that housed the Farmer's Advocate. [Hilda Vanstone, Photographer; PG F276, Ivey Family London Room, London Public Library, London, ON]

we saw before, incorporation would have been unnecessarily complex, costly, and time consuming. Regardless, everything still points to the House of Weld. And whether it used personal or commercial funds, only one man could have led the charge: John "The Chief" Weld.

John "The Chief" Weld

Sources describe John Weld as squared-faced, rugged-featured, and broad-shouldered. He possessed an indomitable temperament. His father groomed him to take over the family businesses. He rose to the rank of foreman at the London *Free Press* and later worked at the New York *Sun*. He also journeyed to Chicago, then to Saskatchewan, where he pioneered a farming homestead. He finally returned home to apprentice under his father's tutelage.

John became general manager of the William Weld Company. He eventually held many titles simultaneously: president of the London Printing and Lithographic Co., president of the Bryant Press in Toronto, and president of the Farmer's Advocate Press in Winnipeg. Friends and colleagues viewed him as a force of nature. They all called him "The Chief." He was also the

Weld clan's decision maker and ultimate arbiter. His family's companies, while still of modest size in 1901, prospered enormously under his guidance. He possessed a "nose for news" and an affinity for "opportunities for leadership." His editorial approach stated that "no expense should be spared in the securing of worthwhile material." He suffered a heat stroke at an airshow in 1931 and died a few days later at his London home. At the time of his passing, the Weld consortium ranked among the "first half dozen similar businesses in the Dominion."[330]

Like his father before him, John had become a farmer–publisher. He managed to combine the two vocations into a profitable business model. With his hand on the tiller, a keen eye for news, and a decisive temperament, he may have jumped at the chance to finance Simpson's search in 1901. Perhaps a successful treasure hunt in remote New Brunswick would have made for a good story in the *Farmer's Advocate*.

John's presence at the London Rowing Club on October 9, 1901, proves beyond all doubt he did not travel to Moncton. However, he was most likely the master sponsor of Simpson's efforts that year. And he could have delegated his younger brother, Corbin, to Irishtown to act as his surrogate.

We still lack a smoking gun. Yet chances are high that Corbin Weld journeyed to Irishtown. Another Weld brother, possibly Thomas Saxon, perhaps also made the trip. But determining which Weld(s) travelled to Moncton is secondary unless it can help us unmask Simpson. No one Weld brother could fund the quest on his own. We know there were "other parties financially interested in the search." The House of Weld, whether in private or corporate form, likely funded the 1901 attempt. And John "The Chief" must have been the man in charge.

Our investigation's progress is undeniable. Nevertheless, we need more evidence to crack open the case. Our protagonist's identity appears achingly close, but it remains elusive. The *Farmer's Advocate* never published an account of Simpson's saga. The Welds, more than anyone, had the means to immortalize the story. Maybe they feared that, empty-handed despite their efforts, no good could come from publicizing their involvement in a wild goose chase.

The Weld lead was our best chance to pick up Simpson's trail in Southwestern Ontario. Our hopes of pinning down our gold seeker have taken a blow. All we can do now is ask how John "The Chief" made Simpson's acquaintance.

Could the answer lie in the maiden name of his wife, Florence *Simpson*?[331]

The Guns of Fort Folly

HISTORICAL · CONTEXT ·

Blakeny's tale depicts a French pay ship docking at Grindstone Island, an islet in Shepody Bay near the Petitcodiac's estuary. Such a vessel would have few reasons to sail these particular waters, though an escape scenario is in line with Acadie's long history of British men-of-war patrolling its coastline. But does the theme of a naval chase fit the legend? Blakeny's words read differently: "The country was over-run with the British at the time and the French were taking every precaution. Realizing it was useless to try to get their ship up the [Petitcodiac] river past the British guns they left it at Grindstone Island, at the mouth, and transferred to dories. Even the small boats were sighted, however, and the French, pursued by a large force, had to take to the woods."

Blakeny makes no mention of a British warship. Shepody Bay is also too confined for one vessel to hunt another. Instead, Blakeny recounts, a French pay ship sailed undetected to Grindstone Island, but British defences—ones presumably based on land—closed off the Petitcodiac. As it turns out, such land-based defences did exist. Only, not in the right era.

Shepody Bay remained under France's nominal control until the mid-1750s. Le Rouge's 1755 map captures the period well: It shows the French "Fort Shepody" (opposite Grindstone Island) and the "Chemin de Québec" linking the Memramcook and Petitcodiac, among several features.[332]

Word of mouth puts a French fortlet at Fort Folly Point where the Petitcodiac and Memramcook rivers meet.[333] The encampment reportedly shelled an attacking British party, led by Major Joseph Frye, during the Battle of Petitcodiac in 1755. The story goes that the British destroyed it that same night and threw its two bronze cannons into the waters below. Early twentieth-century accounts testify that the guns still protruded from the bay's muddy banks at low tide.[334] Yet no hard evidence supports French defences at Fort Folly Point. Certain to keep rumours alive, though, is a 1753 letter from William Shirley, then Governor of Massachusetts, who wrote about "the small French Fort on the point of Land between the Rivers Amrancook [Memramcook], and Petcoject [Petitcodiac]."[335]

In 1776, twenty years after the fall of Acadie, the British erected an outpost at Fort Folly Point, and not a moment too soon. An American revolutionary force led by Jonathan Eddy took the redoubt the following month and likely used it as a supply depot.[336] The British repulsed Eddy's group after it mounted a final assault on Fort Cumberland (formerly Fort Beauséjour). Fort Folly Point became a Mi'kmaw First Nation reserve in 1840. Authorities built a now vanished lighthouse in 1899 on top of whatever ruins still stood.[337] Precisely what the name "Fort Folly" memorializes—French fortlet, British outpost, American depot—remains unclear.[338]

In the late 1800s, as the origins of Fort Folly receded in the mists of time, the designation itself inspired rumours of buried treasure. One such Mi'kmaw legend tells of gold coins found near Fort Folly Point on the shores of the Petitcodiac River.[339] Only, it is all too easy to conflate one historical period with another. If Blakeny's tale insists on British land guns guarding the Petitcodiac, then no French pay ship could have been around to try and send gold upriver.

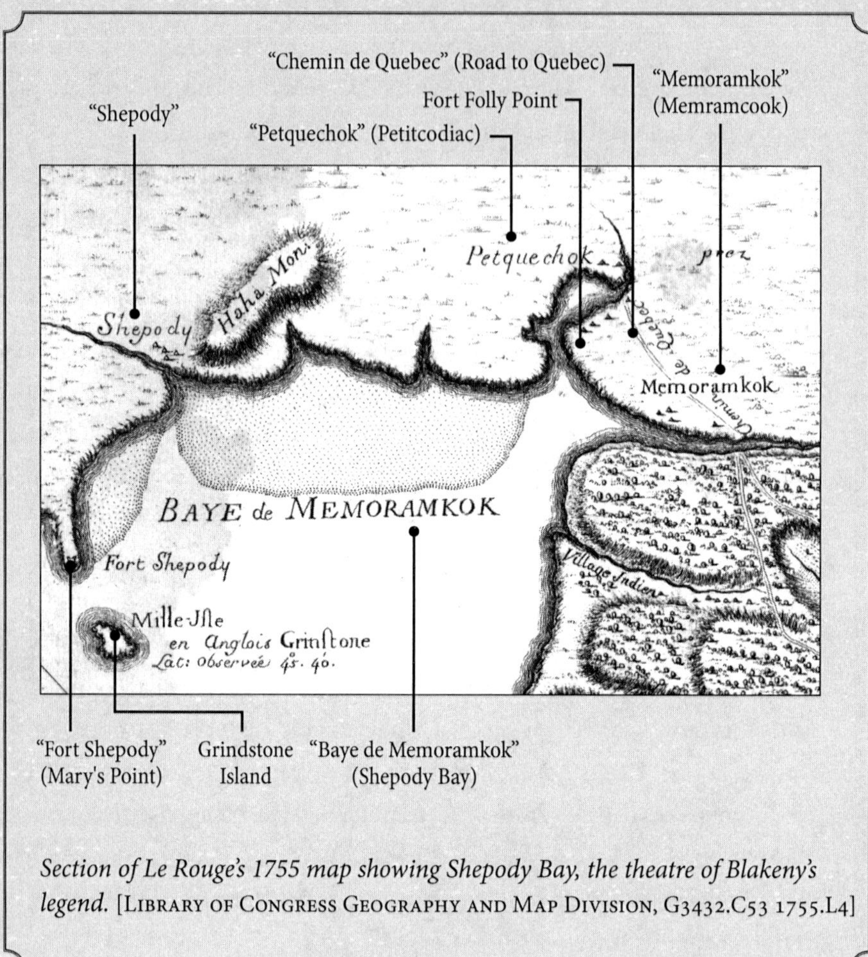

Section of Le Rouge's 1755 map showing Shepody Bay, the theatre of Blakeny's legend. [Library of Congress Geography and Map Division, G3432.C53 1755.L4]

Chapter 13
The Three Simpsons

Never touch your idols: the gilding will stick to your fingers.
– Gustave Flaubert, *Madame Bovary*

In *Madame Bovary*, Flaubert warns us not to meet our heroes, lest their aura be dimmed. But when it comes to Simpson, we may have no choice but to disregard the advice.

In 1903, a Mrs. Young from Loughboro, Ontario, charged her husband with blacking her eye. John Simpson Jr., a farmer and long-serving town clerk and Justice of the Peace in Kingston Township (Frontenac County, ON), adjudicated the case. He was also the father of Florence Simpson Weld and therefore the father-in-law of John "The Chief" Weld, the enterprising London publisher of the *Farmer's Advocate*.[340] The defendant, who pleaded guilty, sought lenience on account of extreme provocation: "Your Worship," he argued, "you have heard her tongue and neither you nor my lawyer have been able to stop her. Do you wonder that I do not go home at night 'til she is asleep." Simpson levied the lowest possible fine. He further made it clear he would have preferred to sentence Mrs. Young for her garrulity instead.

In the search for our Simpson, we must entertain the possibility that our protagonist's values may run counter to our own. John Simpson Jr. trivialized domestic violence. He mocked Mrs. Young and publicly humiliated her in the press. Newspapers published the verdict no doubt because their male-heavy readership would find humour in the cruel plot twist. Nonetheless, though tainted by misogyny, is John Simpson Jr. our treasure hunter?

So far, we have inferred several identities—the McSweeneys, the Welds—by process of elimination. Yet how can we sift through, say, the 245 males named "Simpson" with ages between fifty and seventy-five who, in 1901, were domiciled in Ontario?[341] Ties to Southwestern Ontario offer no guarantee that our man resided there. John Weld's father-in-law lived over four hundred kilometres from London and could still be our treasure hunter. Even if our Simpson were from London or surrounding Middlesex County, we would have at least twenty-three Simpsons on our list.[342] Without positive evidence linking a particular individual to the Irishtown dig, we are condemned to play the elimination game. But ruling out all but one person among hundreds is easier said than done. Simpson's identity seems to be slipping from our grasp.

Still, let us not give up without a fight.

The problem is that we are too ill-equipped to recognize our Simpson even if we crossed his path. With too many candidates and too few leads, how can we hope to unmask him? If standard practice in law enforcement is any guide, it would first have us build a forensic profile. Such a profile, in turn, should help us reduce our long list of Simpsons to a handful of likely contenders. That is the objective we will pursue in this chapter and the next.

The Three Simpsons

Composite sketching, a well-known forensic tool, involves depicting unidentified suspects through a witness's careful selection of facial features, including eyes, noses, and mouths.[343] A visual description of our Simpson, if we had one, would be of limited use in our case. Fortunately for us, profiling can also use other identifying constraints, such as probable age, income, location, psychology, life choices, etc. The overarching point is that the whole should be more recognizable than the sum of its parts; for that reason, the approach cannot restrict itself only to known facts, and speculation must fill in the blanks. The opportunity, then, is to reflect on the personal qualities and individual circumstances that would have enabled our Simpson to mount a three-year treasure hunt in Irishtown.

So, how should we go about it?

One promising avenue is to seek inspiration from a handful of Simpsons on our list. The idea is to limit ourselves to a small sample and pinpoint, within each individual, attributes that suit our gold seeker well. Instead of starting from scratch, we stand to create a richer, more accurate description of Simpson if we pick out the best-matching biographical bits from his real-life contemporaries.

Out of the 245 Simpsons aged between fifty and seventy-five who resided in Ontario for 1901, let us pick three. Each must be a plausible contender to fill our protagonist's shoes, and best would be three who differ markedly from each other, as there would be little sense in selecting people we could hardly tell apart. In other words, in order to forge our profile, we need a palette of attributes that spans a reasonable gamut.

We cannot neglect John Simpson Jr., the Justice from Cataraqui who happened to be John Weld's father-in-law. We will also dwell on William Simpson, a hotel owner and tavern keeper who migrated from the northern outskirts of London to the city proper. Finally, we will scrutinize Joseph James Wesley Simpson, a restless estate auctioneer whose nomadic ways brought him back to his home in Southwestern Ontario.

John Simpson Jr.

John Simpson Jr., John Weld's father-in-law, was born in Ireland in 1829 and emigrated to Canada with his parents around 1838. By 1851, he had settled in Cataraqui (Frontenac, ON) in Kingston Township. He resided there all his life with his wife, Eliza Ovens.[344]

John Jr. was a farmer who possessed aptitudes for official responsibilities. He filled oaths, bonds, ordinances, and resolutions in his capacity as township clerk. He became Justice of the Peace by 1867. He compiled vital statistics (births, marriage, and deaths) and presided over minor cases.[345] He would have received a small stipend or charged modest fees for this part-time work. His position in the community would have been one of prestige, not one of wealth.[346] His temperament, as we saw, did not always rise above the prejudices of his era.

John Jr.'s duties included recording the deaths of his fellow citizens. Mirroring the drip-drip of the grim tally, his entries were matter-of-fact and timely. He made two poignant notes in 1887. In the first, he registered the death of his son, Ernest, and simply wrote "My Son." He reported the loss

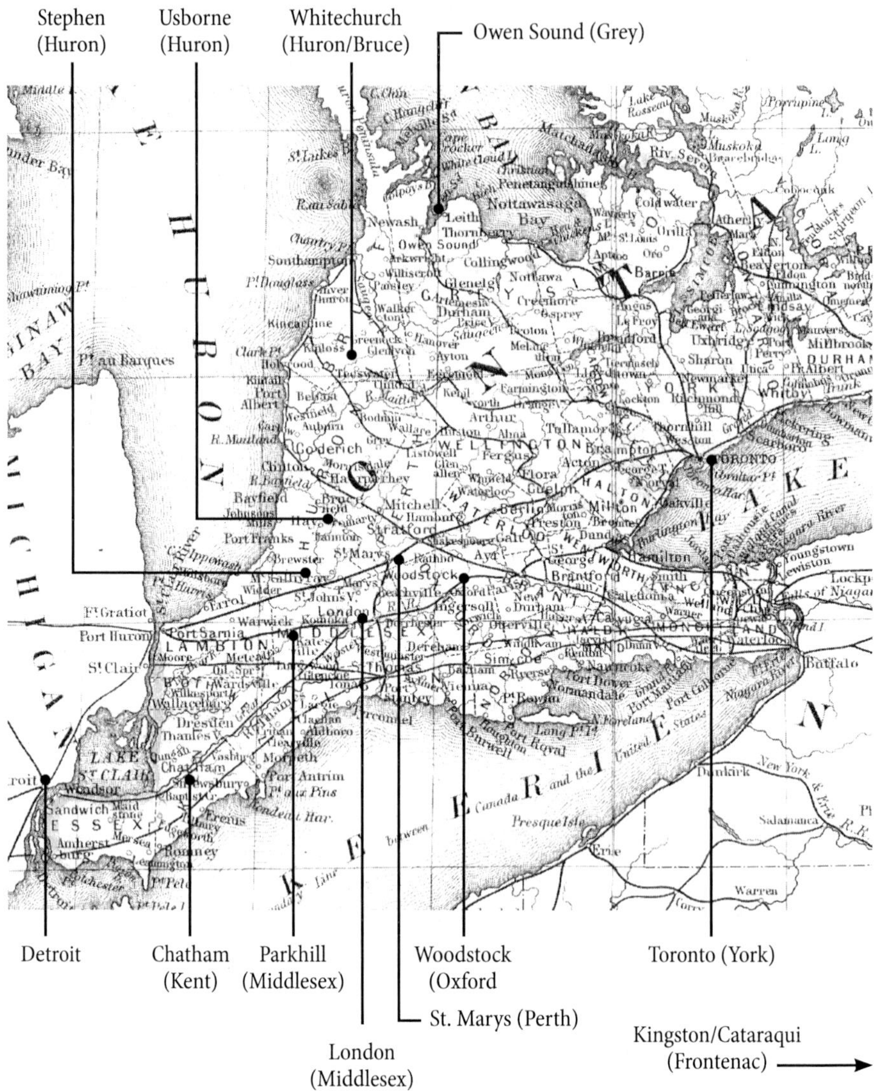

An 1897 map of Southwestern Ontario counties showing key locations. [S. AUGUSTUS MITCHELL, PUBLIC DOMAIN, VIA WIKIMEDIA COMMONS]

of his daughter Ada in the very next slot. Twice bereaved, he penned and underlined "My Darling Daughter" in the remarks section.[347]

John Jr.'s surviving daughter, Florence, married John Weld in 1889. The ceremony unfolded in John Jr.'s hometown of Cataraqui.[348] The groom and bride's respective fathers likely attended. Still, no hard evidence puts John Jr. and John "The Chief" Weld in the same room together.

Life unfolded predictably for John Jr. He remained a public servant until at least 1905, when age and failing health were catching up.[349] His son took over the family farm, but it proved insufficient. By 1911, his daughter Florence had travelled from London to lend further assistance—presumably a temporary arrangement.[350] John Jr. passed away in 1915 from pneumonia at eighty-six.[351] Florence returned to London with her widowed mother in tow.[352]

John Jr. was already seventy in 1901—a decade older than "about sixty" or "sixty or over." But, if he kept working well into the 1900s, his appearance may not have betrayed his years. It does not help matters that he resided over four hundred kilometres from London, the apparent Ontario epicentre of the treasure hunt. He was likely not down to his bottom dollar as a farmer and part-time official when the 1899 Irishtown dig got under way. He was also not the adventurous type, if his sedentary lifestyle and staid occupations are any indication.

John Jr. may not be the most promising stand-in for our Simpson. But his daughter's marriage to John Weld would have granted him a level of trust within the Weld clan to which no one else on our list could possibly have aspired. Millions of dollars in gold were supposedly at stake. Family ties may have trumped all other concerns.

William Simpson

Born in 1841 in Scotland, William Simpson emigrated to Canada as a child and grew up in Usborne (Huron County, ON).[353] He married Rebecca McCann in 1866 and, like many of his countrymen, migrated progressively toward London.[354] By 1871, he had settled in the township of Stephen (Huron County, ON), where he cut his teeth as a hotelkeeper.[355]

William later gravitated to Parkhill (Middlesex County, ON), a small community in London's more immediate periphery.[356] There, he ran, in turn, the Powell House and the Central Hotel, which he purchased in 1889.[357] His establishment also doubled as a saloon.[358]

An armed robbery in 1889 targeted William's Parkhill hotel. W. H. Hollands, the establishment's bartender, foiled the attack. He literally dodged a bullet and responded with two shots of his own, one of which wounded the assailant in the neck.[359] Having risked life and limb, Hollands surely endeared himself to his employer. The act of bravery did not go unnoticed by William's daughter, Laura, who married Hollands in 1891.[360] But then, tragedy struck.

In 1893, William's wife passed away from a stomach ulcer, an uncurable disease until the 1980s.[361] Her death exacerbated the prior loss of two adult sons, Willliam George and Benjamin, and destabilized the family.[362] She was pulling double duty tending to both hotel and home. Her bereaved husband borrowed a large sum only one month after the event.[363]

William took Sarah Ann Page (née Olver) as his second wife in 1894.[364] Page, herself a widowed innkeeper, owned the Metropolitan Hotel in nearby Exeter (Huron County, ON). The couple split its time between Parkhill and Exeter. They briefly ran a dining hall in Grand Bend (Lambton County, ON) in the summer of 1897.[365] However, the two struggled to reimburse accumulating debts.[366] By late 1897, they received a ten-day loan-repayment notice.[367] William saw lenders repossess his Central Hotel shortly thereafter.[368] In September 1898, his son-in-law, W. H. Hollands, relocated to London, where he worked as a wine clerk and hotel bartender.[369] By then, William's marriage to Sarah was on the rocks.

William and Sarah had moved in together in Exeter in April 1898, presumably out of financial necessity.[370] By October 1898, Sarah was living alone in neighbouring Hensall. Tellingly, the local press no longer called her "Mrs. Simpson."[371] William appears on Exeter tax assessments between 1895 and 1898, but he is absent from the 1899 edition onward. Conversely, the 1899 registry lists Sarah for the first time in several years.[372] We have no evidence that the couple ever filed for divorce. Still, it is apparent that, by late 1898, they had split up.[373]

William's trail becomes more difficult to follow from there on. In October 1900, the London *Advertiser* announced the death of "Miss Fannie Simpson, eldest daughter of Mr. Wm. Simpson, *of this city*, formerly of Parkhill" (emphasis added).[374] The 1901 London directory puts William (no profession) as residing in his son-in-law's home.[375] Similarly, the 1901 Canadian census records him as a retired boarder living as part of the Hollands household.[376] William passed away in 1906 at sixty-eight. He suffered from chronic neuritis and severe rheumatism. A stroke left him paralyzed for the last three years or so.[377]

We know little about William's character. But as a hotelier and tavern keeper, he could not have done without some social skills and an entrepreneurial spirit. He is also a promising suspect in terms of age, finances, lifestyle, and location. He would have been fifty-nine in 1901. Widowed after a first marriage and separated after a second, he had few obligations and only a bit of money to his name. William's stay in London coincides with the Irishtown dig. The sparse documentation on his whereabouts during this time proves little; the city, because of its size, afforded more anonymity as well as reprieve from small-town newspaper gossip.

Joseph James Wesley Simpson

Joseph James Wesley (JJW) Simpson was born in 1843 in Whitechurch (Bruce County, ON). By 1861, his father, a mill owner, had relocated his family to St. Marys (Perth County, ON), some forty kilometres from London. The eighteen-year-old JJW was baptized in Nissouri that same year. He married Sarah Birtch two years later.[378] Nothing in these unremarkable beginnings hints at the colourful life he would later lead.

We can find few traces of JJW immediately following his wedding. The births of two children, one in 1867 and one in 1869, tell us he spent time in Maine, USA. Perhaps he studied at Wesleyan Seminary (Kent Hill, ME); an alumni yearbook from the right time and place lists a "J. J. W. Simpson."[379] Either way, after about four years, he returned to Ontario an enlightened man. He soon embarked on a lecture tour promoting alcohol temperance. In an 1876 address, he proclaimed, "I can take every liquor dealer by the hand as a brother, but his business I cannot recognize as an honourable one."[380] JJW and his speeches received wide-spread approval.[381] His introduction at another public appearance noted his title of Provincial Deputy Grand Worthy Patriarch of the Sons of Temperance organization.[382] He further expressed moral outrage in opinion pieces.[383] Still, high-mindedness put little bread on the table.

JJW worked as a sales agent.[384] He resettled in Owen Sound (Grey County, ON), where he founded *The Tribune*, a newspaper pro-reform on politics and pro-temperance on values.[385] The gazette folded two years later.[386] These must have been uncertain times for JJW. In 1880, he posted an ad seeking to acquire a horse wagon in exchange for "a new first-class Cabinet Organ or Piano, or a second-hand Organ."[387]

By 1884, JJW was in Toronto selling music instruments.[388] He had sewing machines on offer the next year.[389] He formed Simpson & Burge in 1886 and supplied musical and sewing equipment.[390] He turned to property auctioneering the following year.[391] Then, in 1888, he established Simpson, Ross & Co., a company specializing in property brokerage, valuation, and auctioneering.[392] The year after that, he put together Simpson, Barkwell & Co., which provided real estate services, such as brokerage, estate auction, rental, insurance, and financing.[393] He launched Furness, Simpson & Co. in 1890 and ran a property clearing house called The Land Mart.[394]

Adding to his already busy life, JJW took on the job of agent and publisher. In 1890, he obtained the rights to a pamphlet authored by Wilford Hall. The monograph, edited and printed by JJW's own Simpson Publishing Co., is utter nonsense. For instance, it strains to identify the sigmoid colon as the "citadel of constipation." It also prescribes water enemas as miracle cure-alls for every ill.[395] Trouble started when JJW's book deal with Hall fell through. Feeling cheated, JJW repackaged the leaflet in a naked attempt at circumventing copyright.[396] Against all odds, it succeeded; Hall sued but lost. JJW subsequently wrote a triumphant newspaper tirade in which he accused Hall of conspiracy. He even had a writ for $30,000 ($1.1M) issued against the New-York based Hall & Co. for criminal and malicious prosecution.[397] Hall reportedly cowered in his office for fear of acknowledging receipt.[398]

By 1893, JJW slogged it as a travelling salesman. He represented various interests between 1894 and 1897.[399] He never seems to have gotten very far ahead despite decades of intense activity. He dropped in at a political rally in 1894, still in a lecturing mood. There, he impressed his audience with a comment on—of all things—the dire straits of Ontario's experimental farms. A journalist estimated that "Mr. J. J. Wesley Simpson, of Toronto, made the longest, strongest, broadest, and deepest speech of the afternoon."[400]

By 1898, JJW had relocated to Woodstock, a mid-sized town some forty-five kilometres east of London. There he worked as investment commissioner and real estate auctioneer.[401] The move also marked a comeback to his native Southwestern Ontario, where he resided with his wife and four grown daughters.[402] He remained involved in property valuation over the following two decades.[403] He died in 1919 in Toronto from stomach cancer.[404]

JJW's life is a confusing kaleidoscope of events. Still, he represents an attractive stand-in for our elusive gold seeker. He was nearly sixty when Simpson's quest got under way. London was an easy day trip from Woodstock. And the timing of JJW's return to Southwestern Ontario coincides with the Irishtown treasure hunt. He had a flexible schedule as a realtor and only some money to his name. Manifestly, he hopped from one thing to the next with gusto. People found him convincing, charismatic, and sincere. JJW also perfectly captures our Simpson's ability to form new partnerships on a yearly basis.

The three Simpsons—John Jr., William, and JJW—provide a window into our treasure hunter's time and place as well as into the lives and minds of his Victorian contemporaries. The trio will supply the raw material for creating our treasure hunter's forensic profile. A helpful analogy that anticipates our approach is the mixing of primary colours. In the same way that red, yellow, and blue paint can combine with each other to form any other colour, so too should a careful blend of attributes from the three Simpsons form an impression of our gold seeker.

As it turns out, the profile will take on a noticeable yellowish hue.

Acadian Resistance

HISTORICAL · CONTEXT ·

In 1755, immediately after the fall of Fort Beauséjour, Britain began a decade-long scheme of forced Acadian removal. Many Acadian families were caught helpless. Anglo-American forces laid waste to their homes and shepherded them aboard ships. But the depiction of a powerless people deported to faraway lands masks another reality.[405] When given a chance, many Acadians pushed back. The most militant among them chose armed resistance.[406]

Lionized today as leader of the Acadian uprising, Joseph Broussard (Brossard) *dit* Beausoleil took matters into his own hands.[407] He settled south of Le Coude at Le Cran (near Stoney Creek, NB) around 1740. From there, he agitated against British presence. His participation in an attack on a British detachment at Grand-Pré (near Wolfville, NS) made him an outlaw. It is believed that he later joined Abbé Le Loutre's guerillas to drive their shared enemy from the country. The French, British, and Indigenous Peoples alike practised scalping, an all-too-frequent occurrence in frontier warfare. Acadian irregulars were not above the fray.[408]

Broussard fought during the siege of Beauséjour in 1755 and retreated west of Le Coude (near Boundary Creek, NB). From there, he supported Acadian refugees and preyed on British forces. He outfitted a small privateer with Quebec's help and harassed British ships in the Bay of Fundy.[409] One British colonel wrote, "These people are Spirited up in their obstinacy by one Beausoleil."[410] Broussard, reduced by forced famine, surrendered in 1761, along with his companions. In 1765, he led a handful of Acadians to Saint-Domingue (now Haiti) and then Louisiana. There, he became a militia captain and commandant of the "Acadians of the Attackapas." He died soon after.[411]

Other examples of Acadian resistance abound. In December 1755, for instance, a group of 232 Acadian detainees boarded the *Pembroke* at Annapolis Royal. The 140-ton scow, operated by an eight-man crew, formed part of a deportation convoy bound for New England.[412] Charles Belliveau, one of the Acadian prisoners, devised a plan to seize the boat. Opportunity arose when strong winds separated the *Pembroke* from its sister ships. Only six Acadians were permitted on deck at a time. During a switchover, Belliveau overpowered his captors with the help of his comrades. He turned the *Pembroke* around and headed for the Saint John River. His group evaded British search parties and travelled overland to Boishébert's encampment on the North Shore.

Boishébert, while not Acadian himself, remains inextricably tied to the Acadian resistance. A French-Canadian officer sent to guard the Saint John River, he later sheltered Acadian expatriates while keeping the British at bay. All the more impressive is that he relied mostly on Acadian militiamen and Indigenous irregulars to confront a professional army. Like Broussard, he reportedly "made the English tremble more than all the cannons of Beauséjour."[413]

In September 1755, British forces began raiding continental Acadie's villages. Boishébert ambushed an enemy detachment at Petitcodiac (near Hillsborough, NB) and inflicted heavy losses. He set up a refugee camp at Cocagne in 1755–56 and Miramichi in 1757 to deal with the influx of Acadian exiles. Poor provisioning by Quebec led to appalling conditions.[414] Acadians of all ages, especially children, perished by the hundreds, weakened by hunger and disease.[415] Still, resistance continued.

The British did not strike Acadian settlements on the upper Petitcodiac until 1758. On July 1, in the closest analog to Blakeny's story of a battle near Le Coude, a British sloop lured into the open forty Acadian fighters headed by Broussard.[416] The militia, unaware that New England rangers hid in the woods, unwittingly revealed its position.[417] The rangers pounced and "took nine prisoners, killed and scalped three, drove fourteen into the river, ten of whom were drowned, four swam across the river, and the rest made their escape, under cover of a large dike in the marsh."[418] The following November, an operation overseen by Major George Scott and rangers Benoni Danks and Joseph Gorham removed most of the Acadian presence along the Petitcodiac, including the Broussards' home near present-day Salisbury, NB.[419] The rangers, it is said, "have left a reputation more enviable for efficiency than for humanity."[420]

History celebrates the victorious more than the defeated. The Acadian resistance features unheralded leaders, such as Joseph-Nicolas Gauthier *dit* Bellair, Joseph Godin *dit* Bellefontaine *dit* Beauséjour, and Joseph LeBlanc *dit* le Maigre, to cite only a few.[421] Still, none reached the legendary status of Beausoleil Broussard, the charismatic Acadian rebel who sailed the waters of the Petitcodiac River and trekked through the wilderness, musket in hand, in search of compatriots to rescue or British to harass.

As for Blakeny's tale, bits of the Acadian resistance may be filtering through his distorted accounts of a battle near Le Coude, of small French boats going up the Petitcodiac, and of French soldiers pursued through the woods.[422] Even at their most fantastic, popular myths rely on semi-truths that recall shades of an otherwise forgotten past.

Chapter 14
Simpson's Sketch

The principles of true art is not to portray, but to evoke.
– Jerzy Kosinski

A FORENSIC PROFILE OF OUR TREASURE SEEKER SHOULD HELP US SIFT THROUGH our long list of candidates and narrow down probable Simpson contenders. The biographies of our chosen three—John Jr., William, and Joseph James Wesley—present a rich array of real-life attributes akin to colours on a painter's palette. We now have a blank canvas before us. Despite its limitations, the painting metaphor points to a sensible sequence of steps: Define the subject's outline, fill in the coarser features, and add in the finer details.

Let us follow suit.

Profile Outline

Consider what the three Simpsons had in common. These were older men living in Ontario during the late 1800s. They were born as waves of immigration settled large swaths of the province. Railway expansion in the 1850s consolidated Ontario's status as Canada's economic engine. Still, family farms endured, and city dwellers were in the minority.[423] Unsurprisingly, then, each of the three Simpsons grew up in a rural or semi-rural context between the 1840s and 1860s. There is every chance our Simpson did as well.

Mechanization in the second half of the nineteenth century increased agricultural productivity and ushered in a manufacturing boom. Canada's equivalent of the Industrial Revolution, which drove a mass countryside exodus toward city centres, presented both challenges and opportunities. During the 1860s and 1870s, young men, such as the three Simpsons, could decide between a rural or an urban way of life.

Career choice remains our treasure hunter's biggest question mark. The three Simpsons vary widely in this respect. Yet possibilities narrowed for the elderly. There was no state support to provide for retirement. The less fortunate boarded with family, friends, or strangers. If their health permitted it, many never stopped working at all. In the early 1900s, sixty-year-old males had an average life expentancy of about seventy-two. Our Simpson likely passed away between the 1900s and the 1920s, most probably in the 1910s.[424]

The outline of our forensic profile has come into view. Let us now layer in some of its features by emphasizing key differences between the three Simpsons.

Profile Features

John Jr.—John Weld's father-in-law from Cataraqui—was a decade older than the other two Simpsons. That is perhaps why he never abandoned his agricultural ways. For his part, William—the hotelkeeper from Parkhill—broke with his family's agrarian past and worked in small-town hospitality for over a quarter-century. Meanwhile, JJW—the Woodstock estate auctioneer—forswore his pastoral roots and pursued an event-filled career in large city centres. So, did our Simpson adopt a rural or urban lifestyle?

In 1871, over 80 percent of Canadians made their home in the countryside. By 1901, that proportion had shrunk to 52 percent.[425] Still, chances are high that our Simpson did not reside on an Ontario farm during his treasure-hunting years. For one, his 1899 and 1901 search efforts coincided with the fall harvest. This critical period demanded that everyone—including children and the elderly—lend a hand. A senior but otherwise able-bodied Simpson would be no exception. That would go double for our gold seeker, who reportedly struggled to save for old age. In short, it is not obvious to place our Simpson in an Ontario hinterland from where he could repeatedly travel for faraway, inopportune, months-long quests.

So what about city life?

John Jr. persisted in his rural ways despite his part-time occupation as town clerk and Justice of the Peace. The other two Simpsons became proper townsfolk, but their respective experiences of city life differed markedly. Single and unemployed, William boarded in the modest house of his daughter and son-in-law, W. H. Hollands. The latter worked as a salaried wine clerk and likely possessed little leverage to help his father-in-law earn extra cash. William was bankrupt after the recent repossession of his Parkhill hotel. He was in no position to launch a new business. Moreover, it would have been more difficult for him to compete for jobs against younger, more productive men. In a word, he may have fallen into an urban retirement trap.

JJW no doubt found his time in Woodstock more enjoyable. Married, head of his family, father of four stay-at-home daughters, and active professionally, he pursued projects that only large agglomerations made possible. He also would have been more in control of his schedule as a realtor. For many, urban living came with a certain freedom untethered from the never-ending demands of farming duties. Importantly, then, a city-based Simpson would have been more at liberty to embark on repeated, prolonged, remote treasure hunts.

Our gold seeker, we know, had strong links to Southwestern Ontario and to London in particular. John Jr. remained on the outskirts of Kingston some 440 kilometres from downtown London. JJW settled in Woodstock, a small burg about 45 kilometres away from the centre of London. William, for his part, resided in the heart of London itself. But how close to London did our Simpson need to be?

In the late 1800s, a one-day round trip could cover at most one hundred kilometres. The distance corresponds roughly to travel from London's far periphery to its downtown core and back. The journey, whether by horse and buggy or by rail, would prove costly and time consuming. Overnighting in London would add to expenses and stretch the absence from home. At best, such trips to the city would only buy our Simpson mere hours or days to find and sell potential partners on a New Brunswick treasure hunt, let alone plan for one. Telegram was not secure. Telephone was unreliable. Mail was cumbersome. In short, placing our Simpson in London's far periphery compounds a string of impediments. And while JJW did live closer to the city than John Jr. by a factor of ten, it hardly would have mattered in practice. So what about the city's near periphery?

Suburbia as we know it today is a post-Second World War phenomenon made possible by fast cars, trains, and buses. Before then, only a few kilometres separated home and work, as no one could travel farther on a routine basis. Urban cores were more concentrated. Cities' limits were more sharply defined.[426] In the late 1800s, a fifteen-kilometre commute was as unthinkable as a fifty-kilometre one. Having to journey repeatedly to London from its periphery—whether near or far—would create a logistical nightmare for Simpson's quest.

Placing our Simpson in London itself simplifies his difficulties to such an extent that we cannot justify imagining him anywhere else. And, if he lived in the heart of the city, our man could have met his future partners through sheer dumb luck. One such partner, for instance, could have been John Lewis—the septuagenarian owner of London's Huron House guesthouse—who retired and put up his establishment for sale in the weeks leading up to the 1901 Irishtown dig.[427] Nothing definitively ties John Lewis to our story. But a London-based Simpson would have had months if not years to approach him.

Let us now compare the three Simpsons' temperaments. The contrast between the cool-headed John Jr., the amiable William, and the impetuous JJW is striking. Gold fever aside, our treasure hunter came across as guarded, persistent, unflappable, and organized. John Jr. may have shared some of these character traits, but his staid dispositions made him ill suited for a far-flung expedition to New Brunswick. Were we in the market for a colourful protagonist, we could do worse than an excitable Woodstock auctioneer. Still, JJW's thunderous personality and verbose inclinations are incompatible with those of "a man of action rather than talk." William, conversely, appears to be neither a homebody nor a thrill seeker. His experience as a hotel and tavern owner shows he could deal with all manner of people and practicalities. He also felt the pinch of precarity more keenly than John Jr. or JJW likely ever did. Hopes of unearthing gold can motivate anyone, but thoughts of escaping poverty can add extra incentive. William, it seems, fits our Simpson's mental makeup rather well.

Probable elements of Simpson's story—lifestyle, whereabouts, and temperament—have begun to emerge. But the three Simpsons are contributing unevenly to our forensic profile. If we assigned the colours red, yellow, and blue to John Jr., William, and JJW respectively, our portrait would take on a pronounced yellow tint. William—the insolvent, well-rounded Parkhill hotelkeeper turned lonely London retiree—overshadows the other two men. This is not to say that we have pinned down our treasure seeker. So far, our composite sketch reveals only that William offers a better model for our Simpson than either John Jr. or JJW—no more, no less.

If we followed our painting metaphor to a T, putting the final touches on our profile of Simpson would involve adding more details to a likeness already dominated by William. Unfortunately, data are scarce. What we can do, though, is push William's case and see how well the shoe fits.

Profile Details

In line with his noted reserve, our Simpson divulged to the *Daily Times* reporter only that he hailed from Ontario. But if our forensic profile is to put him in London, it must also allow that his answer reflected how he genuinely perceived himself. William may help us understand why.

William migrated from rural Ontario to semi-rural Parkhill to urban London. The journey could explain our Simpson's own sense of self. William only came to London as he neared his sixties. Accordingly, we would expect him to still identify with his countryside and small-town roots.

We know William gravitated from Parkhill to Exeter by mid 1898. He ended up in London by no later than October 1900. But his whereabouts for 1899—a period encapsulating much of the Irishtown treasure hunt—remain puzzling. He appears in the 1901 London directory, yet he is absent from the 1898–99 and 1900 editions as well as from listings and voter records for that period.[428] He may have chosen temporary accommodations in the city. Or perhaps he resided elsewhere for most of 1899. We can interpret the 1900 London directory that way, as it relied on canvassing done the year before. Our Simpson, for his part, was in Moncton both in the spring and in the fall of 1899 and possibly also in between.

William's move from Parkhill to London could also explain our Simpson's involvement with John Walton Mohan, the hotelier from Chatham, Southwestern Ontario, who accompanied Simpson to Moncton in 1899. The two shuttered their respective establishments at roughly the same time. It would have been natural for John Walton—an ex-Londoner with personal and professional ties to the city—to escape his Chatham troubles by retreating to his previous home. William's son-in-law, W. H. Hollands, moved to London in September 1898 and worked as a bartender at the city's Tecumseh Hotel. The venue would have been ideal for William and John Walton—two former innkeepers and tavern owners themselves—to meet each other. Furthermore, the two men potentially knew each other already, as they lived within fifteen kilometres—and never more than fifty kilometres—of each other until John Walton transferred to Chatham in 1890. They would also have had much in common with Moncton hoteliers Théophile B. LeBlanc and George McSweeney.

Forced retirement would have left William with little to do once he moved into his daughter and son-in-law's London household. He may have sought opportunities to regain his independence, financial and otherwise. Widowed in 1893 and separated in 1898, he may have adopted a nothing-to-lose mindset to stave off feelings of loneliness and uselessness. An ancient French parchment seemingly pointing to buried gold in New Brunswick could have infused him with a sense of purpose.

William's shoe, it appears, could hardly fit our Simpson's foot any better.

Zeroing In

Our forensic profile of Simpson is now complete. We pushed William's case as far as it would go. The former Parkhill hotelkeeper emerges as a tantalizing template. Consider how poor our likeness would be had either John Jr. or JJW served as our only source of inspiration. Too old, too remote, too rural, too busy, and too affluent to be our man, John Jr. cannot embody our treasure seeker on account of age (seventy-two), location (Kingston), lifestyle (farmer), relative freedom (married, children), and income (middle class or higher). The argument for JJW is not as clear-cut. Yet we would first need to explain how he could regularly travel to London while residing in its far periphery, take repeated leaves of absence while caring for his large family, and work actively in real estate while having few means at his disposal. In a word, John Jr. and JJW help us reflect on who Simpson *cannot* be; William, on the other hand, shows us who Simpson *could* be.

Let us now begin to screen our list of candidates for Simpson lookalikes.

By the Numbers

We began our search with 245 possible candidates—Ontario men between fifty and seventy-five named "Simpson"—enumerated in the 1901 Canada census. The tally's timing is fortunate: Canvassing took place in the spring, and everything suggests our gold seeker resided in Ontario before his fall 1899 expedition. Nothing guarantees that our Simpson figures on the list. Still, Canada's decadal survey remains the most complete, detailed, uniform, and trustworthy source by far. If there is a chance to bag our treasure hunter, the 1901 census is it.

Let us first summarize our Simpson's forensic profile with five simple descriptors: age (approximately sixty or over), location (in or very near London), lifestyle (non-farmer), income (poor to middle class), and freedom (retired, few responsibilities, no dependents, widowed/living alone, etc.). Next, we can build a model that sifts through our catalogue of candidates and computes the probability of a match for each entry. The exercise is not as difficult as it sounds. In a nutshell, we can assign each individual a barcode of five numbers corresponding to approximate age (in years), location (distance from London in km), yearly income (in dollars), lifestyle (between farmer = 0% and non-farmer = 100%), and freedom (between busy = 0% and free = 100%). We can then compare each barcode to our idealized Simpson's own barcode—also five numbers that best capture our forensic profile. By design, the resulting likelihood scores range between 0% (a complete mismatch) and 100% (a perfect match).[429]

The table below shows the top twelve Simpsons rank-ordered from high to low according to their likelihood scores. The chart also lists relevant data for each candidate. We added two familiar Simpsons—John Jr. and JJW—for reference.

Given Name	Age	County/Ward	km from London	Profession	$/Year (*estimated)	Lifestyle Score (%)	Freedom Score (%)	Likelihood (%)
William	59	London (City) Ward No. 1	0.0	Retired hotelier	300	100	100	90.5
William	61	London (City) Ward No. 4	0.0	Farmer (retired)	500*	100	50	72.3
John	73	Middlesex (East) London (City) Ward No. 2	0.0	Bookkeeper (part-time)	200	100	75	58.8
Robert (Sampson)	54	Middlesex (South) Westminster	11.0	Commercial Traveller	1500	100	50	57.7
Joseph B.	75	London (City) Ward No. 1	0.0	Prof. of Medicine (quack/ peddler)	150	100	50	42.7
Caleb S.	72	London (City) Ward No. 4	0.0	Barrister	800	100	50	28.7
Alexander	53	London (City) Ward No. 4	0.0	CPR Turner	650	100	0	25.8
James	59	Middlesex (South) Westminster	11.0	Farmer	250*	0	0	25.8
James	64	Middlesex (North) McGillivray	19.0	Farmer	500*	0	50	25.8
Herbert C.	54	Middlesex (East) London (City) Wards No. 3 and 4	0.0	Contractor	800	100	0	19.7

John W.	64	Middlesex (East) Dorchester (South/Sud)	17.0	Farmer	500*	0	0	19.3
J. J. Wesley	57	Oxford (North) Woodstock (City)	44.0	Auctioneer / Real Estate	500	100	0	0.6
George	68	Middlesex (South) Caradoc	28.0	Lumberman	200*	100	50	0.5
John (Jr.)	72	Frontenac Kingston	441.0	Farmer (also town clerk and Justice of the Peace)	650*	0	50	0.0

William tops our list with a likelihood of 90.5 percent. Results could hardly have turned out differently because the former Parkhill hotelkeeper informs much of our composite sketch. Still, he does not register as a perfect match, and for good reason. At fifty-nine, he is slightly on the younger side of "sixty or over," although there is reason to believe he was closer to sixty-three at the time.[430] His income of $300—more than what many working people earned at the time—clashes with Blakeny's description of a man down to his last dollar. No one is more promising as a candidate in practice. But our model still allows someone else to fit our Simpson even better in theory.

Our next suspect, another William, was a retired farmer who moved from nearby Lambton County to downtown London with his wife in the late-nineteenth century. He reported no revenue on the 1901 survey. But his large London domicile—515 Adelaide Street—shows he had done well for himself. His score of 72.3 percent makes him less of a contender due to his greater affluence and lesser freedom.

Third down, with a likelihood of 58.8 percent, is John, a seventy-three-year-old, married, part-time London bookkeeper of modest means. He occasionally filled in as town clerk for West London before its amalgamation with the city in 1897. He was involved in compiling official census and voter data. He was also active in Masonic circles. He would narrowly top our list had he been a decade younger.

Likelihoods for remaining individuals tail off quickly. A major reason for this decline is our specification that our Simpson should live in downtown London or very near it. Residing farther away from the urban core also increases the chances of a farming lifestyle. Age, income, and freedom are similarly intertwined in complex ways that subtly affect rankings.[431]

From an initial count of 245 possible Simpsons, we are now down to a more manageable handful. Our model should also help us better direct our research efforts because it plays the odds. For example, William Simpson—the Parkhill hotelkeeper—is over 150 times more likely than JJW to be our treasure seeker.

Our search now has a clear path forward.

Our very next order of business is to revisit William Simpson—the retired Parkhill hotelkeeper—who tops our list by a considerable margin. Unfortunately, none of his direct descendants I could reach were aware of a nineteenth-century, gold-seeking expedition to Irishtown. What they did have, though, stuffed amid handed-down family papers, was something that we should perhaps describe in their own words.

It was an old French treasure map pointing to New Brunswick's Moncton area.

Paper Money

Bad money drives out good.

– Gresham's Law

HISTORICAL · CONTEXT ·

In 1685, the intendant of New France, Jacques de Meulles, was in a real pickle. France had sent over soldiers but had neglected to include the necessary funds.[432] De Meulles soon ran out of money. He managed to cover expenses until June by drawing from personal reserves and borrowing from friends. Still, he required a quick solution to a deep-rooted problem.

New France always bought more than it sold. The imbalance was no accident. European powers had yet to discover the benefits of free trade. Mercantilist optics viewed the world economy as a zero-sum game in which nations prospered by siphoning wealth from one another. Countries guarded their respective monopolies and pressed their colonies to import commodities only from the motherland. France restricted New France's output mostly to fur and fish. It also prohibited activities that competed with its own domestic production.[433]

De Meulles decried how New France's chronic deficit affected its cash flow.[434] In a word, he needed money fast. The year before, the colony had again brought in more than it shipped. It therefore had sent more currency abroad than it had received in return. Specie was scarce. The unpredictable arrival of new coins only compounded the issue. Merchants could wait until the next pay ship; soldiers were not so accommodating. So how did de Meulles solve his problem?

He invented the first paper money in North America.

De Meulles distributed promissory notes written on the back of common playing cards. He then compelled inhabitants to accept the notes at face value and pledged to honour them upon presentation for redemption. The populace grew accustomed to the idea. In fact, cards soon rivalled coins as the favoured medium of exchange.[435] Bad money drives out good, states Gresham's law. In other words, people understandably preferred spending dubious paper and hoarding dependable metal than the reverse. But de Meulle's innovation also had unforeseen side effects.[436]

Versailles was none too pleased with de Meulles's monetary experiment. It complained that the practice invited counterfeiting and threatened budgets. Prices rose as card supply outstripped demand. Yet the benefits of a notional currency were too great to ignore. France would no longer have to send specie across the Atlantic, where it risked foundering at sea or, worse, falling into enemy hands.[437] Given that not everyone redeemed cards in their possession, New France could also increase expenditures beyond what coins would normally permit. Unbeknownst to the intendant himself, de Meulle's short-term expedient helped stimulate the economy.[438]

Rampant inflation in 1717 forced the discontinuation of card money. The ensuing scarcity of legal tender triggered a deep recession. The introduction of copper tokens in 1722 proved a spectacular failure. Nonetheless, the loss of *Le Chameau* in 1725 drove home the advantages of paper over metal. In 1729, authorities delivered promissory notes for the purchase of goods or bills of exchange—instruments one could swap for coins, but only in France. Specie payments in New France dwindled by the early 1750s. By 1757, two years before the fall of Quebec, the practice had largely ceased.[439]

Acadie had its own form of currency from 1750 onward. Officers issued so-called *billets de l'Acadie* to buy local commodities and services. Boishébert explained that "the latter [*billets*] was the de facto tender, authorized by the prince, for lack of specie that was in very little quantity in the colony."[440] Quebec encouraged the *billets* to remain in Acadie by imposing a two-sevenths reduction on their face value when redeemed outside their intended region.[441]

As for French soldiers, they received certificates they could convert into proper denominations upon their return to the mother country.

The risk of carrying precious metal into war zones was simply too great.[442]

The prevailing assumption in popular lore is that New France ran a purely coin-based economy. To be sure, small amounts of specie did circulate in Acadie during the 1740s and 1750s. Unusual circumstances also led to some hoarding, albeit on a modest scale.[443] But Blakeny's legend—nine leather bags of gold buried by French troops in mid-eighteenth-century Acadie—goes against the grain. The near complete transition to paper money by 1750 is perhaps the most damning indictment of claims that such a cache ever existed. The same historical reality also casts a dark cloud over Simpson's alleged treasure map. Indeed, the document could not refer to a fortune that most likely never was.

If Simpson's chart was genuine, it probably pointed to something else.

Chapter 15
Two Birds, One Stone

Dreams are the touchstones of our character.
– Henry David Thoreau

There is no getting used to phoning people about a century-old treasure hunt in New Brunswick. Jane Regent, from Bonnechere Valley (Renfrew County, ON) was gracious enough not to hang up.[444] Brian Hollands, her late husband, had passed away six months before. He was a fifth-generation descendant of William Simpson, the former Parkhill hotelkeeper, who retired in the London home of his son-in-law and daughter, W. H. Hollands and Laura Simpson. The couple went on to become Brian's great-grandparents. William did not have many descendants; Brian was therefore one of the few potential recipients for William's legacy.

Within minutes, Jane retrieved genealogy notes that Brian's father, Frank "Bud" Tallack Hollands Jr., had compiled over the years. She confirmed several details about William Simpson's life. New tidbits about W. H. Hollands also came to light. Still, the family's oral history could not recall anything about an Irishtown treasure hunt. There are no words, then, to describe the whirlwind Jane unleashed when she added a fateful "but...."

A Mystery Document

Brian and his wife were self-described pack rats who had accumulated boxes' worth of heirlooms over time. About a decade ago, Jane said, Brian noticed a folded, pocket-sized, letter-like manuscript while ferreting through family files. It clashed with the rest of the pile. He showed it to her. She recalled thinking, upon opening it, "Oh my God! It's a treasure map! It's for real!"[445]

The parchment was no modern stationary; according to Jane, it looked ancient, genuine, and odd. Old-fashioned, "spidery," quill-penned handwriting graced the page. "It wasn't done twenty years ago!" she emphasized. The faded blueish ink contrasted with the weathered paper's greyish buff tinge. There were also no drawings of any kind, just French text. She remarked that the word *chevaux* (French for *horses*) had initially struck her eye. She and Brian only knew basic-level French, but they managed to decipher other fragments: "we offloaded the boat," "we got some horses," "we carried the thing upriver." She later remembered reading "soldiers getting ready for battle."

Jane was also adamant that she and Brian concluded the manuscript pointed to the greater Moncton region, though she could not exactly recollect why: "Yes, that was clear to me for some reason. I definitely believed it should be [the] Moncton area."[446] If the chart indicated a particular spot, she said, it was through instructions, as in three paces to the east, ten paces to the north, etc. Brian and Jane, both incredulous and excited, joked about travelling to New Brunswick to look for the cache themselves. "Oh no, it was definitely a treasure map! No doubt about that!" Jane protested. Still, her memories of the parchment are fuzzy. "It was more than ten years ago that we would've last seen this piece of paper. I think I only had it in my hand maybe once or twice."

Sadly, we must describe the odd letter through Jane's eyes for a reason. Brian took it out of a pile of documents, but he never put it back in. What has happened to it since then is anyone's guess. Jane raised the possibility that Brian believed it was a prank and simply discarded it. Instead, she prefers to trust his pack rat instincts and remains hopeful the letter lies misplaced somewhere in his vast stash of books and records. As of this writing, she continues to comb through his belongings. She has vowed to keep searching, intrigued by what could constitute an extraordinary family legacy. The mystery parchment may yet turn up. So far, it has not.[447]

A Reckoning

There is no reason to doubt Jane's good faith. Yet we must remain clear-eyed. We will cover the ins and outs of her account later. First, though, let us celebrate the obvious. What are the odds that, while searching for a would-be French treasure map referencing Acadie's Le Coude area, we stumble on someone in Ontario making the unprompted claim of having precisely such a thing? No need for likelihood scores here.

William Simpson, the former Parkhill hotelkeeper, must be our Simpson. And Brian's letter must be his precious chart.

Of course, nothing proves that the parchment led to buried gold or that it was even genuine. Old-looking does not necessarily mean centuries-old. Directions from A to B do not, in themselves, imply a cache of hidden riches. In short, we would do well to avoid treating Brian's letter as a real treasure map unless incontrovertible evidence forces our hand. What Jane's story does do, however, is add to our understanding of Simpson's document.

More Than Words

How can we reconcile ourselves with the notion that Simpson's manuscript consisted of text only? The terms *map* and *chart* can evoke cartography—two-dimensional drawings outlining terrain features. But squaring the circle may come down to semantics. Jane and Brian themselves, in full knowledge it contained only words, immediately thought of the letter as a "treasure map." Others, including the Blakenys and Moncton reporters, could have resorted to similar language. We already have descriptions of Simpson's map from multiple sources. So how well do these fit with Jane's account of a parchment devoid of any imagery? Let us revisit the characterizations and keep an eye out for hints of illustrations. Key terms appear in bold.

Blakeny recalled in 1937: "That **chart** was the oldest **document** I ever saw. It was all in French." He added, in the same interview: "We did find landmarks **shown** on the **chart**—a south running stream and a spring. It **showed** the treasure as being buried behind a big rock..."

The Moncton *Daily Times* claimed on October 17, 1901: "The **chart** **designates** a starting point on the old French road leading in the direction of Shediac, and **states** that the treasure was buried on the east bank of a south running stream; and, according to the best interpretation of the **plan**,..."

Hanford remarked in his 1960 autobiography, "He and my father gathered about the table in the kitchen, in the dim light of the oil lamp, to examine the

map. It was an old and faded **parchment** with compass **inscriptions written** in French. I recall the **marks indicating** the location of the big rock which was supposed to have the picture of a frog carved on the bottom."

Sources use expressions such as *chart*, *document*, *plan*, *map*, and *parchment* to refer to Simpson's manuscript. But *map* and *chart* could be surrogates for "list of directions" or analogous mouthfuls. The term *chart* can also invoke a less pictorial way of presenting information (e.g., bullet points, a series, a table). The word *plan* is similarly less committed to imagery. Otherwise, Simpson's document contained *inscriptions* and *marks*. It was said to *show*, *designate*, *state*, and *indicate*. Crucially, though, nowhere is there the irrefutable mention of an illustration. Nor are there phrases, such as *draw*, *portray*, *depict*, *picture*, or *sketch*, that would point to one.

Our purpose here is not to reject the possibility of drawings on Simpson's map. On the contrary, it is simply that we cannot find unequivocal references to any graphic element of any kind. We can only settle the matter with our own eyes. Until then, we can take comfort in knowing that a word-only manuscript is at least compatible with all the evidence at hand.

But the exclusive use of text also explains much more.

Simpson's map alluded to "the old French road leading in the direction of Shediac." The abandoned trackway has since disappeared. Memories of its location had long vanished by the time our treasure seeker arrived in Moncton. That would be less of an issue had the parchment depicted the Irishtown area in minute detail. But words are more problematic. Disagreements between Blakeny's engineers become more understandable if inscriptions were all they had to work with. Moreover, an all-text document changes the game. Jane and Brian's deciphering, however incomplete, suggests that Simpson's manuscript was self-explanatory. More letter-like than cartographical, it referred to offloading a boat, to carrying something upriver, to fetching horses, and to soldiers readying for battle. It is difficult not to see in such snippets the ghost of Blakeny's legend: gold transferred from a French ship onto dories; precious cargo taken up the Petitcodiac River by French troops on the run; booty hauled inland and buried to evade British seizure.

Extraordinarily, and to my own surprise, Simpson's map seems to have told its own story.

The provenance of Simpson's parchment would matter less to Simpson's prospective partners should the document speak for itself. Physical aspects, such as weathering, material, ink, and handwriting, could allay concerns about forgery. But content, just as much as appearance, would sway opinions regarding the manuscript's authenticity. The text's mention of the old French road to Shediac may have been the clincher. Other narrative details, including the document's purpose, would add layers of credibility. If Simpson's chart recounted its genesis, it may well have answered enough questions to warrant a search effort.

A Dreamer's Eulogy

We should not toss Simpson aside as if his only purpose had been to lead us to his map. The mystery manuscript, no matter its nature, could not foretell the passions it would later ignite. Simpson remains a vital part of our story. His life is worth revisiting in light of his newly revealed identity.

Mary Simpson, William's sister, provided a glimpse of her brother's early life in a 1935 newspaper interview she granted at the age of ninety-three.[448] Growing up in the 1850s while homesteading a Southwestern Ontario lot was no picnic. The Simpson family dug up the land by spade and seeded it by hand. Kids walked half a mile barefoot in the snow to milk the cows. There was no money for months. Interest rates reached 50 percent. William's father, William Sr., once walked a bushel of wheat thirty miles to London to have it milled into flour. In 1873, he wrote an autobiographical poem, "Sketch of the Life of William Simpson," testifying to similar hardships.

Mary also recalled that she and her siblings received no gifts or sweets. Nothing but pork turnovers brightened Christmas Day. "Those were the happy days when we only had a crust of bread in the house," she remarked. The clan ate mostly porridge for weeks on end. The Simpsons made their beds out of rope and filled their mattresses with straw. An open fireplace is all that heated their small log cabin. Makeshift candles—pieces of rag dipped in tallow—were their only other source of light. The family crafted its own soap, shoes, and clothes.[449]

William's childhood, which his sister Mary characterized as "plain living" and "hard times," may appear unimaginably difficult to us. Still, it was not the exception in rural mid-nineteenth-century Canada. Blakeny had had a similar upbringing in New Brunswick. Perhaps he saw bits of himself in our gold seeker.

William had already lived through most of his life's tragic arc by 1899. He had been a father who lost two sons, Willliam George and Benjamin, in 1889 and 1890 respectively, a husband who lost his first wife, Rebecca, in 1893, and an innkeeper who lost his business in 1897. He found brief solace with his second wife, Sarah Ann, before they parted ways in 1898. Yet he could visualize a happier future even in his seventh decade. He embarked on a multi-year treasure hunt in New Brunswick when, presumably, he could have stayed put at his son-in-law's London household. That, in itself, speaks of a man whose inner flame still burned.

William rose time and again. Even the death of his daughter Fannie in 1900 did not stop him from mounting another effort that year and the next. Soon thereafter, a stroke robbed him of his power to continue his search. He passed away in 1906 at sixty-eight and lies buried in Exeter Cemetery.[450] I was unable to locate any succession documents (a will, a letter of probate, an affidavit, or estate papers) in the Archives of Ontario.[451] None were likely ever filed. The eulogy pronounced at William's funeral service may well have made no mention of his Irishtown quest at all. And yet.

While others eschewed, he dreamed. While others watched, he acted. While others quit, he persisted.

William never unearthed the concealed riches he pined for. But, while he kept his hopes alive, he perhaps found camaraderie, joy, and purpose. In short, he was not the spectral figure depicted by Blakeny in 1937. Our gold seeker was of Scottish descent and possessed modest roots from Southwestern Ontario. He was someone with a name, an identity, and an eventful existence, if at times a heartbreaking one. Behind Simpson's shadowy facade, we now know, lay William's humanity.

William could not have foreseen that his Irishtown dig would be the very thing to revive his memory in the twenty-first century. His reserve around Moncton reporters—the simple withholding of his given name—nearly threw off his scent more than a hundred years later. His quest adds another chapter to Canada's already storied East Coast. If he took to his grave the origins of his chart, then we are the poorer for it. While he searched for the yellow metal, he may have had figurative gold in his hands all along. Despite his failure—or perhaps because of it—he succeeded in firing the imagination of generations.

The tenuous string of evidence that led us to Simpson threatened to snap on more than one occasion. But we can now point the finger at William—the former Parkhill hotelkeeper—as our elusive protagonist. We have solved nothing short of a real-life whodunnit from another century. That is no small victory. Perhaps the revelation of Simpson's identity will take on special significance for the Hollands-Simpson family. Who among us is so lucky as to have a Victorian ancestor who embarked on a treasure hunt for French gold buried in the mid 1700s? Her grief still fresh, Jane Regent has helped cement her deceased husband's extraordinary legacy.

Momentous though the unmasking of Simpson may be, the near rediscovery of his map is the bigger news. We had no right to expect that we would track down the puzzling chart to a great-great-grandson's stack of old papers. A fateful two-birds-one-stone phone call both pinned down our man and brought us almost within reach of his enigmatic document. Had Brian been alive, we might have pulled off the unimaginable and cracked our story's most enduring and perplexing mystery then and there.

Jane's description of Simpson's manuscript—an ancient French text relating its own origins in terms eerily reminiscent of Blakeny's legend—has altered our thinking. And yet, unable to inspect it for ourselves, we remain with many of the same fundamental questions. What was its nature and purpose? What and where did it point to? When was it created? Was it genuine? What other information did it contain? How should we interpret it?

Simpson's lead has been good to us. But it is now out of our hands. We cannot substitute for Jane in her ongoing efforts to locate Simpson's map. Whatever she finds will be hers to share. However, this is not the end of the line for our story. The previous few chapters have neglected clues closer to its roots in New Brunswick. Local memories passed down generations may add important elements.

What a ninety-four-year-old Irishtown farmer would do, though, is not so much contribute to our investigation—he would rock its very foundations.

A Barrel of Gold

In 1758, John Bradstreet sailed across Lake Ontario and once again came within view of Fort Frontenac (Kingston, ON). The British officer had failed to defeat the French outpost a month earlier.[452] But now, after having corralled a force of over 3,000 men, victory was at hand. His French counterpart, Pierre-Jacques Payen de Noyan et de Chavoy, commanded a garrison of only 110 soldiers and surrendered on the spot.[453] Bradstreet ransacked the compound, seized nine vessels berthing in its harbour, and set the place alight.

The Battle of Fort Frontenac happened a world away from Acadie, but a legend of buried treasure is tied to the event.

Rumour has it that, as his fleet neared Fort Frontenac, Bradstreet sighted a French gunboat beating against the wind. He dispatched two ships to intercept. The French boat, which reportedly carried a barrel of gold, could no longer reach the relative safety of the fort. It changed tack and headed downwind to escape. Bradstreet's ships gave chase. A race ensued for thirty miles. As the distance closed, the French rounded Salmon Point, sailed up "the Outlet," and made landfall. Once ashore on the beach, they sank the precious cargo deep in the sand. They then burned their own vessel and marched toward Fort Frontenac. C. H. Widdifield immortalized the tale in 1892.[454]

There are uncanny similarities between Widdifield's story and Blakeny's, but with more specific names, places, and dates, Widdifield's yarn seems to best Blakeny's in terms of credibility. Only, details are a rumour's Achilles heel. Indeed, we can find a blow-by-blow account of the Battle of Fort Frontenac in none other than Bradstreet's personal campaign journal. The context, and even some of the events, are broadly compatible with Widdifield's fable. Yet Bradstreet's diary, which he published in 1759, makes no mention of a fleeing French gunboat laden with gold.[455]

Folk tales are difficult to dissect because their very haziness shields them from the harsh glare of scrutiny. For us, Bradstreet's writings do more than debunk Widdifield's improbable narrative. Ontario and Acadie, though separated by a thousand kilometres, have a long, common history of Franco-British hostilities. The two regions therefore inherited similar period archetypes. Understandably, then, they interwove shared bits of truth into their own local lore.

Blakeny's legend, it seems, is not so unique.

Chapter 16
Rocks of Ages

The eye sees only what the mind is prepared to comprehend.
– Robertson Davies

In 1894, a packed Moncton courtroom awaited Justice Cowling's verdict. The two-day trial opposed Irishtowners George Budd (the plaintiff) and Richard Anketell (the defendant). The dispute involved competing claims to a curious boulder. The object, a witness said, was four feet long by about twenty inches square and came from "one of the crude formations that went to make up the farm owned by Mr. John Bishop fifty years ago."[456]

During the 1860s, someone took the stone from Bishop's property and placed it on nearby public land that later became Budd's farmstead. Budd fenced in the rock at first to protect its suspected value as an old relic. He eventually moved it to the roadside. A few summers afterward, Anketell grabbed the stone for himself on advice from his neighbour, John Bishop. Irked, Budd sued Anketell for $8 (~$280). He claimed that the item was his alone and that it would "be used for a special purpose some time in the future." Justice Cowling found for the plaintiff and awarded him a 50¢ (~$18) pittance.[457] The low-stake litigation offered both cheap entertainment and gossip fodder for the proceedings' many onlookers.

Readers left shaking their heads at the odd squabble are in good company. The boulder had few distinguishing attributes. It also appeared to have little utility or meaning. Perhaps it served as a proxy for a territorial cockfight between two feuding villagers. To be sure, nobody particularly seemed to want the object. But no one could bring themselves to ignore or discard it either. Such is the fascination with rocks.

Throughout the ages, stone has been a material of choice for creating landmarks and has provided an ideal medium for telling and preserving stories. But stonework can become positively enigmatic when it outlives its creator. Worse, it is all too easy to fool ourselves into interpreting natural rock features—bumps, crevices, patterns, or even placement—as the result of human intent. The significance of George Budd's boulder, if it had any, was already lost on late-nineteenth-century Irishtowners. Nothing suggests the object corresponds to Simpson's missing frog-carved stone.

As far as strange rocks go, though, Irishtown appears to be full of them.

More Stones

In 1924, the Moncton *Transcript* reported on a treasure hunt in the northern part of the city. The transcription appears here in full:

> Treasure Hunt On Near City
>
> Boulders Bearing Inscriptions Lead to Search for Buried Gold
>
> In the northern part of the city, digging operations have been underway for sometime [*sic*]. There is something of the mysterious attached to them but it is understood that there is a search for treasure going on. In the near vicinity are three large boulders which, it is claimed, bear certain marks that would lead to the belief that there is gold below or not far away from them. On one are the initials "O. B.," supposed to mean "on the bend," on the second "O. H.," standing for "on the hill," and on the third, "7" meaning seven paces. In fact it is maintained by the discoverers of the marks that there are certain inscriptions which can be read only with the aid of a mirror which look like a crude attempt to write "steps."
>
> Already three large holes have been dug and it is said that down several feet a layer of birch bark has been discovered, which it is believed by the excavator, was placed there to keep the moisture off the cases which contain the gold.
>
> The treasure itself is supposed to have been left there by the French who were making their way to Quebec from Nova Scotia

> and who buried it when they discovered that they were being followed by the British forces. The man in charge of the work is very reticent about where the information came from which led him to believe that the gold was buried in this section of the country.[458]

William Simpson, long since dead, could not have been the "very reticent man" who led the 1924 excavation. Yet its location—somewhere "near [the] city" or "in the northern part of the city"—is suggestive. Moncton's north–south axis stretched only a few blocks at the time.[459] Automobiles further shrank distances. The old Bishop farm lies only five kilometres north of Moncton as the crow flies. Could it be the site of the 1924 dig? The article's backstory matches Blakeny's legend point for point, minus again the naval component. So what is the connection?

One possibility is that Simpson's descendants revived their ancestor's quest. William's map, we now know, stayed in the family. Still, the 1924 column made no mention of a document guiding the operation. Plus, the effort was downright amateurish. Deciphering markings with the use of a mirror may seem silly enough. Even more questionable were English solutions—"on the bend" for "O. B.," "on the hill" for "O. H.," etc.—to crack a code allegedly written in French.

Another possibility is that locals got wind of Simpson's prior searches. Without Simpson's chart, however, the new seekers could do nothing else but follow in the old seeker's footsteps. Thus handcuffed, they would have little choice but to look near—or even possibly *on*—the Bishop farm. The three boulders engraved with *O. B.*, *O. H.*, and *7* could therefore lie in the vicinity of Simpson's earlier dig. What could the symbols represent under this scenario?

The 1924 treasure hunters were no doubt on the lookout for telltale signs. But everything is a nail to a hammer, goes the saying. The inscriptions *O. B.*, *O. H.*, and *7*, should they prove of human origin, could constitute evidence of a previous excavation rather than clues about hidden wealth. The distinction between *searcher* and *depositor* activity is essential in the jargon that characterizes the TV series *The Curse of Oak Island*. Perhaps Simpson carved the markings himself as a shorthand for staking out his operation's progress. Similarly, why should birch bark rediscovered several feet down by the 1924 operation imply concealed riches? Blakeny's labourers, for instance, could have placed the material there themselves to provide better traction for their workhorses. As always, we must first rule out more likely explanations.

Here is the crux of the problem.

Anyone looking for mid-eighteenth-century French gold buried in New Brunswick is holding out for a highly improbable truth. Wishful thinking can play tricks with our own sense of reality. It is all too easy to mistake natural features for clues. It can also be tempting to interpret human-made artifacts—including previous searcher activity—as indications of nearby treasure. In short, mindset conditions the eye. Put another way, the heart sees what it wants.

These are words worth remembering. We will need them.

Local Lore

John "Jack" Bishop was born in Digby, Nova Scotia. He came to New Brunswick in 1831. A naval carpenter like his father, he worked in the Moncton shipyards until at least 1851. He resettled in Irishtown following the industry's collapse, as did his younger brother George. The Bishops, along with the neighbouring Blakenys, pioneered a new life in the area. The region abounded with raw materials. Cleared forests provided timber for housing and land for crops. Rocks dotting the fields ended up in enclosures, foundations, and hearths.[460]

George Bishop had only one child and ran a simple farmstead. His sibling Jack had eleven offspring and built a large dairy operation. He later turned over the business to his son John A. Jr. If treasure stories are in need of a so-called "peg-legged" character, then we are in luck. John A. Jr.'s white hair and ginger beard no doubt attracted attention, but his wooden leg made the greatest impression of all.[461] He was "a well-known and prosperous farmer" and "a man of many sterling qualities and a kindly disposition."[462] Still, he was not without flaws. For example, authorities arrested him in 1896 after a dispute with John J. McDonald over a land purchase. He broke into McDonald's dwelling, smashed through doors and windows, and discharged a gun while evicting its occupants.[463] The incident earned him a thirty-day jail sentence.[464]

Period court dockets show that Irishtown was no stranger to frontier justice.

Little were the Bishops aware at the time that a retired Ontario hotelkeeper would disrupt their lives. But surprise soon gave way to habit: For three years running, if not more, they had a front-row seat to Simpson's operation. In 1901, John A. Jr. and his uncle George were themselves active participants in the treasure hunt. So did traces of Simpson's quest persist in Bishop family lore?

In 2020, at the age of ninety-five, Alma Margaret Stiles (née Bishop) could still recall her paternal grandfather, John A. Jr., recounting tales of past treasure hunts on his property. She remembers once walking along Lynch's Brook during her youth and coming across large, dug-up holes. Her childhood memories are blurry, and she cannot recollect much else.[465] Jackie Tilton (née Richards), one of John A. Jr.'s great-granddaughters, spent summer vacations at her ancestors' farm. There, her great-grandfather regaled her with anecdotes. In one story, he told her that a map once pointed to a fortune a group of Acadians had buried at the back of his field before the Great Expulsion. In another account, he relayed to her how he lost his leg: He fell into one of the several pits that gold seekers had excavated on his estate.[466]

We were less successful with Richard Anketell, Bishop's immediate neighbour to the south. He had Irish origins and was one of Jack Bishop's fellow boatbuilders at the Moncton shipyards. He moved to Irishtown during the late 1850s. His son Richard Jr. eventually inherited the property.[467] Undoubtedly, the junior Anketell must be the one Simpson approached for permission to dig on the family's land. The ranks of the Anketells, once numerous, have since thinned. I could find no direct descendants to interview. The Anketell farm was put up for sale in 1993 and subdivided for redevelopment.[168]

Simpson's quest has left few traces in the written record. John Edward "Ned" Belliveau—journalist, author, and great-grandson of Richard Anketell Jr.—made no mention of it in his anecdote-filled books.[469] Moncton chroniclers Lloyd Alexander Machum and Edward William "Ned" Larracey are also silent on the topic.[470] Charles Alex Pincombe, another Moncton-born historian, briefly evoked Simpson's operation in his works. His source, though, was none other than Sherman Blakeny's 1937 interview by Ian Sclanders. Pincombe remained skeptical about buried gold. He tackled Blakeny's tale only to challenge its account of a Franco-British battle at Le Coude (see Appendix B).

Irishtown genealogist Linda Donovan Evans had never heard of Simpson's endeavour. She, in turn, queried her near-centenarian mother, who offered the same answer. The latter, once informed that the search had spilled over to the Anketells, reportedly quipped to her daughter, "If there was treasure on the Anketell property, it was probably a cache of moonshine!"[471] Shirley Landry Cail, who also wrote about the Tankville area, was similarly unaware of the story.[472]

We can either celebrate or lament what little has survived of Simpson's quest in local lore. At the time, perhaps, it seemed unimportant to the present and irrelevant to the future. But for us in the twenty-first century, the treasure hunt carries mystique and elements of a deeper, unresolved mystery. Simpson may have failed to find buried gold. But that does not explain why he and so many others believed it was there for the taking.

Today, the old Bishop farmstead is no longer in the family's hands. But its current owner did have something to add.

Tidd Bits

His quivering voice betrays his age. Yet, as of this writing, Ernest Tidd—a ninety-four-year-old Irishtown farmer—remains remarkably fit both of body and mind. He is a practical and affable man of kindly dispositions. He still tends to the former Bishop property he has owned for the past half-century.[473] Born in Massachusetts but of New Brunswick descent, he resettled to Canada when he was a child.[474] He inherited the Bishop land in 1971 from his aunt and uncle, who purchased it in 1948.[475] Tidd is much too young to have witnessed Simpson's search first-hand. Crucially, though, did he know anything about it?

In a word, no.

Tidd expressed muted interest at the news. He declared himself unaware of events from 120 years ago. And, as it so happens, he does not hold treasure seekers in high regard and wishes they directed their energies elsewhere instead. His opinion, however, stems from personal experience.

One summer day during his teens, Tidd took a stroll by Lynch's Brook on the old Bishop farm. There, he came across two Americans scanning the ground with "Geiger counters." He said the two men had heard stories about French gold buried in the vicinity. Thinking nothing of it, he pressed on with his walk. He remembered being fourteen at the time of his 1942 encounter.[476] Manifestly, rumours of riches concealed on Bishop's land near Lynch's Brook never truly died. But Americans? In 1942? With Geiger counters?

Tidd's stated date of 1942 agrees with the rest of his chronology. For instance, he recalled living across from the Bishops when he had his odd encounter with the two Americans. The Bishops, for their part, sold their property in 1945.[477] Tidd also recollected that several years had passed between his chance meeting and the purchase of the old Bishop farm by his aunt and uncle in 1948.[478]

Portable Geiger counters did not appear before the end of the Second World War. They were initially restricted to military and medical applications. Only in the late 1940s did they become available to the public. Moreover, such devices are worthless for pinpointing refined gold. Dubious advertising touted their ability to locate radioactive ores commonly associated with natural deposits of the yellow element. If the two Americans did carry Geiger counters, as Tidd insists, they were employing the wrong technology for their purpose.[479]

Otherwise, detecting metal through radio frequencies had been a known principle since the 1870s. In 1881, Alexander Graham Bell used it to try and extract a bullet lodged in President Garfield's chest following an assassination attempt. America kept the science under wraps for decades due to its wartime potential. Expensive, heavy, cumbersome, and prone to failure, the first portable metal detectors began selling around 1931; however, they made virtually no inroads into the consumer market. Not before the 1950s, with the advent of the transistor, did hand-held metal detectors reach casual hobbyists.[480] So how could metal detectorists be searching by Lynch's Brook in 1942, as Tidd claimed?

One possibility stands out. That same year, Canada joined Allied assaults on Nazi-occupied France. Moncton bustled with military activity.[481] The nearby Scoudouc airfield serviced long-range Second World War aircrafts, including the anti-submarine Consolidated B-24 Liberator and the Avro Lancaster. Canadian Forces Base (CFB) Moncton housed army units and handled logistics throughout the Maritimes. War material bound for Europe travelled by train via Moncton to the ports of Saint John and Halifax.[482] In Europe, Allied forces deployed countermeasures, including Geiger counters and metal detectors, against feared radiation attacks and minefields left behind by retreating German troops. Is it conceivable, then, that Tidd came across two American servicemen playing with their new wartime gadgets?

We may never know the truth.

Yet More Stones

Tidd recalled a peculiar rock sitting high up on the eastern bank of Lynch's Brook. Two to three feet in diameter, it stuck out less than a foot above ground. It had three weathered, thumb-sized holes drilled into it.[483] Bernard Gray, Tidd's neighbour, said he had noticed it as well. In 2019, at my behest, Gray tried but failed to locate the stone amid the tall grass. He made another attempt in 2020 with Charles Després, a local metal detectorist. Still, the object remained elusive. What the two did discover in the same general area, though, were several other rocks marked with strange cuts, grooves, and notches. They also found a small nineteenth-century axe head and a wrought-iron bar. Could these artifacts be remnants of Simpson's operation?

Després suggested to me that the carved boulders and iron rods could have worked in tandem as anchors supporting a chain-and-pulley system. Perhaps the rig could have helped both guide and draw Blakeny's horses as they trudged on the brook's steep-slopped bank. The axe could represent further evidence of tree-felling—a necessary step before digging. Després ran a metal-detector along the eastern side of Lynch's Brook and the egg-shaped feature on the adjacent plateau. All he unearthed was a lone present-day horseshoe and bits of modern scrap.

No Doubting Thomas

Tidd's uncle, Albert Davidson Thomas, led a treasure hunt of his own on the old Bishop farmstead. He purchased the land in 1948. Soon after, he asked a bulldozer crew to straighten the path of Lynch's Brook on the property's very northern edge. Diverting the brook, Tidd said, allowed his relative to look where no one ever did, namely underwater.

Artifacts by Lynch's Brook. Above: View of the eastern bank of Lynch's Brook. An iron bar fits within a horizontal groove in the sandstone. A vertical groove could allow a rope or chain to pass through. Below: A nineteenth-century axe head found nearby. [Charles Després]

Tidd had no clue what could have sparked the idea in his uncle's mind. Perhaps Thomas thought that if the pipeline somehow altered the course of Lynch's Brook, then riches hidden nearby long ago could later lie submerged. Waterways are also inherently dynamic, and their route can change naturally over time. Tidd suggested that a looping meander—an oxbow—could have led water to pool over the cache. Thomas could access the formerly dry spot simply by draining it. He never found what he was seeking. When asked why he declined to join him, Tidd replied half-jokingly, "I guess I was a little smarter than he was!" But Thomas was not alone in dreaming of undiscovered wealth.

Tidd recalled that a retired sailor from Prince Edward Island came to Irishtown in the 1950s to search for treasure. Consumed by a severe case of gold fever, the old sea dog talked endlessly with Thomas about buried booty. He toiled from dawn to dusk on the eastern bank of Lynch's Brook, armed only with a pick and a shovel. The spectacle unfolded over the course of a summer, often in sweltering heat. Tidd wanted no part of it. But he could not ignore the sight of the man who dug hole after hole "like a gopher."

As he watched the bulldozer divert Lynch's Brook, Tidd could not understand his uncle's rationale. Why should a cache lie so low in the riverbed? The stream amounts to little more than a trickle today. Yet it was once four or five feet deep—enough for Tidd to remember his own children jumping into the water from the branch of a bordering elm tree. Surely, Tidd thought, burying treasure on the creek's bank would be a non-starter, because fluctuating levels could put the gold out of reach all too easily.

No doubting Thomas, Tidd's uncle, like Simpson before him, remained undeterred.

The Eye of the Beholder

Nowhere is the curious egg-shaped feature on the former Bishop farmstead more pronounced than in an aerial photograph taken in June 1945. But not all readers will perceive the image in the same way.

The direction of incident light can alter the appearance of objects in overhead imagery even if things remain unchanged on the ground. Viewers may perceive the egg-shaped feature either as a hole or a hill in the June 1945 shot.

The sensation may flip from one impression to the other simply by rotating the picture on its side or upside down. Such visual illusions, like Moncton's famed Magnetic Hill, remind us that our senses are far from foolproof. So which impression—hole or hill—is the correct one?

The long westerly shadows cast by the trees indicate that the 1945 photograph was taken while the sun was rising in the east. The shadow cast by the egg-shaped feature is shorter and also points west. Together, these two clues reveal that the object was a small hill at most a few metres high. The mound

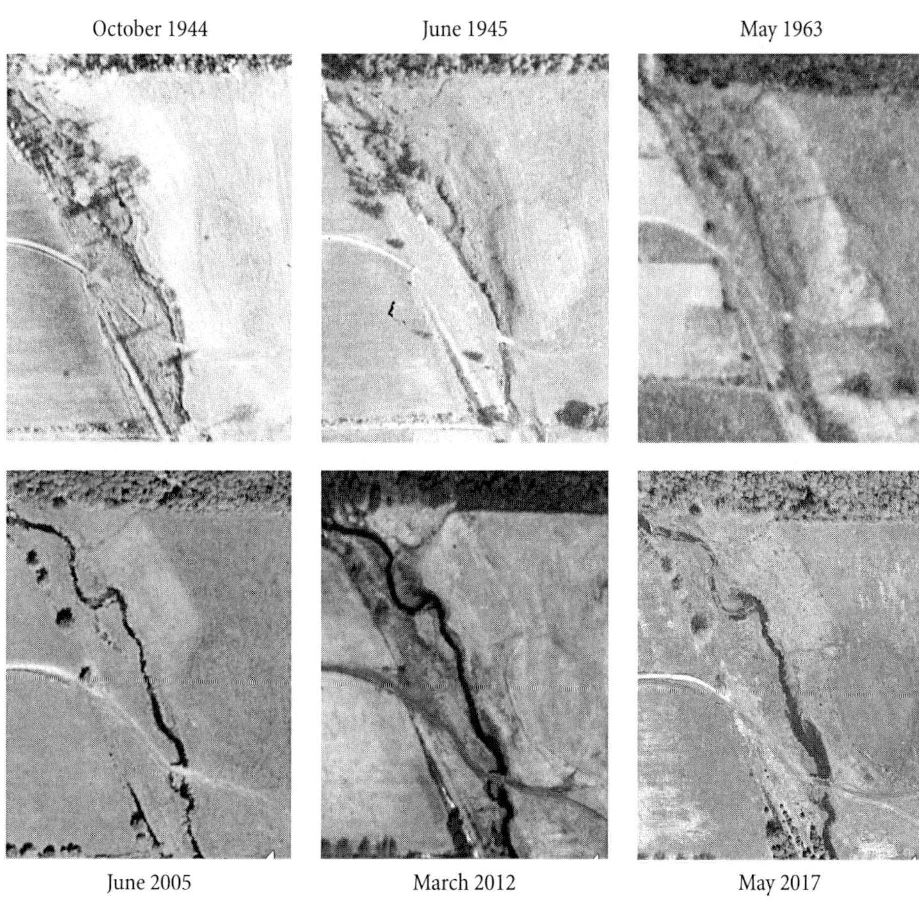

Aerial and satellite photographs of the old Bishop farm show the evolution of Lynch's Brook over the years. Above, left to right: Aerial shots from 1944, 1945, and 1963. [National Air Photo Library] *Below, left to right: An overhead view of Lynch's Brook in 2005, 2012, and 2017.* [Map data ©2005, ©2012, and ©2017 Google]

appears less prominent in later imagery. It is barely noticeable on the ground today. The plow has likely levelled it over time.

Simpson was not the last to seek a cache of riches by Lynch's Brook. Search efforts from the 1920s, 1940s, and 1950s attest that rumours of French gold buried north of Moncton persisted well after Simpson's visit. The theme of the present chapter—that expectation affects interpretation—could not be more topical in a book on treasure hunting. And objects, including George Budd's odd stone, do not always yield their secrets in unambiguous, straightforward terms. Readers may have experienced for themselves that simple holes and hills can play tricks with the mind. I myself, while investigating Simpson's dig site, struggled to entertain other alternatives. The meaning we give to words, images, and the rest often betrays our own preferred understanding.

Tidd, the ever-skeptical, no-nonsense pragmatist, offers a refreshing counterpoint to a story dominated by dreamers. But that has not stopped the old farmer from passing along precious memories. These, in turn, have expanded this book's universe. Under various guises, this chapter warns us that the heart can cloud the mind and colour what the eye sees. And we should heed that advice going forward.

Because Tidd, unbeknownst to even himself, had saved his best for last.

The Lost Treasure of Louisbourg

With a few ifs, one could put Paris in a bottle.
– old French saying

Founded in 1713 on Isle Royale (Cape Breton, NS), Louisbourg grew ex nihilo into one of North America's busiest harbours. New France's preeminent settlement on the Atlantic oceanfront met several imperatives, namely countering British expansionism, guarding French-held territories, protecting routes to Quebec, sustaining cod fisheries, fostering a "nursery of seamen," boosting trade with the West Indies, and providing a base for navy vessels and privateers.[484] Troops and ramparts turned the community into a veritable stronghold.[485] Large infusions of crown and private funds stimulated local entrepreneurs, including shipowners, merchants, craftsmen, and innkeepers.[486] But the colony's relative prosperity adds a wrinkle to our story.

Because, at Louisbourg, gold coins circulated until the end.[487]

The benefits of bills of exchange, promissory notes, and various legal instruments were not lost on Louisbourg's inhabitants. Uniquely, however, Isle Royale never resorted to paper money.[488] Its per capita subsidies dwarfed those of other French colonies.[489] It also abounded with coinage, including during periods when currency shortages afflicted the rest of New France.[490] Its capture by Britain in 1745 did not stop its use of metal denominations. After France won back control in early 1749, its commissaire-ordonnateur, Jacques Prevost de La Croix, returned with 450,000 livres (~$10M) in specie to jump-start its economy.[491] From 1755 onward, Louisbourg paid its troupes de Terre directly in silver and gold.[492]

Isle Royale owed part of its monetary influx to commerce, both legitimate and contraband. It tended to run a positive trade balance and often conducted business on a cash basis. Privateers rounded out its supply of specie. Between August and October 1757, for instance, Louisbourg-based corsairs seized thirty-nine enemy vessels valued at over 800,000 livres (~$17.8M).[493] Ultimately, estate inventories and government papers attest to the presence in the colony of gold coins, such as French louis d'or and Spanish pistoles.[494]

Thus, rumours of a lost Louisbourg treasure endure. Persistent legends involve corrupt French bureaucrats hiding their wealth in a secret vault or sending money to safety before Britain's 1758 siege.[495] Louisbourg's administrators treated the king's treasury as a personal slush fund and rewarded subordinates with patronage. They also blurred the line between the public and private spheres by engaging in commercial ventures to supplement their salaries. They amassed fortunes in the process.[496]

Vague talk of an undiscovered hoard would remain just that were it not for the claim by one former French official that such a cache, in fact, did exist. In 1730, Jean Laborde rose to the rank of secretary to Louisbourg's commissaire-ordonnateur. By 1750, the one-time protege of François Bigot had accumulated the titles of royal notary, attorney general of Isle Royale's Conseil Supérieur, and treasurers' agent for the Marine and Colonies services. It is in the latter capacity that Laborde wielded enormous influence in distributing the colossal subsidies the mother country sent to the colony. Controversially, he also leveraged crown funds to bankroll his personal involvement in transatlantic shipping, international brokerage, and high-seas privateering, all while using his position to steer the king's business toward his own. Merchants in France's port city of Saint Malo complained that Laborde had cornered Isle Royale's market. He netted 165,000 livres (~$3.7M) from 1755 to 1758 alone by supplying troops with molasses. He further pocketed 150,000 livres (~$3.3M) from raids by the *Vigilant*, one of five corsairs that scoured the Atlantic on his behalf. He returned to France after the fortress's final capture in 1758 and worked at reconciling his account books.

His ledgers, though, came up several hundred thousand livres short.[497]

Laborde attributed the discrepancies to documents he had left behind at Louisbourg along with a strongbox filled with money. He sought power of attorney to recover evidence from the colony's post-conquest British governor and sent his son to London to expedite matters. French authorities remained unconvinced. They later accused him of having fabricated the story to expunge his debts. They jailed him in 1763 and released him the following year, but not before stripping him of his remaining assets, or 336,104 livres (~$7.5M).[498]

Reliability aside, Laborde's statement shows how Louisbourg easily lends itself to fanciful tales. With a few "ifs," we could even tie rumours of Louisbourg's lost treasure to Blakeny's own yarn. Indeed, Britain disrupted France's sea routes in the North Atlantic during the lead-up to the 1758 siege. But journeying between Isle Royale and Quebec remained possible via a combination of portages and small-boat coasting through Le Coude's general area.[499] Still, plans to send away the fortress's riches to safety would have been rife with difficulties.[500] Venturing beyond Louisbourg's walls—let alone reaching Quebec—would have meant eluding watchful British forces on high alert for sorties.[501] And with Quebec as Britain's next obvious target, the capital of New France was no place to safeguard vast quantities of gold.

Laborde's story, while unsubstantiated, carries another important subtext: A strongbox of money left behind at Louisbourg comes across as an oddity—an exception to the rule that France had otherwise repatriated such funds from Isle Royale. As for the colony's wealthy elite, it did not take well to the inclement weather. It regularly shipped savings to the motherland, where it hoped to soon retire.[502] In short, there were few incentives to hoard large amounts of crown or private assets at Louisbourg before the 1758 siege, much less in a form that could be lost, stolen, or seized. The most probable scenario also remains the most sensible: Whatever gold there was at Louisbourg returned home to France.[503]

Chapter 17
A Stone Left Unturned

When you have eliminated the impossible, whatever is left, however improbable, must be the truth.
– Sir Arthur Conan Doyle,
Sherlock Holmes, The Sign of Four

Tidd is the ultimate pragmatist. The ninety-four-year-old farmer remained unperturbed when told of a massive, late-nineteenth-century excavation on his Irishtown property. A laconic "Is that so?" is all that greeted the news.

Then, silence.

Treasure hunting, we know, is not Tidd's cup of tea. But no matter how well-meaning his replies, he was mostly aware only of events he had witnessed himself. His passed-on memories did not stretch to Simpson's time. Otherwise, he felt he had little to add. What he said next, then, came as even more of a shock. Mindful not to leave anything out, he revealed that a strange boulder lay embedded in the Bishop house's old cellar.

The rock, Tidd remarked, "was a large stone with a frog cut into it."[504]

When Less Is More

It is best to share as few details as possible during an investigation. Withholding information shields us from steering witnesses toward hoped-for answers or planting ideas they could later come to regard as their own. Up to that point in the interview, I had not told Tidd about Simpson's so-called treasure map. Nor had I ever alluded to a frog carved into a rock.

Tidd's stunning declaration appeared out of the blue.

Readers shaken by Tidd's bombshell are not alone. Could there be a real-life counterpart to the engraved boulder mentioned on Simpson's chart? Could the old Bishop cellar contain the stone that Simpson had sought in vain? And would finding such an object validate his quest as well as Blakeny's legend? To subsequent questions, Tidd replied he had no clue where the rock came from, who sculpted it, why it lies on his property, or what it symbolizes. We ourselves would have remained in the dark had it not been for one source.

Hanford Blakeny was ten years old in 1899 when he and his father welcomed Simpson into their Sunny Brae home. That evening, in the dim light of the oil lamp, Hanford saw the two men pour over the document laid out on the kitchen table. He wrote sixty years later: "I recall the marks indicating the location of the big rock which was supposed to have the picture of a frog carved on the bottom."

Hanford's extraordinary footnote stands as the only known account that references the engraved boulder on Simpson's chart. Blakeny's son printed at most a few dozen copies of his memoir. Nothing about the book advertises that it tackles Simpson's quest in its last few pages. The autobiography reads as a work of dutiful remembrance that caters largely to family, friends, and local historians. One such historian, Dan Soucoup, cited the footnote verbatim in a 2003 follow-up to a short article he had written about Simpson's search in the Moncton *Times & Transcript*.[505] But this is the exception that proves the rule. Without Hanford's personal comment, Tidd's mention of a frog-carved stone would carry no more meaning for us than for anyone else.

The less Tidd understood, the more intriguing things got.

The Plot Thickens

Pressed about the strange boulder's location, Tidd said the old Bishop cellar now lies buried under his own backyard. Tidd inherited the property in 1971, and he demolished the dwelling's floating summer kitchen soon after. He then pushed back the main section, which was still supported by its original rectangular stone foundations, forty metres to the east, rested it on a concrete slab, and converted it into a storage shed. Finally, he backfilled the old gaping basement flush with his lawn. A few of the structure's top stones still protrude

Aerial photography showing the old Bishop house in 1963 (above) and 2017 (below). Tidd moved the house east by forty metres and backfilled the old stone cellar between those two dates. [Above: National Air Photo Library, Natural Resources Canada; Below: Map data ©2025 Google]

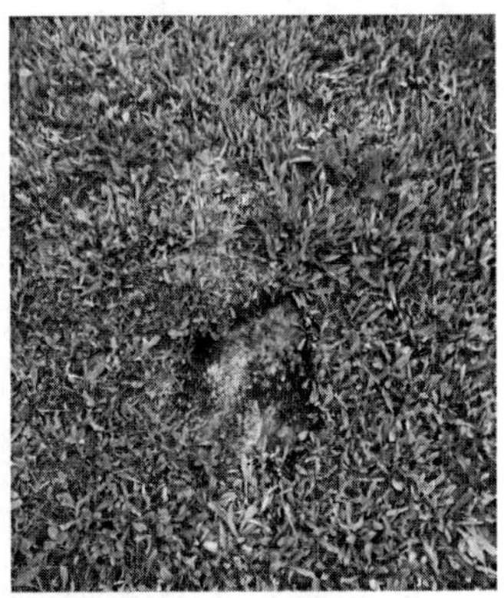

Ernest Tidd's backyard. Top left: The old Bishop house originally sat on stone foundations. Top right: Stones from the old Bishop cellar poking through Tidd's lawn. Bottom: East-looking view of Tidd's backyard. The old Bishop cellar lies under the lawn in the foreground. [AUTHOR]

through the grass today. Frustratingly, like Simpson's map, it seems Tidd's frog rock lies just beyond our grasp. The plight of Tantalus springs to mind, as do legends of treasures that vanish the moment they appear to come within reach.

Disappointingly, Tidd claims he never saw the frog rock himself. In fact, he only *heard* about the odd boulder from none other than his uncle Thomas. So why did Tidd neglect to look for the strange stone before he filled in the exposed foundations? The ever practical farmer admits he had more pressing things to worry about. He never so much as glanced at the cellar's walls.[506] In his defence, he did not know then what we know now. A curious boulder nestled in the old Bishop basement meant nothing to him. Still, the bombshell revelation remains unsettling. And, as the plot thickens, we have to consider trading the pen for the shovel.

But first, the past is trying to speak.

Echoes From the Past

We have every reason to trust Ernest Tidd, the elderly farmer, whose very name evokes honesty. Of greater concern is Thomas, the source of Tidd's second-hand information. Tidd's uncle was not as grounded as his nephew. We must take his frog-rock claim with a pinch of salt and proceed carefully. The burning question, of course, is whether Thomas's statement is accurate. Still, we have no choice but to approach the problem from the side. That is, in Thomas's mind, did the carved stone lead to buried gold?

Tidd insists that his uncle Thomas never spoke of the frog rock and hidden booty in the same breath.[507] Perhaps Thomas failed to make the connection. Under that scenario, a strange boulder found in the Bishop cellar would constitute a meaningless curiosity for him, just as it did for his nephew. The other possibility is that Thomas kept his thoughts to himself. Tidd's disinterest in lost riches was no conversation starter. That, surely, is why he is unable to elaborate on his uncle's rationale. Either way, if Thomas somehow got wind

Left: Ernest Tidd, the current owner of the old Bishop farm. Right: Albert Thomas, Tidd's uncle and previous owner of the Bishop farm. [ANGÈLE GRAY]

that an engraved stone indicated concealed wealth, the game would change on a profound level. Again, mindset is everything.

And Thomas did not need much proof to believe.

Thomas's treasure-seeking days date back to his early years in Kent County. There, as a young man, he dug for rumoured gold under an oak tree near a river's edge.[508] It should come as no surprise, then, to find him scouring for a missing hoard on the Bishop farm he acquired years later. More intriguing is that Tidd's uncle diverted Lynch's Brook in virtually the same spot where Simpson had begun his own search half a century before. Manifestly, Thomas knew much about the elderly Ontarian's quest. He may even have been aware of the frog rock indicated on his map. But if a carved stone—real or imagined—led him to march in Simpson's footsteps, how did he come to learn what the boulder could symbolize?

The most likely source is John A. Bishop Jr.[509] Because, it turns out, Bishop was Thomas's next-door neighbour.

Thomas and his wife, Florence, returned to their native Canada after a lengthy stay in Massachusetts. In 1941, they moved directly across from John A. Bishop Jr.[510] Bishop died the following year, still the owner of his family's farm. In the interim, Thomas lived shoulder-to-shoulder with one of Simpson's closest collaborators. And though unrelated to Bishop by blood, Thomas had links to him by marriage.[511]

At first, Tidd claimed to be unaware of a century-old treasure hunt on his land. But he later recalled that the Bishops themselves had searched for gold on the property. Tidd could add nothing more except that he likely learned the fact from his uncle.[512] He also remembered the elderly Bishop as "quite the storyteller." Tidd's remarks reinforce the idea of social proximity between the neighbouring Thomas and Bishop. And if Thomas knew much about Simpson's quest, it could only be because of privileged intelligence that few others than Bishop himself could have passed on.

From Simpson to Bishop to Thomas to Tidd to us—the mention of a frog rock could be a chain of reverberating echoes from the past. The Thomas-to-Tidd link appears to be the one where the most information was lost. In the end, evidence suggests Thomas was aware of Simpson's map and of the association between a carved stone and buried gold.

It is just that he never shared it with his nephew.

A Rock and a Hard Place

Believing and seeing are two different things. Maybe Thomas did spot a frog rock in the Bishop cellar. Alternatively, maybe he just simply wished one into existence. Let us examine which scenario—genuine vs. imagined stone—passes muster.

A physical frog rock would have far-reaching implications for our story. Simpson would have leaped for joy at the sight of the odd boulder under the Bishop house. His confidence that "the money is on the Bishop property or it is nowhere" would appear more understandable. Blakeny even described the mechanism by which stones on the bank of Lynch's Brook could have ended up as part of the Bishop basement: "We did find landmarks shown on the chart—a south running stream and a spring. It showed the treasure as being buried behind a big rock but a lot of building stone had been taken out of the place and the rock was gone, so that wasn't any help."

And therein lies the problem. How could Thomas have casually stumbled upon a carved stone that so many had actively sought but somehow missed? And how could the Bishops themselves be unaware of a strange boulder embedded in their own house's cellar? Jack Bishop—John A. Jr.'s father—had erected the foundations himself, and he was still alive and well during Simpson's visit.[513] The rediscovery of the odd stone—the one tangible piece of evidence that would lend credence to Simpson's chart—should feature prominently in Blakeny's story. Yet Blakeny confesses instead that he never laid eyes on it, much less recovered it. We can draw only one conclusion: Rather than witness an actual frog rock, Thomas merely *believed* in one.

But how did he come to imagine such an object in the old Bishop cellar?

According to Blakeny, builders incorporated stones taken from Lynch's Brook into nearby structures. That alone could have led Simpson to assume that his chart's missing frog rock had ended up in the Bishop basement. The boulder's sculpted face could even lie hidden from view, depending on its orientation and placement within the walls. Putting faith into something that cannot be proved false—out-of-sight stone or out-of-reach gold—is an inviting mental shelter for treasure hunters unwilling to question the validity of their quest. In short, Tidd's bombshell could be a figment of Simpson's wishful imagination, passed on from one generation to another. But our credo of leaving no stone unturned puts us between a rock and a hard place.

We have to dig up the old Bishop cellar.

Would the ever-skeptical Tidd allow it? It was only fair that we briefed him on the significance of his frog-rock comment. “I don’t want you to do it!” was Tidd’s frank reply. His decision was no knee-jerk reaction either. Excavating the Bishop foundations, he said, would risk killing the proud elm tree that stands nearby. The elderly farmer is under no obligation to let us ruin his backyard. We can only thank him for the stories he helped us immortalize.

This is the end of the line for the frog-rock lead. We must leave the proverbial stone unturned. For what it is worth, Tidd does not have high hopes that a frog rock lies buried in the old Bishop cellar. He spent decades rubbing shoulders with his treasure-seeking uncle. And while he does not say it so overtly, he leans on the side of deluded relative rather than meaningful object.

Our investigation is coming full circle. We have met much of the Aristotelian who-what-when-where-why-how challenge. But the “what” jumps out. Our story’s true main character, its unifying thread, and its original big bang, the ultimate “what” is also the most befuddling. Simply put, what was Simpson’s chart?

A genuine treasure map can be no more probable than real treasure itself. And so we must look at alternatives. Clever con? Misread memo? Unable to inspect Simpson’s parchment for ourselves, we can only speculate. But, before we tackle what Simpson’s manuscript could be, let us reflect on what it most likely is not.

The clever-con angle runs into problems. A paper’s weathered appearance would require counterfeiting know-how. Content, though, remains the more troubling aspect. Why prefer words over imagery? Why write in French when an English text—say, one referencing Captain Kidd’s supposed buried treasure—would be more accessible and thought-provoking? And how could a nineteenth-century forger accurately reference a long-forgotten French portage trail? Plus, a dishonest mapmaker must carry out not one act of deception but two. The first is to craft a convincing document. The second is to invent a credible backstory. An elaborate hoax suggests profit as a motive. Finding a gullible yet resourceful buyer is no sure-fire proposition.

The map's provenance also remains nebulous. Blakeny addressed it in these words:

> His [Simpson's] story was that a man whom he had helped had given him a chart—the chart—which had been made by those who buried the payroll.
>
> There was a romantic tale attached to it—how a French soldier had secretly preserved it hoping to return himself and reclaim the treasure and how, wounded and on his deathbed, he had given it to a friend, and how, at last, it had fallen into the hands of the man who gave it to Mr. Simpson.

In Simpson's eyes, the document dated back 150 years before his time. It then quietly passed down a chain of obscure acquaintances and agonizing confidants. The backstory matches a well-worn literary trope, and it is probably apocryphal on this ground alone.[514] Short of finding gold, Simpson could never have been certain of it himself. Yet it appears he had his reasons to trust the chart's pedigree. Indeed, according to Blakeny, the prized object had been a gift rather than a purchase.

No matter which aspects we scrutinize—appearance, content, or provenance—the fakery angle makes for a hard sell. The manuscript, it would seem, is neither a genuine treasure map nor a forgery.

So what in the world could Simpson's parchment possibly be?

The *Monckton*'s Escape

HISTORICAL • CONTEXT •

In 1759, two British vessels—the *Monckton* and a small sloop—berthed at Grindstone Island. Gunshots rang out the next day. The sloop had been hijacked the night before, possibly by Beausoleil Broussard and his followers. It bore down on the *Monckton*. "Take care of yourselves, we are all prisoners here," a cry shouted. Then a summon, "Lower your main sail, we are all French, and will give you good quarter." The

Monckton, rather than comply, returned fire.

Then, the wind picked up.

The *Monckton* seized its chance and headed for Fort Edward (Windsor, NS). The boats traded salvos during a five-hour chase across the Bay of Fundy. The *Monckton* did not escape unscathed: A boy lost his life, and two men suffered injuries. Initially bound for Fort Cumberland (formerly Fort Beauséjour), the *Monckton* carried "a considerable charge of money" overseen by a paymaster. The abductors never found the stash of $600 (~$18,500) hidden aboard. They later ransomed the sloop for $1,500 (~$46,200).[515]

A stopover at Grindstone Island, near the mouth of the Petitcodiac. A period-accurate naval pursuit between French and British forces. A secret cash reserve for troop salaries. The *Monckton*'s getaway is no match for Blakeny's legend, but it may have inspired more fanciful accounts.

The story of the *Monckton* appeared in a war journal written by John Knox.[516] The Irish lieutenant served in the British army during the Seven Years War. The world's first global conflict ended with the 1763 Treaty of Paris. Soon after, Planters from New England settled on lands vacated by the Acadian deportation. In 1784, Britain split continental and peninsular Acadie into the colonies of New Brunswick and Nova Scotia respectively.[517] The partition, some argued, made New Brunswick's capital of Fredericton less remote than Halifax. It also gave more political representation to the new territory's many British Loyalists who had fled the American War of Independence.[518]

David Blakeny, Sherman Blakeny's great-great-grandfather, emigrated from Northern Ireland to South Carolina in 1767. There, he and his British sympathies became the target of persecution. He left America in 1782. He put down roots in Petitcodiac (Salisbury Parish, NB) in 1786.[519] He and his descendants likely learned about local history from a Loyalist perspective. Sherman Blakeny himself apparently took a keen interest in the region's mythology.[520]

Chapter 18
The Riddle of Skull Island

Reality leaves a lot to the imagination.
– John Lennon

Reason catches up with emotion. Fact catches up with fantasy. And the past catches up with the present. This book's historical context reminds us that Blakeny's legend—nine leather bags of gold concealed by French troops near Le Coude during the 1750s—is out of step with the story of Acadie. Our tussle with Tidd's frog rock also shows that proving a negative is no easy task. In the case of Blakeny's tale, however, we may well have achieved just that.

Blakeny's yarn, though unique in its specifics, is not unique in its genre. Popular lore and published fiction made use of similar elements during the late nineteenth century. Plot devices included treasure maps leading to booty offloaded from ships and hastily buried on land. Blakeny's account also evokes a French supply vessel (where there was none) sent to pay French units (where there were none) with gold (that never was) that eluded British guns (where there were none) and evaded British soldiers (where there were none). Moreover, the silence from New France's administrators is deafening. Archived records—letters, reports, and inventories—and subsequent memoirs show that no large sum of money vanished in Acadie for the period in play. The loss of *Le Chameau*'s precious payload, while comparable to Blakeny's nine missing bags of gold, generated voluminous correspondence chronicling the disaster and its repercussions.[521] Evidence points to only one outcome: Unexceptional. Unworkable. Unsupported. Blakeny's legend is as good as dead.

The demise of Blakeny's tale, while perhaps demoralizing to dreamers, is a necessary rite of passage for truth seekers. Previously, we put low odds on a forged treasure map and lower odds still on a real one. More probable, we argued, is that Simpson's chart was a genuine mid-eighteenth-century French document misconstrued by romantic, late-nineteenth-century eyes. Nothing less than seeing the manuscript with our own eyes will settle the issue. Short of that, readers will decide for themselves which scenario—clever con or misread memo—is more plausible. The clever-con alternative already got its fair shake. The misread-memo option now deserves a shot of its own.

As we begin tackling the mystery that is Simpson's parchment, let us keep two ideas in mind: Truth can be stranger than fiction, and some things can be worth more than gold.

Map Meets Legend

We must now autopsy Blakeny's deceased fable for clues. Our first task is to peel back the Sunny Brae excavator's interpretation of Simpson's chart and sneak a speculative glance at the odd document ourselves.

Simpson and Blakeny were perfect strangers until the former knocked on the latter's door. Never before seen by Blakeny, Simpson's manuscript contained French text pointing to present-day Moncton and recounting its own origins. Blakeny, for his part, recalled a local myth in which mid-eighteenth-century French troops concealed gold near Le Coude. So, did the two treasure seekers find their respective accounts matched up point for point?

Not a chance.

Folk tales evolve from one retelling to another.[522] The odds are therefore vanishingly small that Blakeny possessed *the* version that would have corroborated Simpson's document word for word. Ian Sclanders himself introduced Blakeny's yarn as mere backdrop. Only later, in a single stroke, did he establish a connection between map and legend: "His [Simpson's] story was that a man whom he had helped had given him a chart—the chart—which had been made by those who buried the payroll."

Sclanders's brilliant style ties *a* chart (Simpson's) with *the* chart (the legend's). But the link could not be more tenuous. Simpson and Blakeny may have played up similarities and downplayed differences as they compared notes. Perhaps vague rumours of gold concealed near Le Coude helped paper over their clashing narratives. Yet something has to give when immovable object meets unstoppable force. To be sure, local lore must have influenced the understanding of Simpson's manuscript.

But, inversely, did the chart also cause Blakeny to reinterpret his home-grown legend?

Blakeny was awestruck by the "oldest document" he had ever witnessed. The parchment, we now know, contained only words. By the same token, it may also have been correspondingly light on place names. Moreover, it evoked travel over water. But while we have come across several retellings of the legend, only Blakeny's version includes a maritime element. So, could the Sunny Brae excavator have injected a naval component into a countryside yarn to reconcile Simpson's chart with landlocked Irishtown? Grindstone Island and the Petitcodiac River would have been natural choices for him to fill in the blanks.

Simpson and Blakeny no doubt saw what they wanted to see in a French text alluding to a bygone era. Peering beyond Blakeny's own interpretation carries risk. At this stage, however, speculation only requires us to clear a very low bar. As we begin imagining more plausible alternatives, we need not even be right. We only need to be less wrong.

The End of the Road

To our knowledge, Blakeny's yarn is the only source to explicitly mention Grindstone Island and the Petitcodiac River. The legend's very geography is now in doubt, and we must therefore shift its epicentre accordingly. With little certainty about landmarks other than the general area of Le Coude, we risk entering an interpretative free-for-all divorced from hard data. But that would be discounting the 1901 *Daily Times*'s extraordinary reveal: "The chart designates a starting point on the old French road leading in the direction of Shediac." It remains unclear how the ancient pathway ties into our story. Still, rather than look south of Le Coude, as Blakeny did, indications are that we should search east toward Shediac for the answers we seek. The change in geographical perspective comes with intriguing possibilities.

We know from French engineer De Léry's 1750 memoir that France made strategic but fleeting use of a portage path linking Shediac to Le Coude.[523] Indigenous Peoples had blazed the shortcut between the Bay of Fundy and the North Shore centuries before.[524] The trail also helped desperate Acadian families flee peninsular Acadie.[525] But where, exactly, does the old French road lie?

No definitive evidence pins down the location of the now forgotten trackway. Enthusiasts have pondered its whereabouts for over a hundred years. William Francis Ganong, the indefatigable New Brunswick explorer, ranks as chief among these. In his 1899 monograph, he was unaware of De Léry's 1750 report. He summed up his understanding of the old French road in these words: "The only reference to this portage known to me is in a document of 1756 given by Rameau de St. Père."[526]

The 1756 text recounts a harrowing winter journey undertaken by Acadian Pierre Gauthier over nearly seven hundred kilometres of frozen lands and rivers to deliver mission-critical correspondence—or *paquets de la Cour*—from Louisbourg to Quebec. The account explains: "It is a portage of six leagues [~23 km] from one place [Shediac] to the other [Petitcodiac], and a good road. There are at the said [Petitcodiac] river six or eight French homes."[527]

Ganong's 1899 monograph proves that the old French road's location remained a mystery even at the time of Simpson's visit. Perhaps local rumours—or possibly Simpson's map itself—left no doubt as to the trail's whereabouts. We, however, have no such luxury. Three potential paths—a northern, a middle, and a southern one—have emerged. And one path in particular serves up food for thought.

Ganong, once aware of De Léry's work, proposed the middle path in 1928. His itinerary links Humphreys Brook—the eastern branch of Halls Creek in Moncton—with the French *magazin* (storehouse) on De Léry's map at the Shediac River's head of tide. The trail forms a straight line between the two endpoints. By definition, it is the most direct. Its lengthy portage section, though, makes it especially arduous.[528]

The archaeologist Kevin Leonard suggested the southern path as part of his 2001 Shediac survey. The hypothetical route, which connects the same

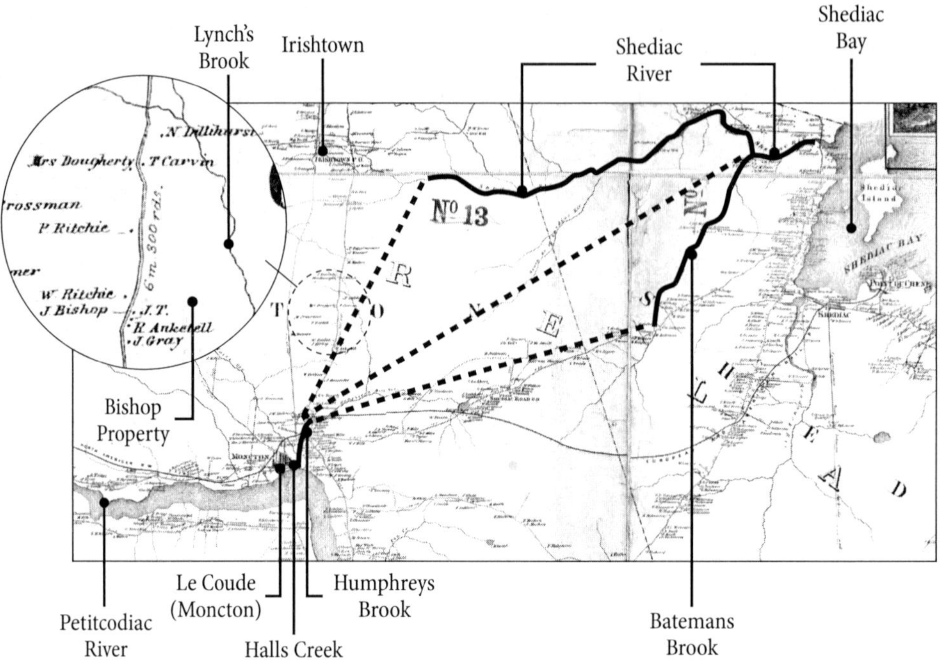

The old French Road to Shediac. The road's exact path is unknown. Various routes—a northern, middle, and southern path—have been suggested. Solid lines show potentially navigable sections, dashed lines show possible portage sections. [06_01_011670, Norman B. Leventhal Map & Education Center, Boston Public Library]

endpoints as Ganong's, leverages Batemans Brook, a shallow tributary of the Shediac River.[529] Because it exploits waterways, the route cuts down the distance covered on foot. Still, it would only be viable if, unlike today, the navigable portion of Batemans Brook extended far upstream at the time.[530]

Finally, historian John Clarence Webster put forward the northern path in 1928. According to his sketch, it begins at Humphreys Brook and proceeds toward the Shediac River's headwaters near Irishtown. From there, the Shediac River would have provided navigable access to the inland *magazins* on De Léry's map and to the coast of Shediac Bay. The itinerary is the longest overall. However, it is also the easiest because its overland segment is the shortest. Webster wrote that the Shediac River road "was probably the early path used by the Indians and French between the North Shore and the Petitcodiac."[531]

Robert Doyle, a modern-day woodsman and canoeist, supports Webster's intuition. His lifelong work of charting out lost Indigenous Peoples' and

French portages throughout New Brunswick leverages state-of-the-art technology. His on-the-ground reconnaissance around Irishtown lends credence to the northern-path hypothesis. But it also serves up a surprise: According to Doyle, the old French route cuts directly across the former Bishop farm.[532]

Doyle's proposed track heads due north from Humphreys Brook. His GPS waypoint #11 falls squarely inside the Bishop property. From there, the itinerary trends north-northeasterly and meets Lynch's Brook near the Moncton reservoir.[533] Finally, it reaches the Shediac River's closest navigable jumping-off point at the intersection of Cape Breton Road and Caledonia Road, about 4.5 km east of Irishtown.[534]

Given everything we know, there is an objective basis to suggest that Simpson's quest was not wrong to concentrate on Irishtown and on Lynch's Brook specifically. If we imagine "a starting point on the old French road leading in the direction of Shediac," only the northern path appears compatible with a "south running stream"—Lynch's Brook—in Moncton's vicinity.

We have made progress linking a mid-eighteenth-century French portage trail to our story. And more clues await us at the end of the road.

Skull Island

French and Acadian explorers from the seventeenth and eighteenth centuries visited the Shediac region. The area remained exclusively populated by the Mi'kmaq until the late 1740s.[535] In 1749, Quebec chose the site to build a small outpost. It dispatched Louis Chevalier de La Corne, a veteran of past Acadie campaigns, to carry out the plan. The mission, which mirrored Boishébert's task at the Saint John River, consisted in reasserting France's control over continental Acadie, relocating peninsular Acadians, securing allegiances, organizing militias, and denying entry to the British, by force if necessary.[536]

In November 1749, La Corne and his detachment of seventy men arrived at Shediac after a difficult journey at sea. Their ship's cargo, which totalled 34,062 French livres (~$800,000), included textiles, cauldrons, nails, saws, planks, knives, hourglasses, salted lard, gunflints, etc.[537] The stockpiles were intended for the fort and its inhabitants, for Acadian exiles, and possibly for Abbé Le Loutre and his warriors.[538]

La Corne established a presence along the Petitcodiac, Chipoudie, and Memramcook Rivers. He also stationed soldiers on the Isthmus of Chignecto. Soon, he requested hundreds more troops.[539] By the summer of 1750, Shediac had become a cornerstone of France's efforts in continental Acadie. The settlement was at once a headquarters, a harbour, a shortcut, a deterrent, a lifeline, and a resupply base. Why, then, was the outpost abandoned in 1751 after having operated for little more than a year? And can France's flash-in-the-pan stay in the region yield clues about Simpson's chart?

Shediac lay more than fifty kilometres from the Missaguash River, the boundary between French- and British-held Acadie. The Bay of Shediac was also reputedly unsuitable for oceangoing vessels. De Léry wrote in his 1750 report:

> The port of Ejetdaik [Shediac] can be useful only to small ships, which will be able to go no farther than the small island, which is in the middle of the port. The port is not advantageous, the channel is narrow between the island and land south of the said island. There are two fathoms [~3 metres] and two-and-a-half fathoms [~4 metres], hard sand bottom, and water is no deeper two leagues [~8 km] out to sea. North of this island, which is 3/4 leagues [~3 km] long, there is no channel. The said island forms the port of Ejetdaik.[540]

A navigable channel did allow inward progress. But De Léry noted that Shediac Bay's waters were so shallow that even small boats could sail no farther than Shediac Island.[541] Crucially, then, where did ships dock?

De Léry's report, which describes the Shediac outpost without specifying its location, offers no clear answer.[542] The fort's whereabouts, like the Shediac portage road, have since vanished in the mists of time. But the most probable site is also the most thought-provoking.

De Léry's crude map places La Corne's operation on the mainland somewhere south of the Shediac River.[543] Still, there are grounds to doubt its accuracy. D'Anville's 1755 chart, for instance, puts French fortifications immediately north of the Shediac River.[544] The two documents cannot both be right, of course, but they could be wrong in the same way. That is, they may both be conveying the settlement's existence rather than its precise spot. Also, De Léry writes a final cryptic remark: "The said island forms the port of Ejetdaik."

Could La Corne's outpost be *on* Shediac Island?

In 1897, Ganong investigated the ditch-and-rampart ruins of what locals called Fort Sauvage on Skull Island, the tiny islet next to Shediac Island.[545] Oral tradition has it that the Mi'kmaq constructed the stronghold for protection against the British and the Kanien'kehá (Mohawk). De Léry made no mention of Skull Island, nor did he have any reason to. At the time, it formed a peninsula tied to Shediac Island. A sandbar linking the two land masses is still visible today at low tide.[546] Coastal erosion has washed away much of it, along with Skull Island's shoreline and portions of the fort itself.[547]

Ganong found that the Skull Island fortifications were small and lacked access to fresh water. He concluded, on this basis, that the site did not correspond to La Corne's settlement. The earthworks, he argued, were more likely those of Indigenous Peoples. Yet the fort's walls are similar both in shape and in size to other French stockades in Acadie. The buildings listed in De Léry's account would easily fit within them. As for the absence of drinkable water, it would have taxed the fort's occupants no matter who they were. Also, an archaeological investigation uncovered a fully cocked flintlock from an early eighteenth-century French musket on the beach below the encampment's ramparts. We need more evidence, but the leading theory is that the Mi'kmaq took over La Corne's facilities after he abandoned them in 1751.[548]

Additional clues also favour Skull Island as the site of La Corne's outpost. Maritime charts of Shediac Bay—both old and new—show that seagoing vessels could only approach the mainland several kilometres away from the Shediac River.[549] It would make little sense, then, for La Corne to erect his stronghold so far from the river. Stores brought in by ship would have to travel great distances overland just to reach the riverway meant to ease such shipping.[550] Skull Island offers a better alternative: Its surrounding waters are not only some of the deepest in Shediac Bay, but also some of the nearest to the Shediac River's mouth. A submerged structure protruding from the island's southwestern tip—possibly an old wharf—could be further evidence of the fort's location.[551]

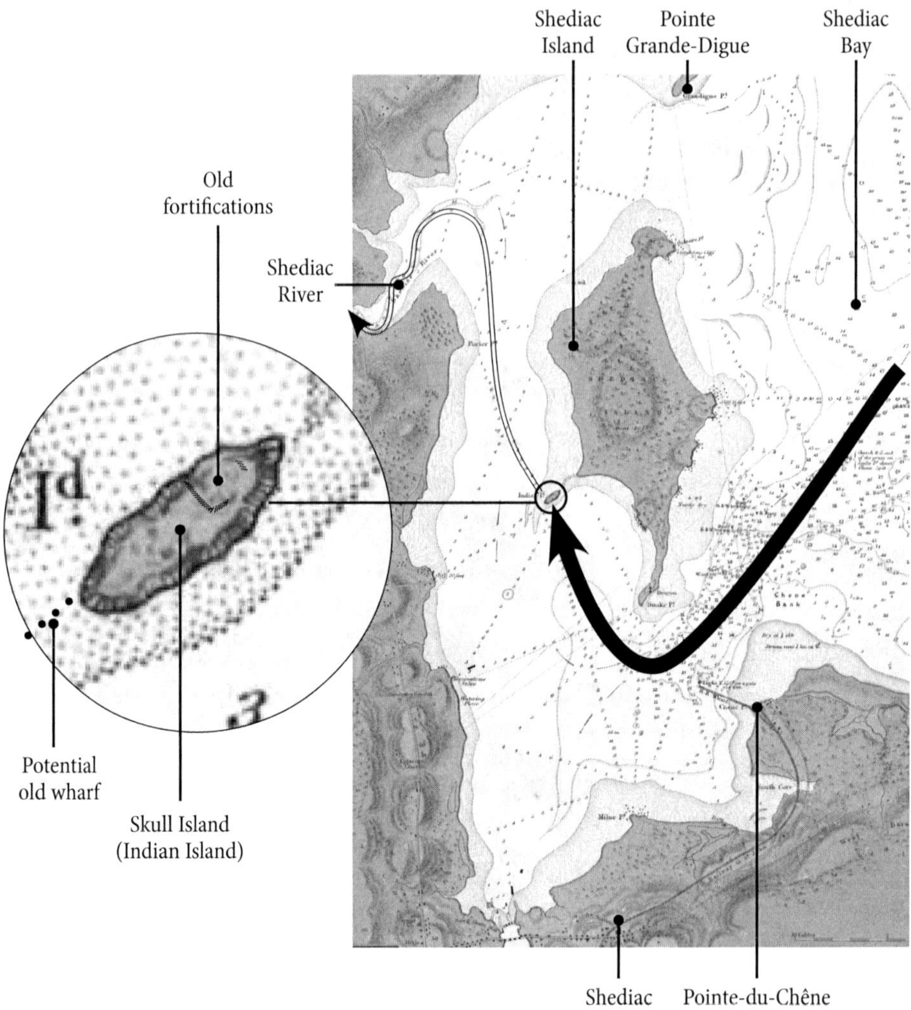

Shediac Bay (1749–1751). Old fortifications (⁄⁄⁄⁄⁄ to scale) and a potential former wharf (dotted line) on Skull Island. French ships (thick line) could have docked at Skull Island. Supplies intended for inland portage could be put onboard small boats (double line) and travel up the Shediac River. [UNITED KINGDOM HYDROGRAPHIC OFFICE, PUBLIC DOMAIN VIA WIKIMEDIA COMMONS]

Our Shediac lead suggests a narrative with strong ties to Simpson's map. Vessels from Quebec and Louisbourg would dock at Skull Island to resupply La Corne's encampment. Small boats or canoes would then ferry the stockpiles upstream to the storage *magazin* situated at the Shediac River's head of tide.[552] From there, the wares would transit to Le Coude via a portage cutting across modern-day Irishtown.

It is no surprise, in hindsight, that La Corne's Shediac operation was short-lived. Difficulties in transferring people and material to and from Shediac Bay were simply too great. Fort Gaspareaux came into service at Baie Verte in 1751 and spelled the end for the Shediac settlement. Its location offered a deepwater port and a shorter, more practicable route to nascent Fort Beauséjour.[553]

So, what about Simpson's "map"?

Limited in time and purpose, the Shediac outpost and its road to Le Coude tie Simpson's chart to a specific historical context. And, once put in that context, words from Simpson's manuscript—"we offloaded the boat," "we carried the thing upriver"—do not appear so outlandish. Unloading French supply ships at a nearby island and transporting wares upstream in small rafts seems to have been the norm in Shediac between 1749 and 1751. If Grindstone Island and the Petitcodiac River were merely Blakeny's best guesses for unnamed features on Simpson's document, then Skull Island and the Shediac River provide more compelling substitutes.[554]

Shediac's past may even hint at grains of truth in Blakeny's legend. Indeed, the folk tale is correct in evoking French cargo travelling via Le Coude during the mid 1700s to avoid detection by British forces. But, in that time and place, French stockpiles did not proceed from Grindstone Island up the Petitcodiac River, as in Blakeny's yarn. Instead, they headed downstream along the Petitcodiac after having journeyed from Shediac to Le Coude. For deciders in Quebec, Shediac was not so much a destination as a vital if fleeting access point to the rest of Acadie.

And Shediac is where our own interpretation of Simpson's map begins.

No Ordinary Document

Did Simpson and Blakeny misread a French period memo detailing the transfer of unremarkable supplies from Shediac to Le Coude? In other words, did they mistake a routine report for a treasure map? The explanation holds some appeal. But such a vanilla account remains unsatisfying on several counts.

For one, Simpson's chart seems to retell a one-off happening. Jane Regent recalled thinking, "Oh my God! It's a treasure map! It's for real!" as she inspected the faded parchment. "Oh no, it was definitely a treasure map! No doubt about that!" she said when pressed further. Contents, as much as appearance, gave the document its treasure-map flavour. What struck Jane the most was the letter's singular narrative: waypoints (seas, rivers), means of transportation (boats and horses), a sense of urgency (soldiers readying for battle), and the ferrying of cargo (something carried upstream). Such fragments do not add up to a treasure map, of course. But they are more in line with an unusual expedition than a run-of-the-mill transit.

Simpson's map also evokes a journey via unexplored terrain. By all accounts, the manuscript dwells on wayfinding details—landmarks (rivers, creeks, springs, rocks) and cardinal directions (east, south)—that would serve no purpose in reports of travel along well-worn paths. Period references to the old French trackway do not bother with such minutiae. But while the 1901 *Daily Times* does tie Simpson's map to the Shediac portage, it identifies the route only as the chart's "starting point." The document, it seems, alluded to a new, unbeaten course that deviated from the more customary one.

Jane vividly recalled the parchment's mention of horses. The beasts of burden, in turn, imply the haulage of a heavy load. De Léry himself evoked horses trudging over the trail's muddy surface in his 1750 memoir. But while Europeans did march in the Indigenous Peoples' footsteps, they also adapted the roads to their own needs.[555] Conceivably, then, Simpson's manuscript relates the transport of a hefty cargo along a one-off, horse-assisted itinerary that bypassed riverways—perhaps something akin to Ganong's middle path.[556]

Lastly, Jane Regent could not pin down the all-important "thing" being carried upriver. Did the drafter of Simpson's map have obfuscation in mind? Secrecy would be key for any document telling of soldiers readying for battle. Intercepted messages were as damaging as they were common. Good practice demanded that written exchanges remain evasive about particulars already shared between friends and allies, as in you-know-who sent you-know-what to you-know-where.[557] If Simpson's chart offered no explanation for the "thing," only a reader already in the know could recover the parchment's full meaning.

Evidence, while sparse, is that Simpson's chart could be a genuine period text describing the one-time, difficult, vital, horse-aided, and covert transfer of a heavy haul over unfamiliar terrain between Shediac and Le Coude. And even if our interpretation only captured part of the underlying truth, we can still reach one conclusion: Simpson's map appears to be no ordinary document.

The reflex of seeing a treasure map in what appears to be an unusual, mid-eighteenth-century, French parchment is understandable. Imagination and romanticism beg to fill in the blanks. That would go double if the letter's author willfully omitted key details. There are no guarantees that we ourselves, despite our skepticism, would resist the pull of fantasy should we one day stumble on the mysterious document. Nature abhors a vacuum. Inquisitive minds are no different. Without a concrete alternative to indulge our need for closure, the "thing" evoked by Simpson's chart risks forever tormenting us with a haunting thought: If not gold, then what?

Chapter 19
A Last Hurrah

Extraordinary claims require extraordinary evidence.
– Carl Sagan

On May 1, 1751, La Jonquière shipped an urgent letter briefing Versailles on the last tumultuous six months in Acadie.[558] La Corne, the leading officer at Shediac, had been ailing and returned to Quebec. Pierre-Roch de Saint-Ours Deschaillons, his second-in-command, stepped up.[559] The freshly appointed Saint-Ours faced the daunting task of erecting new fortifications on the Isthmus of Chignecto: Fort Beauséjour on the Bay of Fundy and Fort Gaspareaux at Baie Verte.[560] France's grasp over continental Acadie hung in the balance. Time was not on Saint-Ours's side.

Events from the year before had exacerbated tensions. In April 1750, British forces headed by Charles Lawrence landed near the Acadian village of Beaubassin (see "Historical Context: Halifax" at the end of chapter 6). Saint-Ours's predecessor stymied Lawrence's aims. His action, though, only delayed the inevitable. In September, after routing a band of Acadian and Mi'kmaw irregulars, Lawrence prevailed. British troops, once firmly entrenched at the Missaguash River, were within striking distance of continental Acadie. Alarmed, Quebec rushed plans to build massive defences in the area.[561] And, critically, the shifting military landscape has important ramifications for our story.

Almost overnight, the Shediac outpost went from essential to expendable.

Unfortunately, we know precious little about France's short-lived operations in Shediac. Even less well understood are events surrounding the decommissioning of the encampment. But two recently uncovered documents may change all that.

And with them our outlook on Simpson's map.

A Last Hurrah

La Jonquière devoted only a single sentence to the Shediac stronghold in his news-filled letter from 1751: "As for the Ejedaick [Shediac] outpost, the S. de St-Ours will leave one officer and a few soldiers to keep watch on the magazins [storehouses]."[562]

La Jonquière's pithy statement intimated that planning for the fort's decommissioning had been well under way. Contributing to the encampment's demise was de Léry's late-1750 report highlighting its deficiencies. Britain's campaign in Chignecto had provoked France into redeploying its resources. Shediac, once the linchpin of continental Acadie, would henceforth constitute little more than a biscuit cache guarded by a few unlucky servicemen.[563] France abandoned the site altogether in the following months.[564]

But the Shediac outpost did not go away quietly.

France urgently needed new fortifications in Chignecto after Lawrence's incursion. Still, these would take time to erect. British presence also complicated France's access to the isthmus. Ships could bring men and material intended for Fort Beauséjour and Fort Gaspareaux via Baie Verte. But the strategy was not without risk. Deciders in Quebec were understandably skittish about naval transport after Britain's recent capture of *Le London* and the *Saint-François*.[565]

The prudent course of action for France would be to leverage the Shediac outpost as the safer alternative. As before, smaller vessels would dock in its more secure harbour. From there, rather than travel by sea, people and provisions would journey overland to Le Coude, sail down the Petitcodiac River, and reach Chignecto unmolested. Besides, La Jonquière could ill afford to cast aside any assets before the isthmus's defences had become minimally operational. The Shediac stronghold, perhaps more than ever, could have played a pivotal role in funnelling France's resources into Acadie. So, did the encampment serve as a staging ground for France's military buildup before its decommission? And could such a final event—call it Shediac's last hurrah—shed any light on Simpson's map?

To date, no account has surfaced describing the wind-down of France's Shediac activities. New France's relevant archives—the *magasins du Roi*, the *bureau de contrôle de la Marine*, and the various *munitionnaires du Roi*—were lost in the wake of the British conquest.[566] Much of what remains consists of intendant decrees and other high-level correspondence. Surviving records, because of their summary nature, shy away from details such as France's latter days in the region. Still, some rare specifics do live on.

In November 1750, for instance, La Jonquière briefed his superiors that he had been unable to dispatch the *Saint-Joseph de Nantes* to Shediac, along with the additional 230 men and 6 officers he had promised Saint-Ours.[567] The draft of the ship, he explained, was too deep to navigate Shediac Bay's shallow waters. Instead, he sent two smaller vessels with only 82 men. So, does La Jonquière's troop surge correspond to the outpost's last hurrah?

Not exactly. For one, nothing ties La Jonquière's Shediac troop surge to the erection of Fort Beauséjour and Fort Gaspareaux. If anything, La Jonquière had already announced the personnel uptick in business-as-usual terms in a letter predating Lawrence's latest actions in Chignecto. Also, he spelled out in his May 1751 memo that he ordered the buildup of fortifications at Chignecto on November 8, 1750, more than a month after he had decided on assigning more soldiers to Shediac. La Jonquière's request for strongholds on the isthmus only reached Saint-Ours during the winter of 1750. Construction began the following spring.[568] To be fair, rumblings about British fortifications at Baie Verte had been circulating. Similarly, France had considered establishing defences at Chignecto as early as 1748.[569] Lawrence's attacks in Beaubassin upset the status quo and changed the calculus. Still, the point remains: No hard evidence implicates the Shediac outpost in the erection of Fort Beauséjour and Fort Gaspareaux.

That is, until now.

While sifting through archives, I identified two period documents showing that Shediac did not sink quietly into oblivion. Instead, the papers reveal the encampment's vital role in the building of Chignecto stockades. In the end, Shediac did have its last hurrah.

And Simpson's map may have been a witness to it.

A Tale of Two Storekeepers

Shediac could never have singlehandedly managed all the resources intended for Chignecto. Despite the danger, Quebec did send most of its cargo vessels to Baie Verte. The only question is whether France made use of a Shediac supply route as well. The Shediac outpost, for all its shortcomings, could have helped La Jonquière hedge his bets. But is there any evidence it was involved in building Chignecto fortifications? And if so, does that evidence shed any light on Simpson's alleged treasure map?

On May 1, 1751, the intendant of New France, François Bigot, penned a *mémoire d'instructions*. The document, preserved in the Bibliothèque et Archives nationales du Québec, outlines the responsibilities of a man named Brassard, the newly appointed storekeeper to the fledgling Fort Beauséjour. It reads:

> The said Sieur [Brassard] will board one of the ships chartered by the King and go to Chedaïk [Shediac] [...] Before he leaves, he will provide a list of foods, munitions, and supplies we are presently sending to the said outpost. Upon his arrival at the said location [Shediac], he will provide a copy of the list to the Sieur Druillhet, storekeeper, who will remain in the said outpost so that he [Druillhet] can receive and verify the said shipments and give leave to the captains of the said ships. The Sieur Druillhet will remain in charge of the stores, which he will send Brassard as and when he needs them. Accordingly, he [Brassard] will go with his seconds to Pointe à Beauséjour where the detachment commanded by M. de S. Ours resides.[570]

Bigot's *mémoire* makes plain that Quebec had not forgotten the Shediac outpost. In fact, the stronghold held its own as late as May 1751 and beyond. Importantly, it was also contributing to Fort Beauséjour's construction, which by then was in full swing.[571] The two storekeepers, Druillhet and Brassard, manned their respective warehouses. In effect, Bigot set up a just-in-time supply chain to deliver material from Shediac to Beauséjour.[572]

The question is, what material?

Bigot does not precisely mention the items Druillhet, the Shediac storekeeper, would dispatch to his Beauséjour counterpart. Yet his three listed categories—foods, munitions, and supplies—show that the wares reaching Shediac were significant both in volume and variety. Druillhet would be sending Brassard more than just biscuits after all.

The shipment of resources from Shediac to Chignecto has obvious repercussions for our investigation. But what could have led to the drafting of a curious, one-off manuscript describing the horse-assisted and possibly secretive transfer of heavy gear to Chignecto along a path deviating from the usual Shediac route? Chances of rediscovering additional period documents are remote.

That is why a fortuitous find came as such a surprise.

The Surprise of *La Louise*

A chance discovery sometimes causes everything to fall into place. Such a breakthrough came in the form of paperwork dated November 4, 1751, signed by François-Marc-Antoine Le Mercier, commander of New France's first artillery company, and countersigned by La Jonquière himself.[573] The ten-page record, conserved in France's Archives nationales d'outre-mer, lists material shipped from Quebec to Acadie for 1751. The inventory, though dry, reveals that Shediac's last hurrah unfolded on an unexpectedly large scale. And, crucially, the document offers a measure of closure for Simpson's saga.

The first three pages of Le Mercier's inventory fall under the heading "Inventory of artillery items that were sent to Chedaick [Shediac] aboard the schooner *La Louise* on May 12, 1751."[574] Listed at the top are twelve iron cannons—four four-pounders, four six-pounders, and four eight-pounders—along with field and marine mounting carriages. Ammunition comprised 400 round cannonballs for each calibre and 240 assorted bags of lead grapeshot. The second and third pages enumerate hardware for handling, firing, and servicing the large guns: iron trails, gunner's ladles, ramrods, gun powder, linstocks, etc. (see Appendix C). But while *La Louise* was Shediac bound, its cargo was only passing through.

Duplicata 12 mai 1751

236

Etat Des Ustancilles Dartillerie qui ont Eté envoyez a Chedaick par la Goelette la louise le 12e may 1751.

Scavoir

4. Canons De fer De . . . . 8.£ De bale

4. Idem. De . . . . 6.

4. Idem. De . . . . 4.

Affuts de Campagne garnies Davant train

4. De . . . . 6.

2. Idem. De . . . . 4.

Affuts Marins garnies de cossins et coins De mire

4. De . . . . 8.

4. De . . . . 6.

4. De . . . . 4.

Boulets ronds

400. De . . . . 8.

400. De 6

400. De . . . . 4.

Sacs de mitraille en plomb

80. De . . . . 8.

80. De . . . . 6.

80. De 4

The first page of a three-page inventory of supplies sent by Quebec to Shediac in 1751 aboard La Louise. [COL C11 A 93, 95-97 ARCHIVES NATIONALES D'OUTRE-MER]

The Shediac outpost had no use for weapons to confront an enemy that lay well beyond its reach. In any event, France abandoned the encampment not long after *La Louise*'s delivery. All the same, La Jonquière confirms that he destined *La Louise*'s artillery for Chignecto. He wrote on May 1, less than two weeks before *La Louise* set off from Quebec, "I must send him [Saint-Ours] 12 cannons, including four of 8 L [French pounds], four of 6, and four of 4, that he will put in those two forts [Beauséjour and Gaspareaux]."[575]

We also have corroboration that six pieces—presumably half of those carried by *La Louise*—arrived in Chignecto during that time frame. Saint-Ours took possession of four eight-pounds and two six-pounds at Beauséjour.[576] But how significant was Shediac's role in funnelling France's armaments into Acadie?

We learn from Le Mercier's inventory that, in the fall of 1751, La Jonquière dispatched six twelve-pound cannons to Baie Verte aboard the *Aimable Catherine*.[577] Dividing shipments between Shediac and Baie Verte was a wise risk-mitigation strategy; transporting the heavier gear via Baie Verte also simplified their transfer to Beauséjour. A report for the following year listed twenty-four guns at Fort Beauséjour—six twelve-pounders, four eight-pounders, and fourteen six-pounders—and four four-pounders at Fort Gaspareaux.[578] All told, then, *La Louise*'s cargo accounted for no less than 43 percent of the arsenal France had sent to Chignecto. The ratio could be as high as 79 percent if Fort Beauséjour's ten remaining six-pound weapons transited through Shediac as well. Tellingly, Fort Gaspareaux received *La Louise*'s four four-pound cannons early; once better protected by the fort's battery, Baie Verte became a safer destination for France's subsequent deliveries.

In the end, Shediac embodies more than just a forgotten, diminutive predecessor to Beauséjour and Gaspareaux. In fact, the outpost played a pivotal midwifing role in the birth of France's Chignecto defences. Its last hurrah is now one for the history books. And bits of Simpson's map also begin making more sense under this new light.

The image of the cannon-laden *La Louise* sailing into Shediac Bay in the spring of 1751 comes as a vivid treat. The ship likely docked at Skull Island, where it transferred its cargo onto dories. The small boats would then have navigated to the mouth of the Shediac River and presumably headed a short distance up the shallow waterway. However, burdened by the massive armament, they could not have gone much farther. The road to Le Coude probably exploited riverways. *La Louise*'s twelve guns, in contrast, would have no choice but to trudge over an unbeaten ground route that bypassed the usual itinerary.

Heavy in their own right, the twelve cannons also required mounting carriages, ammunition, and assorted hardware. A mid-eighteenth-century, eight-pound French iron cannon tipped the scale at over one metric tonne. Mounting carriages weighed just as much. The four hundred eight-pound cannonballs exceeded 1.5 metric tonnes. In other words, transporting *La Louise*'s arsenal from Shediac to Chignecto would be no easy feat. French artillery manuals emphasized horses as indispensable in carrying cumbersome weaponry overland.[579] The same would no doubt apply to lugging *La Louise*'s cannons along the Shediac–Le Coude leg of their trip.

Shediac, unlike Baie Verte, added an element of stealth to France's war efforts. The outpost, tucked away in continental Acadie, acted as a back door for discrete deliveries and as a covert base for clandestine operations in peninsular Acadie. We have already speculated that the drafter of Simpson's document hoped to shield such information from British eyes. Perhaps the cannons of *La Louise* and the curious parchment were part of a common Shediac strategy in which France played its cards closer to the vest.

In our search for a one-time, antebellum, difficult, horse-assisted, and secretive transfer of a heavy, valuable, and consequential load over unexplored terrain between Shediac and Le Coude, the cannons of *La Louise* exceed all but our wildest expectations. And, if we substitute *La Louise*'s twelve iron guns for Blakeny's nine bags of gold, the fog surrounding Simpson's chart begins to lift. We may well have pinned down the "what" on Simpson's manuscript. Still, we need to address a few remaining loose threads.

Simpson's "map," it seems, will bedevil us until the end.

An Instance of the Fingerpost

The journey of *La Louise*'s twelve cannons from Shediac to Le Coude paints a picture of utter misery. Few were more aware of the obstacles involved than French military engineer De Léry. In his 1750 survey of the area, he remarked that he had "never seen such a detestable land." During summer droughts, he complained, horses struggled to pull themselves out of quagmires and had been useless that year. Such was the state of the road, he added, that it was impracticable for wagons.

How much more difficult the task with no road at all.

Previously, we argued that sheer weight would have prevented small boats from carrying *La Louise*'s artillery up the shallow Shediac River. The only alternative would be to portage along an unbeaten track. Hauling heavy weaponry through kilometres of untrodden wilderness borders on the unimaginable. But if *La Louise*'s gear did not follow the conventional itinerary, what route did it take?

One option would be a beeline between Shediac and Le Coude. The proposition, while analogous to Ganong's middle path, is not without problems. Much of the region's interior remained uncharted. Natural obstacles potentially hampered progress. The overriding concern was for *La Louise*'s armament to reach its destination. Blazing a fresh trail through unexplored territory would represent the riskiest choice at the worst possible moment.

A second option would be to hug the Shediac River instead. Skirting the riverbank would entail more distance to cover. Still, it would hold the major advantage of negotiating better-known terrain. Once past the Shediac River, *La Louise*'s guns could then rejoin the usual land portage and head to Le Coude with relative ease. In short, somewhere near modern-day Irishtown, the new route would have met the old.

And, where two roads cross, a fingerpost often points the way.

By the spring of 1751, Saint-Ours's forces had left Shediac and set up camp at Beauséjour. Otherwise, the few Acadian refugees at Shediac had limited resources to spare. It is doubtful that, under such conditions, enough men and horses could have formed a large, single, one-time convoy. In all likelihood, *La Louise*'s artillery journeyed to Le Coude piecemeal instead.[580] To be sure, repeated trips along an unbeaten trail would increase the chances of getting lost or of missing the crucial left-hand turn toward Le Coude.

A well-placed stone marker, though, could help keep the weaponry on track.

The mention of a frog-carved rock on Simpson's map is troubling. But while it is one thing to signal important information, it is another to indicate buried gold. The cannons of *La Louise* suggest a simpler, more plausible explanation. As the armament progressed overland, a conspicuous way finder would reassure guides and allay confusion. In other words, the penultimate object that Simpson sought may have emphasized direction, not location. And if *La Louise*'s arsenal skirted the Shediac River before rejoining the usual portage to Le Coude, the story now practically writes itself.

Our misread-memo scenario is taking shape. Rather than follow the customary road, the guns of *La Louise* may have travelled along new, uncertain, and difficult terrain with the assistance of horses. In this context, a text specifying itinerary, heading, landmarks, and transportation becomes a more natural and likely possibility. If it ever existed, the frog rock on Simpson's map could bear witness to a series of extraordinary events at the heart of France's struggle for Acadie.

The saga, we already know, did not involve nine bags of gold. But it could tell the no-less-consequential tale of twelve French cannons on the move.

The Test of Time

An old French manuscript describing the transfer of *La Louise*'s cannons from Shediac to Le Coude ticks virtually every box. But how could such a text land in Simpson's hands? Archived documents, as they often do, point to a distinct possibility.

During his stint in Acadie, La Corne sent De Léry a letter containing various instructions.[581] Action items included chartering boats, moving crates of rifles back to Shediac, and arranging for the shipment of oxen. But La Corne's behest, while intriguing in itself, stands out mainly for its provenance. That is, rather than go up the chain of command, it went down the pecking order instead. Such messages, which relied on short-haul couriers, highlight the logistical nitty-gritty of France's military adventure in Acadie. Tens if not hundreds of such memos were likely written. Most were discarded once they had fulfilled their purpose.

Why, then, did La Corne's letter fare differently? De Léry, the missive's recipient, preserved it as part of his service papers.[582] The son of Quebec's foremost engineer, he belonged to an ambitious family that tended closely to its legacy. The De Lérys accumulated such correspondence over several

A folded, pocket-sized, quill-penned letter by La Corne, commander of Acadie, to French military engineer De Léry in 1750. [CHAUSSEGROS DE LÉRY FAMILY FUND, 311364, BIBLIOTHÈQUE ET ARCHIVES NATIONALES DU QUÉBEC]

generations. The Archives nationales du Québec acquired the lot in 1973.[583] How many other documents like La Corne's still lie out there, sleeping in private shoeboxes?

La Corne's letter demonstrates that veterans of France's actions in Acadie passed on field orders, campaign journals, and personal notes as meaningful heirlooms. The subsequent migration of French-Canadian families in search of economic opportunities would allow for such documents to turn up virtually anywhere. But the significance of objects—and of language—can fade over time. Could the rediscovery of a worn-out, out-of-context parchment, penned in unfamiliar French and nestled in a pile of old household papers, have sparked dreams of buried gold decades or even centuries later?

I showed La Corne's letter to Jane Regent, the wife of Simpson's great-great-grandson. She recalled that Simpson's map adopted much the same format and may have begun with a similar dear-so-and-so formula. Invited to comment on its appearance, she replied, "Yes, that is how I remember the letter that Brian found, in terms of the spidery handwriting."[584]

Nothing proves Simpson's chart was a lost letter of Acadie. What La Corne's dispatch does bring to the misread-memo scenario, however, is a potential mechanism by which Simpson's prized document could have withstood the test of time and made its way to Southwestern Ontario. Of recent Scottish and Irish extractions, neither William Simpson nor his extended family had any French-Canadian ancestry. If our treasure seeker uncovered a lost letter of Acadie, he seems to have done so outside his immediate circle. The mystery manuscript, whatever its nature, beguiled him. And, as it reaches across the ages, the enigmatic parchment continues to fascinate.

The twelve iron cannons of *La Louise* purchased what nine leather bags of gold never could have. The artillery rewarded Quebec with a timely and potent deterrent. The weaponry helped stave off a British invasion of continental Acadie for the next four years. Had France prevailed, today's New Brunswick could well be called Nouvelle Acadie. The Acadian people might also have met a less tragic fate. History decided otherwise. The fall of Beauséjour in 1755 spelled the end of French control in the region and, by ricochet, in the rest of North America.

We seem closer than ever to cracking the mystery of Simpson's chart. If truth remains elusive, it is because our misread-memo explanation—a lost letter of Acadie describing the transfer of *La Louise*'s heavy guns between Shediac and Le Coude—counts only as informed speculation. We set the goal for ourselves of proposing a "less wrong" interpretation of Simpson's alleged treasure map. We now have proof of concept, but we still lack proof of fact. For all we know, the old Shediac portage road may not cut across Irishtown, the Shediac outpost may not lie on Skull Island, and *La Louise*'s twelve cannons may not have transited through Le Coude. Simpson's parchment refers to a tumultuous era that has not been kind to archival preservation. Any retrospective harking back to mid-eighteenth-century Acadie would presuppose a similarly brittle chain of poorly understood happenings.

Skeptics who prefer the clever-con angle may yet carry the day. As we argued previously, the odds do not favour an outright forgery. However, fraudulent schemes do not always start from scratch, and a swindler need not be a counterfeiter. We tackled the clever-con and misread-memo scenarios separately, but the two ideas are not mutually exclusive. We have seen how period papers can travel across space and time and lose clarity of meaning. Perhaps an estate sale or a rummage through a dusty attic turned up a cryptic, mid-eighteenth-century French manuscript. From that point on, little would get in the way of an unscrupulous seller—or a mischievous jokester—passing off the document as a would-be treasure map to a gullible taker. Simpson's parchment may well have deceived more than one pair of eyes. Perhaps nothing—not even this book—can prevent it from doing so again.

In his 1937 interview with Ian Sclanders, Blakeny pleaded, "But I'm just as certain as I am that I'm standing here that the treasure is there." Yet how could Blakeny be so sure if he failed to showcase the one thing that could have proved him right? No one is more convinced—and convincing—than a dupe. Extraordinary claims require extraordinary evidence. Holding on to unfounded belief goes to the core of the issue. The struggle between the heart's wild wishes and the head's wiser words applies to everyone. The power of imagination over reason is no stranger to legends that later risk being taken as gospel.

From our twenty-first-century perch, we should not render too quick a judgment on Simpson and his companions. They were the products of their time and saw the world through their own imperfect lenses, like every one of us. If fantastic tales captivate audiences today, it is because they offer a link with the past and fill a need for shared mythology. To be sure, the road to truth requires facts and deliberation. Still, desire remains a difficult beast to tame. We should not underestimate the lure of fantasy.

Hope endures that Simpson's map will resurface one day. If it does, we are now better prepared to grasp the document's real significance. Until such a time, we can only ponder how our journey has changed our perception of Blakeny's remarkable story. A self-test of the internal struggle between the head and the heart is in order. Indeed, consider our own reaction should, say, a frog-carved rock turn up on the eastern bank of a south-flowing Irishtown stream. Would we gravitate toward common sense?

Or would we dream instead of nine bags of gold?

Chapter 20
The Peter Pan Within

We are not thinking machines that feel; rather,
we are feeling machines that think.
– Antonio Damasio

Our investigation has showcased its own process of discovery. Instead of hiding all the hard work, *Nine Bags of Gold* opted for a style in which reader and author played detective together. Our journey has been an odd one, if only because it brought a skeptical mindset to a topic—buried treasure—that flirts with delusion and derision. What, then, is the allure? Why tackle Simpson's quest? Why value Blakeny's legend? And why search for explanations that could debunk an improbable but entertaining story? Opinions will vary. Yet few people can contribute a more appropriate insight than a man who has laid eyes on Simpson's alleged map himself.

Hanford Blakeny, it turns out, was something of an armchair philosopher.

A Child's Eyes

For some, the attraction to Simpson's endeavour will boil down to hopes of unearthing French gold buried near Le Coude. Blakeny's son Hanford recalled feeling similarly compelled as a boy. He included this nugget from his childhood in his 1960 autobiography:

> Spanish doubloons, oaken chests filled with diamonds, pearls, and pirate gold beyond the dreams of avarice. To young and old alike

the search for hidden treasure has a fascinating and irresistible lure. At some time in his life every boy has visions of discovering a treasure trove and will search long and ardently to find it.

What more likely place to dig for pirate's gold than on mysterious Crow's Island, a small hill rising from the marshes between Sunny Brae and Moncton, and not far distant from the site of the Old Pumping Station. Legend was that buccaneers from the Spanish Main had sailed up Hall's Creek and at the foot of a great pine tree on the island had buried their treasure chests. Another story was that a ship carrying gold to pay the French troops at Quebec, previous to the Battle of the Plains of Abraham, had been pursued up the Petitcodiac River by a British man-o'-war. To save gold from capture, the French captain had buried it beneath the self-same pine tree.[585]

Hanford's childhood fantasy bears an unmistakable resemblance to his father's mutation-prone yarn. We cannot verify that Simpson's visit influenced the young Hanford's version of the folk tale. But the sequence of events does suggest it. Hanford went on in the next paragraphs:

> What may have been mere legend, was to us boys actual truth. The big tree stump [on Crow's Island] was there to prove it; the ground looked as though it had been worked before because old planking had been found in the diggings.[586] Moreover, some people had said that when they were boys they had found ancient coins in the earth under the great tree-stump.
>
> Among those who searched and dug on Crow's Island, I among the number, were the Steadman street gang. [...] Many were the hours spent in enlarging that hole and in discussing ways and means to find the buried treasure which was surely there. Always the effort ended in failure, but never flagged the belief that we would ultimately succeed.[587]

According to period newspapers, Crow's Island was "a really peculiar and uncanny-looking place."[588] It also had a history of attracting seekers scouring for Captain Kidd's gold.[589] The site, in short, was a natural playground for Steadman Street kids. Hanford implicitly dated his adventures on Crow's Island to the time of Simpson's visit or soon thereafter. He was only a lad in

1899 when the retired Ontario hotelkeeper came to the Blakenys' Sunny Brae household. Later that summer, the Blakenys moved to Moncton's Steadman Street for a four-year stay. With an allusion to his "Steadman street gang," Hanford reveals that his dig on Crow's Island could not have preceded the Irishtown excavation. Maybe he re-enacted Simpson's treasure hunt at the very moment his father carried out the real thing on John Bishop's farmstead.

Previously, we speculated that Blakeny rejigged an Irishtown legend to incorporate references to an unnamed island and river. The young Hanford appears to have done the same by transposing the narrative onto his own universe: Crow's Island instead of Grindstone Island, Halls Creek instead of the Petitcodiac River, and an old tree stump instead of a frog-carved rock. For what it is worth, Halls Creek has a southerly flow, and the now vanished Crow's Island lay on its eastern bank.[590] Imagination is immune to contradictions. But perhaps the Blakenys also felt that Simpson's map afforded some interpretative leeway.

Hanford offers a different take on the elusive parchment as seen through a child's eyes. Mirroring this book's skeptical slant, his recollections also set the stage for his later coming of age.

A Coming of Age

The disparity between Hanford's younger and older selves could not be more striking. Blakeny's son expressed reservations in his later years when he penned, "What may have been mere legend, was to us boys actual truth." Also testifying to his evolution are the words he put down at the end of his extraordinary footnote. In 1960, at seventy-two, Hanford wrote about Simpson's hunt for gold: "Needless to say, the treasure never was found."

Did Hanford still believe in "the treasure" in his eighth decade of existence? He does not rule it out. His "needless to say" lead-in, though, speaks volume. These and other latter-life comments point to an intellectual coming of age during which Hanford's expectations shifted from the fanciful to the sensible. But Hanford's father did not undergo any such conversion. In 1937, also in his eighth decade, Blakeny volunteered words worth repeating here: "But I'm just as certain as I am that I'm standing here that the treasure is there."

Hanford's sober restraint and Blakeny's boastful claim offer a study in contrasts. Hanford's doubts carry the added weight of a man who had seen Simpson's chart for himself. The more we prod Simpson's alleged treasure map, the more it loses its footing and, by the same token, the more our "less wrong" scenario gains traction. Still, this book will have to grapple with an existential question of its own. That is, where does our investigative journey leave us in the end?

Answers will depend on reader persuasions. Starry-eyed romantics may remain unswayed by cold facts and logic. They may instead keep faith with an engrossing treasure hunt that could yet beat the odds. Cautious optimists may fall under a similar spell and welcome new information. On that front, we have confirmed the Irishtown dig, pinpointed its location and time frame, and found that both its scale and duration were greater than the Blakenys themselves seem to have known. We have also identified Simpson himself, not to mention some of his associates, and garnered additional clues about his chart. Though our motivations very much lie elsewhere, we have unearthed plenty of fresh material for anyone wishing to follow in the treasure seeker's footsteps.

Readers whose hopes we first raised and then dashed may file for grievance. Even the disenchanted, though, may see a silver lining in uncovering the lives of diverse characters linked by the oddest of pursuits. We can recall Blakeny's eccentric antics, LeBlanc's wily dodging of temperance law, Mohan's wandering ways, and Bishop's prosthetic leg, to name a few. Our account would also not be the same without the extras—the McSweeneys, the Welds, the other Simpsons, and many more—who fleshed out this book's late-Victorian backdrop. Last but not least, of course, is William Simpson—*our* Simpson—whose tragic journey and inner struggles we have only managed to glimpse. We should also not forget the testimonies of the living, who, like Jane Regent, Ernest Tidd, and several more, inflected our narrative's arc. Treasure or not, human stories have value. The window for capturing their passage is forever growing short.

At the opposite end of the belief spectrum, doubters may find it refreshing to see reason applied to a genre that does not always favour common sense. Dyed-in-the-wool skeptics may appreciate our evidence-driven, no-nonsense elucidation of past mysteries. We have also gained something that neither Simpson nor Blakeny could ever possess, namely a studied grasp of New France's history and Acadie's more specifically. New finds about mid-eighteenth-century Acadie are hard to come by. Amateur sleuths such as ourselves can rejoice at making even modest discoveries.[591] Our quest for truth has placed Simpson's quest for gold in its proper context. And so, for those unperturbed by claims of real treasure maps, Simpson's chart—perhaps a genuine French text from a critical but poorly understood period in Acadie—may take on added value, not less.

The universe of Simpson's saga has grown with our investigation's every step. Simple curiosity and a need for closure have propelled us to this point. We have put on the skeptical squeeze at every turn and passed everything through the historical wringer. Bruised by our cross-examination and stripped of fantasy elements at its core, Simpson's hunt for Acadie's lost gold now lies unflatteringly naked before our eyes. But have we robbed our story of its initial appeal in the process?

Again, Hanford's reflections suggest an answer.

The Peter Pan Within

In the previous chapter, we pondered which part of the mind—reason or emotion—would prevail in the face of questionable but tantalizing clues about buried riches. For most, surely, the answer is a bit of both. Even staunch naysayers may forgive themselves if their heart skipped a beat on word that Simpson's descendant preserved his ancestor's alleged treasure map or that a physical frog rock rests in the old Bishop cellar. What such plot twists expose is the internal tension between rational thought and wishful fantasy. There is no contradiction for skeptics to daydream about Irishtown gold, on the one hand, and to remain grounded by evidence to the contrary on the other. Mark Twain hit the nail on the head when he wrote, "There comes a time in every rightly constructed boy's life when he has a raging desire to go somewhere and dig for hidden treasure."[592] With a knowing wink at his younger self, Twain reminds us that the inner child does not leave as the adult arrives. Reason adds a welcome layer to mental experience, but emotion stands at the core of who we are.[593] The suggestion of concealed riches speaks to the adventurous part of us that never grew up. Solving a mystery can bring intellectual satisfaction, yet it does not always fulfill the Peter Pan within.

In his twilight years, Hanford moved back into his childhood Sunny Brae home at 58 Peter Street. There, he began authoring his memoirs. The walls of the old Blakeny house must have been a fertile source of inspiration for him as he revisited his past. And, to his credit, he gave his inner child a voice. The elderly Hanford expressed fondness, not disapproval, when he recalled the exhilaration of his own youthful treasure hunt on Crow's Island. Similar sentiments animated him as he remembered Simpson's fateful evening visit or later toured the Irishtown dig site for himself. His temperament is a reminder that, at its best, the tug of war between the inner child and the inner adult aims for a fine balance. That balance, after all, allows us to imagine possibilities without taking leave of reality.

Like a corkscrew, time moves forward but has a funny way of circling back. Past is prologue, Hanford remarked.[594] These prophetic words could not have anticipated how his book would lead to mine. If they could talk, the old walls of 58 Peter Street could say much about the visit of a retired Ontario hotelkeeper holding a would-be ancient French treasure map. The same walls could also tell the parallel stories of two young boys—Hanford and myself—who, though separated by a century, grew up to have what Mark Twain might have recognized as rightly constructed lives. In mirrored fates, the two boys eventually left 58 Peter Street. Both returned to it decades afterward to do what, in essence, Simpson and Blakeny had done there themselves in the dim light of the kitchen oil lamp.

In the end, treasure or not, those who pause and listen to their inner Peter Pan are without a doubt the lucky ones.

Epilogue

Readers may recall from chapter 6 that a column entitled "Still on the Hunt" appeared in the September 25, 1899, issue of the Moncton *Daily Times*. The piece made a passing reference to a previous article printed "last spring." I could not search for the earlier report at the time of this book's writing because microfilming in the 1970s failed to process the January-to-June 1899 batch. Library and Archives Canada, in Ottawa, holds the lone paper version I could locate. The collection was inaccessible due to its poor state of preservation, until now.

I put in a request to have the fragile documents restored. The records became available in September 2024 for restricted, in-person consultation. I followed through and uncovered a gem in the edition of May 5, 1899. Quirky and surprising, illuminating and confusing, the text, transcribed below in full, raises as many questions as it answers. Still, the column only marginally impacts my prior interpretations. Readers again have their plates full. But now, in a break from the book's co-investigative tradition, I invite them to draw their own conclusions instead.

In Search of Treasure

Said to Have Been Buried Near Moncton.

The Treasure-Seeker is a Man About Seventy and Has Spent Four Years Looking for Booty Near the Lower City Reservoir.

Many of the older inhabitants of Moncton are quite familiar with the fairy tales that have been so often told about the chests of gold that were supposed to have been buried along the Petitcodiac

River in the vicinity of Moncton by the early Acadian settlers and the immortal Pirate King, Captain Kidd. And some people to this day assert for a fact that pots of money have been unearthed near the city, or within the city limits, not so very long ago. Be that as it may, comparatively few Monctonians have been aware that right in their midst, for the last four years, an aged pilgrim, who has probably seen seventy summers, faithful to the inherent love of gold so strongly implanted in the human anatomy, has been persistently and relentlessly pursuing a methodical course in search of a hidden treasure, said to have been deposited in the earth for safe keeping some thirty-three years ago. The field of operation is near the lower city reservoir, about two or three hundred yards below the dam on the bank of the brook leading from the pond, and naturally enough the people in that vicinity have been more or less interested in the persistent search carried on by the stranger (less enthusiastic, however, as the unfruitful years rolled by) but strange to say very little has been said about it outside of the neighbourhood.

About four years ago a man, who is known as Simpson, made his appearance in the vicinity where he is now operating, and began to excavate, and, at that time it is said, in answer to the curious natives, he stated that he was looking for petrified fish. And, as the locality appeared likely to be more productive in that commodity than any other article of interest, the story satisfied the people for a time. But as Simpson continued his search not only that summer, but the following season, it finally became known that he was in search of a more precious treasure. His labors, however, were not very fruitful, but this eact [*sic*] has not disheartened the treasure-seeker or deterred him from prosecuting a vigorous boring process on a plot of ground about sixty by twenty feet in size on the ast [*sic*] side of the reservoir brook, on the farm of John Bishop. There, Simpson is at work today with an ordinary two inch auger boring every six inches to a depth of about two feet. Last fall the services of a well known Moncton engineer were engaged by Simpson in running lines and giving him certain bearings. He has been at work some weeks already this spring and is accompanied by a young man, who, it is said, supplies the capital required for expenses.

The parties with whom Simpson has ilved [*sic*] while here in the summer months, tell an interesting story in connection with the affair, which is purported to have been told by the treasure-seeker himself. It is said that the treasure he is looking for, is booty buried in that locailty [*sic*] by three men who had robbed a bank some thirty-three years ago. Two of the men, the story goes, are dead, but the third man's fate is a matter of speculation. At the time they are supposed to have come in this direction with their plunder, they camped on the creek along whose bank Simpson is now manœuvering, buried their treasure and made their way out of the country on foot, following the North Shore up into Quebec. The man who is now seeking to bring the slumbering treasure into circulation again, it is alleged, hails from Ontario and has certain data in regard to the hidden wealth, which tends to the belief that he was at least in the confidence of the third imaginary, or real, robber. One of the rules of the search is to overturn and examine very minutely every stone of any size, as the narrative says the money is peacefully resting from its worldly cares beside a rock upon which was carved the image of a frog by one of the burglars, who was a sculptor of some repute. The searcher invariably bores on the west side of the rock.

As previously stated, this treasure hunter is known by the name of Simpson, and whatever there may be in the story about the hidden plunder, he can be seen at work today enthusiastically engaged in his search in the territory designated. He is a man of apparently keen intellect, very tall and of muscular build and by his conversation would not be taken for an individual one would expect to find engaged in digging for a phantom treasure.[595]

Acknowledgements

I WISH TO THANK THE FOLLOWING INDIVIDUALS AND ORGANIZATIONS FOR THEIR support: Angela Mombourquette (Nimbus Publishing), editor Marianne Ward, archivists Robbie Gilmore, Joshua Green, Keith MacKnight, and Melisa Leger (Provincial Archives of New Brunswick), Bridget Murphy, Lawren Campbell, and James Upham (Moncton Museum), François LeBlanc and Bernard Richard (Centre d'études acadiennes Anselme-Chiasson), Anne-Marie Joachim and Manise Young (Library and Archives Canada), Rénald Lessard (Bibliothèque et Archives nationales du Québec), Serge Paquet (Archives of Ontario), Michael Molnar (Huron County Museum and Historic Gaol), Doug Warnock (Middlesex County Library), James Arthur Clowes (New Brunswick Railway Museum), Mylène Bélanger (Exporail—The Canadian Railway Museum), Anne Quirk (University of Western Ontario Archives), and Mark Ranson (London Middlesex Branch Ontario Ancestors).

The following people have kindly provided me with their time and expertise: Ronnie-Gilles LeBlanc, A. J. B. Johnston, Samuel LeBlanc, David R. Elliot, Clément Loubert, Robert Doyle, Jonathan Fowler, Samuel Arsenault, Linda Donovan-Evans, Charles Després, and Jamie Storey. Also deserving of thanks are those who gamely played along or helped in one way or another. They are Jane Regent, Ernest Tidd, Jennifer Mackintosh, Bernard and Angèle Gray, Hugh Wilson and Fran Wilkinson, Brian Rattenbury, Rick DesBrisay, Kathleen Borlase, Elizabeth Richards, Norman Weir, Jackie Tilton (Richards), Judy Tilton, Bill Mohan, Elizabeth Muriel Anderson, Christine Segar, Ron Berry, and Sue and David Hall.

Lastly, my wife, Farah Pérodin, and my mother, Simone LeBlanc-Rainville, offered feedback on early drafts. I am immensely grateful for their support, which naturally extends well beyond the book itself. To those I forgot to mention, I beg forgiveness and hope *Nine Bags of Gold* represents some form of reward.

Appendix A
Chronology

1604	First French settlement in Acadie (Île Sainte-Croix/Dochet Island, Maine)
1605	Founding of Port Royal
1608	Founding of Quebec
1685	First experiment with paper money in New France
1701	Hanging of Captain Kidd
1713	Treaty of Utrecht (peninsular Acadie ceded to Britain)
	Founding of Louisbourg
1725	Sinking of French pay ship *Le Chameau*
c. 1730	Founding of Le Coude (present-day Moncton)
1745	First capture of Louisbourg
1746	Duc d'Anville's expedition
1748	Treaty of Aix-la-Chapelle
	Restitution of Louisbourg
1749	Establishment of Shediac outpost
	Founding of Halifax
1750	De Léry's survey of Chignectou and surrounding area
	Capture of the *Saint-François*
	Paper money introduced in Acadie
	Capture of *Le London*
	Major Lawrence's attacks on Beaubassin
1751	Construction of Fort Beauséjour and Fort Gaspareaux
	Decommissioning of Shediac outpost
1755	Fall of Fort Beauséjour and Fort Gaspareaux
	Battle of Petitcodiac
1755–63	Great Acadian Expulsion and Acadian Resistance
1758	Second capture of Louisbourg
	Battle of Le Coude

1759	Fall of Quebec
	Escape of the *Monckton*
1761	Surrender of Beausoleil Broussard
1763	Treaty of Paris (France cedes several North American colonies to Britain)
1776	Declaration of American Independence
1784	Partition of Nova Scotia (creation of New Brunswick)
1786	Arrival of Loyalist David Blakeny in New Brunswick
1841 (or 1838)	Birth of William Simpson
1865	Birth of Sherman Blakeny
1867	British North America Act (Canadian Confederation)
1884	Worldwide adoption of Greenwich meridian (France abstains)
1888	Birth of Hanford Blakeny
1895–1901	Simpson's treasure hunt in Irishtown (years of activity reported in newspaper articles)
1904	Death of Théophile B. LeBlanc
1906	Death of William Simpson
1910	Death of John Walton Mohan
1912	Death of George McSweeney
1915	Death of John (Jack) Bishop
1921	Death of Peter McSweeney Jr.
	Death of George Bishop
1928	Birth of Ernest Tidd
1934	Death of Havelock H. Warman
1937	Sherman Blakeny's interview with Ian Sclanders
1942	Death of John A. Bishop Jr.
	Death of Corbin Weld
1949	Death of Sherman Blakeny
1960	Publication of Hanford Blakeny's autobiography
1961	Death of Hanford Blakeny
1970	Death of Albert Thomas

Appendix B
A Mysterious Blakeny Quote

In their 1990 book *Resurgo*, Alex Pincombe and Edward Larracey claim to cite a passage from Blakeny's 1937 interview with Sclanders. The excerpt, however, is altogether absent from the original article. The excerpt reads:

> "... the battle was fought right at The Bend; the New Englanders chased the French from what became Outhouse Point to their Chapel, in whose vicinity they buried their dead, of which these skeletons were a part, then they resumed their flight northward. The New Englanders began to gain on them, so they buried their gold from Fort Beauséjour about ten miles due north of Moncton (at the Bend), where the Irishtown Reservoir is now located."[596]

Blakeny appears to specify that the French gold concealed near Le Coude came from Fort Beauséjour. Did Pincombe and Larracey get hold of additional material from Sclanders? The ellipsis at the beginning also suggests the authors only partially relayed the Sunny Brae excavator's remarks.

The solution to the conundrum lies in Pincombe's 1970 master's thesis, which supplies a verbatim copy of the supposed passage.[597] The dissertation employs "the English" in lieu of "the New Englanders"—a dreaded citation bugaboo. But the mystery quote, in fact, is no quote at all. In his thesis, Pincombe clearly uses *his own words* to recount Blakeny's story. Manifestly, he recalled the article from memory and filled in details that are absent in Blakeny's account. The authors of *Resurgo* later compounded the error by wrapping the same passage inside quotation marks, thereby attributing Pincombe's comments to Blakeny instead. The ellipsis, rather than imply additional material, reflects the insertion point for Pincombe's invention.

The misleading quote, while unfortunate, was not intentional. More interesting for us is that Pincombe and Larracey only brought up Blakeny's interview as a straw man: "This account of the battle and the story of the treasure is wholly without foundation and so at variance with the established facts, that no rebuttal is required."

Pincombe and Larracey take issue with Blakeny's claim of hostilities at Le Coude. Yet the two authors themselves document a skirmish between British troops and Acadian insurgents near Le Coude on July 1, 1758. Though perhaps distorted by oral tradition, Blakeny's mention of a battle may yet have merit. Eight years after the expulsion of the Acadians from Le Coude, immigrants from Pennsylvania seized the purged lands. Pierre Belliveau, an Acadian who returned to the region, helped the new colonists adapt. He also shared with them stories of his compatriots who had lived in the area.[598]

Appendix C
Inventory of La Louise
(English translation)

Inventory of artillery material sent to Chedaick [Shediac] aboard the schooner *La Louise* on May 12, 1751.

Namely

4	Iron guns of	8 L shot
4	Same of	6
4	Same of	4
	Gun field carriages and undercarriages	
4	Of	6
2	Of	4
	Gun naval carriages with cannon beds and gunner's sights [quoin]	
4	Of	8
4	Of	6
4	Of	4
	Round shots	
400	Of	8
400	Of	6
400	Of	4
	Bags of lead grapeshot	
80	Of	8
80	Of	6
80	Of	4

5,000 L	Of gunpowder
1005 L	Of match cord
24	Handspikes

	Iron crows	
4	Of 8 weighing together	80 L
4	Of 6 weighing together	60
4	Of 4 weighing together	48
	Gunner's ladles, half of which with [unreadable]	
2	Of	8
2	Of	6
2	Of	4
	Ramrods with bore brushes	
4	Of	8
4	Of	6
4	Of	4
	Paper cartridges	
400	Of	8
400	Of	6
400	Of	4
	Match tubs	
8	Of	8
8	Of	6
8	Of	4

12	Horns with priming powder
12	Linstocks
50 L	Of old pig fat [a lubricant]
1200	Cannon rope wads
4	Double-block pulleys
6	Single-block pulleys
2	Gins with pulleys and sheaves
2	Cannon slings
36	Cannon lines of 10 feet in length and 12 "lignes" (2.7 cm) in diameter
12	Simple extensions of 6 "toises" (11.7 m) in length and 16 "lignes" (3.6 cm) in diameter
4	Double extensions of same diameter and 12 "toises" (23.4 m) in length

4	Gin cables of 12 "toises" (23.4 m) in length each and of one inch and six "lignes" (4.1 cm) in diameter
3	Bales of fishing line
6	"Travers" for balls of 4 "toises" (7.8 m) in length and 10 "lignes" in diameter (2.3 cm)
3	Breeching [or drag ropes] to load and unload pieces of 18 "toises" (35.1 m) in length and one inch and 6 "lignes" (4.1 cm) in diameter
12	Lead plates
6	Dollies to be used as platforms for naval gun carriages

Endnotes

Introduction

[1] Ian Sclanders, "Another Story of a Treasure Hunt For Gold Now Thought Buried Beneath a Moncton Reservoir," *Telegraph-Journal* (Saint John, NB), July 24, 1937, 1, 5.

Chapter 1: The Call of the Unknown

[2] Raoul Dionne, "L'origine acadienne de Moncton: Le Coude." *Revue d'histoire de l'Amérique française* 37, 3 (1983): 399–416; Edward W. Larracey, *Resurgo: The History of Moncton*, vol. 2 (Moncton: City of Moncton, 1990); C. Alexander Pincombe and Edward W. Larracey, Resurgo: *The History of Moncton*, vol. 1 (Moncton: City of Moncton, 1990).

[3] Randall Sullivan, *The Curse of Oak Island: The Story of the World's Longest Treasure Hunt* (New York: First Grove Atlantic, 2018).

[4] Joe Nickell, "Investigative Files—The Secrets of Oak Island," *Skeptical Inquirer*, March/April 2000, 14–19.

[5] "Treasure Hunting Offers Inducement In New Brunswick," *Brandon Daily Sun* (Brandon, Manitoba), January 15, 1938, 3; "Autour et Alentours—Les chasses aux trésors hier et aujourd'hui," *Le Canada* (Montréal), October 5, 1949, 4; W. F. Robb, "Golden Hoard Buried Beneath Irishtown Reservoir, Is Belief," *The Transcript* (Moncton), August 12, 1950, 12; Garnet Basque, "French Gold Near Moncton," in *Canadian Treasure* 1, 2 (1973), 29–31; Alan Cochrane, "Ghosts and Mysteries Around 'the Bend'—Spooky Stories Are Part of Moncton's History," *The Times & Transcript* (Moncton), October 28, 1995, 31; Sandra Devlin, "Open Hearts and Buried Treasure," *The Times & Transcript* (Moncton), June 13, 1998, F3, F8; David Goss, "Buried Treasure Under Reservoir?" *The Times & Transcript* (Moncton), October 21, 2000, G2; Dan Soucoup, "Acadian Gold Rush at Hall's Creek Marsh," *The Times & Transcript* (Moncton), July 29, 2000, H5; Dan Soucoup, "Search for Buried Gold Piques Readers' Interest," *The Times & Transcript* (Moncton), March 25, 2003; Dan Soucoup, *Looking Back: From the Pages of the Times & Transcript* (Halifax: Maritime Lines, 2002); "Forgotten New Brunswick: A Tale of Lost Treasure," *Daily Gleaner* (Fredericton), November 26, 2018, 7.

[6] Ralph Delahaye Paine, *The Book of Buried Treasure* (London: William Heinemann, 1911); David McIntee, *Fortune & Glory—A Treasure Hunter's Handbook* (Oxford: Osprey, 2016). Treasure maps are legion in the literary world. Several works, such Stevenson's classic *Treasure Island*, bill themselves as honest fiction. Wittingly or not, though, too many others pass themselves off as serious nonfiction by blurring the line between fantasy and reality. No matter their provenance or nature, treasure maps have so far proved useless (see Neil Rennie, *Treasure Neverland: Real and Imaginary Pirates* [Oxford: Oxford University Press, 2013]). One such example is the cryptogram allegedly written by Olivier Levasseur, *dit* La Buse (the Buzzard), a notorious eighteenth-century French pirate. Shortly before he was hanged, La Buse reportedly shared an encoded message revealing the location of a cache of gold and diamonds concealed on Île Bourbon (present-day La Réunion) in the Indian Ocean (see de Charles La Roncière, *Le flibustier mystérieux: histoire d'un trésor caché* [Paris: Le Masque, 1934]). The apparent rediscovery of the cryptogram in 1934 caused a stir. But modern-day historians and cipher analysts concur: The cryptogram is most likely a twentieth-century invention (see "The Cipher Foundation," cipherfoundation.org).

[7] R. Lionel Fanthorpe and Patricia Fanthorpe. *The Oak Island Mystery: The World's Greatest Treasure Hunt*. 2nd ed. (Toronto: Dundurn, 2012).

[8] Nickell, "Investigative Files"; Kenneth L. Feder, "Irrationality and Popular Archaeology," *American Antiquity* 49, 3 (1984): 525–41.

[9] Richard Zacks, *The Pirate Hunter: The True Story of Captain Kidd* (London: Hachette, 2003).

[10] Paine, *Book of Buried Treasure*, 61–130; Zacks, *Pirate Hunter*, 245–6; Fredercik De Peyster, *The Life and Administration of Richard, Earl of Bellomont, Governor of the Provinces of New York* (New York Historical Society, 1879).

11 David Goss, "Harbour Treasures Prove Elusive," *Times & Transcript* (Moncton), July 29, 2000, 68; McIntee, *Fortune & Glory*; "Seekers After Buried Treasure," *Daily Telegraph* (Saint John, NB), August 13, 1880, 1.

12 Willard Hallam Bonner, "The Ballad of Captain Kidd," *American Literature* 15, 4 (1944): 362–80.

13 Paine, *Book of Buried Treasure*, 82–86.

14 Paine, *Book of Buried Treasure*, 30.

Chapter 2: The Teller's Tale

15 Edward W. Larracey, *Chocolate River: A Story of the Petitcodiac River From the Beginning of Habitation in the Late 1600s* (Hantsport, NS: Lancelot Press, 1985), 127–59; Charles Hanford Blakeny, *The Story of a Business And Its Founders* (pub. by author, 1960), 72.

16 Larracey, *Chocolate River*, 158.

17 Blakeny, *Story of a Business*, 152. Curiously, unlike other sources, Blakeny's death certificate lists his birthdate as March 13, 1864.

18 Blakeny, *Story of a Business*, 16–17; Daniel K. Glenn, *Parc Nature—Irishtown—Nature Park: Master Plan. Final Report* (Moncton: Daniel K. Glenn, 1996).

19 *New Brunswick County Deed Registry Books, 1780–1930.* Registrar of Deeds, County Office of Service (Fredericton) (55.053, N5, 505, 1889); Blakeny, *Story of a Business*; "Mourn Death of Prominent Merchant," *The Transcript* (Moncton), July 25, 1949, 2; "The Late Mr. Sherman Blakeny," *The Daily Times* (Moncton), July 26, 1949, 4; "City and County Newsy Items," *The Daily Transcript* (Moncton), May 4, 1901, 6.

20 Blakeny, *Story of a Business*, 52–53.

21 Blakeny, *Story of a Business*, 148.

22 Blakeny, *Story of a Business*, 16.

23 Blakeny, *Story of a Business*, 17, 19, 155–7.

24 Blakeny, *Story of a Business*, 21–22, 72–78; "Making River a Highway for Traffic Again," *The Times & Transcript* (Moncton), May 27, 1930, 10.

25 "Collar Bone Fractured," *The Daily Times* (Moncton), February 29, 1904, 7.

26 "Expression of Thanks," *The Daily Times* (Moncton), April 13, 1939, 10.

27 Blakeny, *Story of a Business*, 158.

28 "Westmorland County Court," *Daily Telegraph* (Saint John, NB), December 4, 1899, 1; "County Court," *The Daily Times* (Moncton), December 6, 1899, 1; "$2,528 Damage Suit Begun at Dorchester," *Telegraph Journal* (Saint John, NB), October 31, 1934, 3; "Appeal Court Decides for Defendants," *The Daily Times* (Moncton), June 15, 1935, 10; Larracey, *Chocolate River*, 224–39.

29 Edward W. Larracey, "Flashback on the Petitcodiac—Remembering the River Scows," *The Times & Transcript* (Moncton), June 20, 1987, 17, 37.

30 Blakeny, *Story of a Business*, 28.

31 Blakeny, *Story of a Business*, 28–30.

32 Bona Arsenault and Pascal Alain, *Histoire des Acadiens* (Montréal: Fides, 2004).

33 Marc Lescarbot, *The History of New France*, trans. W. L. Grant (Toronto: Champlain Society, 1907). *Le Théâtre de Neptune* was the first theatrical production in North America. For an account more representative of Indigenous perspectives, see J. D. Belshaw, *Canadian History: Pre-Confederation*, 2nd ed. (Victoria, BC: BCampus, 2020).

34 Arsenault and Alain, *Histoire des Acadiens*.

35 Andrew John Bayly Johnston, "Défricheurs d'eau: An Introduction to Acadian Land Reclamation in a Comparative Context," *Material Culture Review* 66 (2007), 32–41.

36 Naomi E. S. Griffiths, *From Migrant to Acadian: A North American Border People, 1604–1755* (Montreal and Kingston: McGill-Queen's University Press, 2004).

37 Andrew John Bayly Johnston, "Borderland Worries: Loyalty Oaths in Acadie/Nova Scotia, 1654–1755," *French Colonial History* 4, 1 (2003): 31–48; Arsenault and Alain, *Histoire des Acadiens*; Dionne, "L'origine acadienne"; Pincombe and Larracey, *Resurgo*.

38 John Mack Faragher, *A Great and Noble Scheme—The Tragic Story of the Expulsion of the French Acadians From Their American Homeland* (New York: W. W. Norton, 2005).

Chapter 3: An Extraordinary Footnote

39 Blakeny, *Story of a Business*, 105–7; "Economy in All Civic Departments," *The Daily Times* (Moncton), February 4, 1931, 1, 3.

40 Robb, "Golden Hoard Buried."

41 Blakeny, *Story of a Business*, 139.

42 Blakeny, *Story of a Business*, 13–33.

43 Blakeny, *Story of a Business*, 53.

44 Blakeny, *Story of a Business*, 47–103.

45 John Edward Belliveau, *The Monctonians: Scamps, Scholars, and Politicians*, vol. 2 (Hansport, NS: Lancelot Press, 1981), 184.

46 Blakeny, *Story of a Business*, 149–50.

47 "Dr. C. H. Blakeny Dies Here, Age 72," *The Transcript* (Moncton), May 24, 1961, 1–2.

48 Louis J. Robichaud, "Premier's Tribute," *The Transcript* (Moncton), May 24, 1961, 2.

49 Blakeny, *Story of a Business*, 15–16.

50 Hanford's attention to details is also evident in his recollections of European travels—see Charles Hanford Blakeny, *Bits and Pieces: Rambling Through Britain, France, Italy and Switzerland* (pub. by author, 1954); Charles Hanford Blakeny, *Fragments: Impressions of Holland, Belgium, Germany, Austria, Luxembourg, France, Italy, Scotland, and England* (pub. by author, 1956).

51 Deux lettres de monsieur de Mézy à messieurs de Vaudreuil et Bégon sur la perte du Chameau, C11B, vol. 7 (f. 216-219), September 3, 1725; Procès-verbal de la perte du Chameau, C11B, vol. 8 (f. 214-214v), September 9, 1725; J. S. McLennan, *Louisbourg: From Its Foundation to Its Fall, 1713–1758* (London: Macmillan, 1918), 73–75; Mémoire annoté sur le naufrage du Chameau par M. de Mézy et ordre du roi sur le même sujet, C11B, vol. 7 (f. 223-228), September 6, 1725.

52 McLennan, *Louisbourg*, 79.

53 Nicolas Lanoullier de Boisclerc, *État de la situation du sieur* Lanoullier, C11A, vol. 113 (f. 403-404), May 25, 1728.

54 Peter N. Moogk, "When Money Talks: Coinage in New France," *Proceedings of the Meeting of the French Colonial Historical Society*, vol. 12 (East Lansing, MI: Michigan State University Press, 1988), 73, jstor.org/stable/42952181.

55 Alex Storm, *Seaweed and Gold: New Expanded Edition With the Great Louisbourg Treasure of 1758* (Louisbourg, NS: True Canadian Treasure Hunting Adventures, 2011); Neil Genzlinger, "Alex Storm, Finder of Sunken Treasure, Dies at 80," *The New York Times*, August 24, 2018, A21.

56 Allison Lawlor, "Treasure Hunter Alex Storm Struck Gold Off Cape Breton Island," *The Globe and Mail* (Toronto), August 28, 2018; Alan Edmonds, "Treasure! How the Chameau Gave up Its Fortune," *Maclean's*, June 18, 1966.

57 Robert Louis Stevenson, *Treasure Island* (New York: Cassell, 1883); James Fenimore Cooper, *The Sea Lions; Or, the Lost Sealers* (New York: Stringer & Townsend, 1856); Edgar Allen Poe, "The Gold Bug," *Dollar Newspaper* (Philadelphia, PA), June 28, 1843, 1, 4; Washington Irving, "Wolfert Webber, or Golden Dreams," in *Tales of a Traveller* (New York: George P. Putnam, 1852); Simon Garfield, *On the Map—Why the World Looks the Way it Does* (London: Profile Books, 2013), 240–54.

Chapter 4: The Four Financiers

58 Lloyd Alexander Machum, *A History of Moncton Town and City, 1855–1965* (City of Moncton, 1965), 138; *New Brunswick Vital Statistics from Government Records* (RS141)—Provincial Returns of Death, Provincial Archives of New Brunswick, C4, 2525, F18713, 1904.

59 An advertisement listed the following features of LeBlanc's Hotel: "well furnished throughout"; "tables unsurpassed"; "first-class livery stables in connection"; "passengers and baggage free to and from railway station"; and "terms moderate" (*McAlpine's Moncton City Directory,* 1899, 1899, 48).

60 Larracey, *Resurgo*; Machum, *History of Moncton*; Edward W. Larracey, *The First Hundred; A Story of the First 100 Years of Moncton's Existence* (Moncton: Moncton Pub., 1970).

61 Régis Brun, *Les Acadiens à Moncton: un siècle et demi de présence française au Coude* (pub. by author, 1999); Larracey, *Resurgo*, 16–18.

62 "The Death of Mr. T. B. LeBlanc," *The Daily Transcript* (Moncton), July 5, 1904, 8.

63 "Monday's Race on the Driving Park," *The Daily Times* (Moncton), May 23, 1885, 3; "Queen's Birthday Races," *The Daily Transcript* (Moncton), May 23, 1890, 3; "List of Taxpayers," *The Daily Times* (Moncton), July 19, 1884, 2.

64 "Collection of Rare Coins," *The Daily Times* (Moncton), April 6, 1898, 1.

65 "Scott Act," *The Daily Times* (Moncton), October 9, 1886, 4.

66 Greg Marquis, "The History of Policing in the Maritime Provinces: Themes and Prospects," *Urban History Review/Revue d'histoire urbaine* 19, 2 (1990): 84–99; Jacques Couturier, "Prohiber ou contrôler ? L'application de l'Acte de tempérance du Canada à Moncton, N.-B., 1881–1896," *Acadiensis* 17, 2 (1988): 3–26.

67 "Scott Act"; "Paid the Fine," *The Daily Transcript* (Moncton), February 20, 1889, 3; "Scott Act Cases," *The Daily Times* (Moncton), October 18, 1890, 4; Larracey, *Resurgo*, 17.

68 "Scott Act," *The Daily Times* (Moncton), September 13, 1899, 4.

69 "Bourque Sentenced to Seven Years," *The Daily Transcript* (Moncton), September 5, 1900, 1; "Expropriation Arbitration—Expert Testimony as to the Value of Machinery," *The Daily Times* (Moncton), September 11, 1894, 1; "Heavy Crop of Candidates," *The Daily Transcript* (Moncton), October 1, 1888, 3.

70 Dr. Philippe Joseph Benoît LeBlanc, Osithe Surette's cousin, travelled to the Klondike in the late 1890s in search of Yukon gold. He made a fortune there selling high-priced medicine instead. See Brun, "L'or du Klondike"; "Letter from the Klondike"; "In Klondike."

71 "Nouvelles de Moncton," *Le Moniteur Acadien* (Shediac, NB), August 28, 1884, 2; "Expropriation Arbitration—Expert."

72 "Expropriation Arbitration—Expert."

73 "Successful Farming," *The Daily Transcript* (Moncton), September 14, 1899, 4; "Auction Sales," *The Daily Times* (Moncton), October 28, 1904, 5; New Brunswick County Deed (R6, 595, 68.310, 1898); William Henry Irving, *Fundy Family* (Durham, NC: Seeman, 1972); Braesiders, *Sunny Brae: The Town That Was* (Sackville, NB: Tribune, 1985).

74 "The Death of Mr. T. B. LeBlanc."

75 "Elks Honor Mr. H. H. Warman on His 66th Birthday," *The Daily Times* (Moncton), November 26, 1929, 5; "Heart Attack is Fatal to H. H. Warman," *The Transcript* (Moncton), May 8, 1934, 8; lounsburys.com/about-company/; "Lounsbury a Long-Time Resident of Moncton," *The Times & Transcript* (Moncton), June 15, 72.

76 "Heart Attack Is Fatal"; "A Young Girl's Trials," *Daily Telegraph* (Saint John, NB), October 5, 1895, 6; "New Companies That Are Seeking Incorporation," *The Daily Transcript* (Moncton), April 12, 1902, 1.

77 "Horse Race on Saturday," *The Daily Transcript* (Moncton), September 11, 1899, 4.

78 "Heart Attack is Fatal."

79 "Heart Attack is Fatal."

80 "Personal Intelligence," *The Daily Times* (Moncton), July 11, 1899, 4; "Local Miscellany," *The Daily Transcript* (Moncton), September 20, 1900, 4.

81 lounsburys.com/about-company/; *McAlpine's New Brunswick Directory for 1896* (Saint John, NB: McAlpine, 1896), 1220.

82 Alice and Havelock's paternal grandfathers, two brothers, emigrated from the UK and settled next to each other in Kent County, NB. Geographical proximity may have led the two second cousins to forge close bonds.

83 "Recollections of the Olden Time," *The Daily Times* (Moncton), December 11, 1889, 1–15; Pincombe and Larracey, *Resurgo*, 169–72; John Edward Belliveau, *The Monctonians: Citizens, Saints, and Scoundrels*, vol. 1(Hansport, NS: Lancelot Press, 1981), 140–56.

84 *McAlpine's New Brunswick Directory for 1889–1896*, (Saint John, NB: McAlpine & Son, 1889); *McAlpine's NB 1896*; *McAlpine's Moncton 1899*; *McAlpine's Moncton City and Westmorland County Directory*, (Saint John, NB: McAlpine, 1903).

85 "Death of Peter McSweeney, Sr."

86 *McAlpine's Halifax City Directory for 1874–75* (Halifax: McAlpine, Everett, 1874); *Census of 1881*; *Census of 1891*.

87 "Death of Peter McSweeney, Sr.," *The Daily Times* (Moncton), December 2, 1884, 3; Belliveau, *Monctonians: Citizens*, 140–56; "Recollections of the Olden Time"; Pincombe and Larracey, *Resurgo*, 169–72; Machum, *History of Moncton*, 147.

88 Patti Murphy, "Peter McSweeney Co.," *The Times & Transcript* (Moncton), October 7, 1995, F2.

89 Belliveau, *Monctonians: Citizens*, 140–56.

90 The national Temperance Act of 1878 was enforced in Moncton's Westmorland County in 1880. The Act was struck down in 1964, but most local laws were repealed well before. See Marquis, "History of Policing"; Couturier, "Prohiber ou contrôler?"; Rémi Frenette, *La résistance acadienne à la prohibition de l'alcool, 1879—1939*, Département d'histoire et géographie, Faculté des arts et des sciences sociales, vol. M.A. (Moncton: Université de Moncton, 2020).

91 Machum, *History of Moncton*, 149; I. Allen, *Biographical Review* (Boston: Biographical Review, 1900), 176–9.

92 Belliveau, *Monctonians: Citizens*, 140–56.

93 Soucoup, "Acadian Gold Rush."

94 Machum, *History of Moncton*; Pincombe and Larracey, *Resurgo*; Larracey, *First Hundred*.

95 *Census of 1891*.

96 "City and District Newsy Items," *The Transcript* (Moncton), July 21, 1915, 8; "Coming Building Operations in Moncton," *The Daily Trascript* (Moncton), May 17, 1901, 4.

97 *The Canadian Encyclopedia* online, "Contract Law in Canada," by Jean-Louis Baudoin, last edited October 30, 2020, thecanadianencyclopedia.ca/en/article/contract-law.

98 *The Canadian Encyclopedia* online, "Corporation Law," by Roderick J. Wood, last updated December 16, 2013, thecanadianencyclopedia.ca/en/article/corporation-law.

99 Robbie Gilmoure, Public Archives of New Brunswick, personal communication.

100 Paul Murdin, *Full Meridian of Glory: Perilous Adventures in the Competition to Measure the Earth* (New York: Springer, 2009).

101 Laurence Bobis et al., *L'Observatoire de Paris, 350 ans de science* (Paris: Gallimard, 2012).

102 Art Roeland Theo Jonkers, "Parallel Meridians: Diffusion and Change in Early-Modern Oceanic Reckoning," in *Noord-Zuid in Oostindisch perspectief*, ed. J. Parmentier (The Hague: Walburg, 2005), 9–11.

103 Hergé, *Le Trésor de Rackham le Rouge* (Brussels: Casterman, 1945).

104 Margaret Coleman, "Roma, Jean-Pierre," in *Dictionary of Canadian Biography*, vol. 3 (University of Toronto/Université Laval), last revised 1974, biographi.ca/en/bio/roma_jean_pierre_3E.html.

Chapter 5: Dating the Search

[105] Eleanor Rosch, "Cognitive reference points," *Cognitive Psychology* 7, 4 (1975): 532–47.

[106] New Brunswick County Deed (N5, 505, 55.053, June 12, 1889).

[107] Blakeny, *Story of a Business*, 14.

[108] *Census of 1901* (Moncton, 65), 8; *Census of 1891* (Moncton, T-6306, 230), 54; *Census of 1911* (Westmorland, New Brunswick, 180), 21.

[109] Blakeny, *Story of a Business*, 32.

[110] Machum, *History of Moncton*, 183.

[111] Blakeny, *Story of a Business*, 14.

[112] Provincial Archives of New Brunswick, *New Brunswick Vital Statistics from Government Records* (RS141)—Index to Late Registration of Births, (A1b, B92, F18789, 1897).

[113] *New Brunswick Vital Statistics from Government Records* (RS141)—Index to Late Registration of Births (A1b, B73, F18792, 1899).

[114] *McAlpine's Moncton 1903*; *McAlpine's Moncton 1899*, 153. 29 Steadman St. corresponds to 117 Steadman St. today. Blakeny's 16 Peter Street in Sunny Brae became 58 Peter Street as part of a similar civic-address overhaul.

[115] "City Directory for Moncton," *The Daily Times* (Moncton), October 19, 1898, 4.

[116] New Brunswick County Deed (69.926, V6, 245, 1899).

[117] "Epidemic of Fire—A Disastrous Conflagration on Steadman St.," *The Daily Transcript* (Moncton), September 7, 1899, 1.

[118] James Pritchard, *Anatomy of a Naval Disaster: The 1746 French Expedition to North America*, (Montreal and Kingston: McGill-Queen's University Press, 2014), 96–125.

[119] Guy Frégault, "L'expédition du duc d'Anville," *Revue d'histoire de l'Amérique française* 2, 1 (1948): 27–52.

[120] Étienne Taillemite, "La Rochefoucauld de Roye, Jean-Baptiste-Louis-Frédéric de, marquis de Roucy, duc d'Anville," in *Dictionary of Canadian Biography*, vol. 3 (University of Toronto/Université Laval), last revised 1974, biographi.ca/en/bio/la_rochefoucauld_de_roye_jean_baptiste_louis_frederic_de_3E.html.

[121] Étienne Taillemite, "Estourmel, Constantin-Louis d'," in *Dictionary of Canadian Biography*, vol. 3 (University of Toronto/Université Laval), last revised 1974, biographi.ca/en/bio/estourmel_constantin_louis_d_3E.html.

[122] Étienne Taillemite, "Taffanel de La Jonquière, Jacques-Pierre de, marquis de La Jonquière," in *Dictionary of Canadian Biography*, vol. 3 (University of Toronto/Université Laval), last revised 1974, biographi.ca/en/bio/taffanel_de_la_jonquiere_jacques_pierre_de_3E.html.

[123] Frégault, "L'expédition du duc d'Anville," 52.

[124] Pritchard, *Anatomy of a Naval Disaster*, 228–9.The transmission of disease from Europeans to Indigenous Peoples was not always accidental. See Elizabeth A. Fenn, "Biological Warfare in Eighteenth-Century North America: Beyond Jeffery Amherst," *The Journal of American History* 86, 4 (2000): 1553–4 and Barbara Alice Mann, *The Tainted Gift: The Disease Method of Frontier Expansion* (Santa Barbara, CA: EBC-CLIO, 2009).

Chapter 6: A Revelation

[125] "Stray Gossip From Both City and Country," *The Daily Transcript* (Moncton), October 5, 1899, 4.

[126] "Still on the Hunt," *The Daily Times* (Moncton), September 25, 1899, 4.

[127] "Senator McSweeney At Home," *The Daily Transcript* (Moncton), July 22, 1899, 4.

[128] *Daily Times* microfilms at various holding institutions are copies from the same faulty master. Brunswick News Inc. assures me that no copies of the *Daily Times* survive in its archives for the years in play.

[129] Alan Bruce McCullough, *Money and Exchange in Canada to 1900* (Toronto: Dundurn, 1996), 125; McLennan, *Louisbourg*; B. A. Balcom, "For King and Profit: Louisbourg Privateers, 1744," in *Canadian Military History Since the 17th Century*, ed. Y. Tremblay (Ottawa: Department of National Defense, 2001).

[130] Andrew John Bayly Johnston, *Endgame 1758: The Promise, the Glory, and the Despair of Louisbourg's Last Decade* (Lincoln, NE: University of Nebraska, 2007); Faragher, *Great and Noble Scheme*, 245–9.

[131] Thomas Head Raddall, *Halifax, Warden of the North* (Garden City, NY: Doubleday, 1965).

[132] Faragher, *Great and Noble Scheme*, 245–51.

[133] Étienne Taillemite, "Barrin de La Galissonière, Roland-Michel, marquis de," in *Dictionary of Canadian Biography*, vol. 3 (University of Toronto/Université Laval), last revised 1974, biographi.ca/en/bio/barrin_de_la_galissoniere_roland_michel_3E.html.

[134] John Grenier, *The Far Reaches of Empire: War in Nova Scotia, 1710–1760* (Norman, OK: University of Oklahoma, 2008), 146–8; Faragher, *Great and Noble Scheme*, 256–8.

[135] Grenier, *Far Reaches of Empire*, 138–76; Gérard Finn, "Le Loutre, Jean-Louis," in *Dictionary of Canadian Biography*, vol. 4 (University of Toronto/Université Laval), last revised 1979, biographi.ca/en/bio/le_loutre_jean_louis_4E.html.

[136] Dominick Graham, "Lawrence, Charles," in *Dictionary of Canadian Biography*, vol. 3 (University of Toronto/Université Laval), last revised 1974, biographi.ca/en/bio/lawrence_charles_3E.html.

[137] Christopher John Russ, "La Corne, Louis, *dit* le chevalier de La Corne," in *Dictionary of Canadian Biography*, vol. 3 (University of Toronto/Université Laval), last revised 1974, biographi.ca/en/bio/la_corne_louis_de_3E.html.

[138] Grenier, *Far Reaches of Empire*, 155–61. Faragher, *Great and Noble Scheme*, 245–51.

Chapter 7: *X* Marks the Spot

[139] Francis Joseph Rigney, "Think and Grin—Bright Idea," *Boys' Life* (Boy Scouts of America, 1932), 36.

[140] *McAlpine's NB 1896*, 1239; Donovan Evans, Linda. *An Baile Gaelach—An Historical Geography and Genealogical Study of Irishtown, NB.* Published by the author, 2016.

[141] Donovan Evans, *An Baile Gaelach*.

[142] Brenda Orr, "Greater Moncton's Water System—Labor Problems, Delays Marked Early Development," *The Times & Transcript* (Moncton), January 11, 1989, 11; "Moncton's Three Hundred Million Gallon Reservoir About Completed," *The Transcript* (Moncton), July 8, 1914, 1.

[143] Donovan Evans, *An Baile Gaelach*, 305.

[144] Glenn, *Parc Nature*.

[145] Brent Mazerolle, "Sign Recalls Moncton's First Waterworks," *The Times & Transcript* (Moncton), October 22, 2007, A4.

[146] According to hydrographic maps and overhead photography, a now-dry stream once flowed from the reservoir area. The former creek intersects the southeastern portion of the reservoir and was a tributary of Humphreys Brook.

[147] Machum, *History of Moncton*, 109.

[148] Donovan Evans, *An Baile Gaelach*, 167–73; Shirley Landry Cail, *Village of Tankville* (pub. by author, 2004).

[149] New Brunswick Land Grants (58, 0, F16357, 9611, 50 acres, lot Y, south block 12, grant to Eunice Bishop, June 11, 1860).

[150] Kevin Burns, *The Curse of Oak Island*, History Canada, 2014; Sullivan, *Curse of Oak Island*.

[151] Google Earth can display terrain cross-sections along any compass direction.

[152] National Air Photo Library, Energy, Mines, and Resources Canada (Ottawa), A7318-78.

[153] Brenda Orr, "Moncton Area's Water Problems Date Back More Than a Century," *The Times & Transcript* (Moncton), January 9, 1989, 15.

[154] "Water in the Town," *The Daily Times* (Moncton), October 21, 1878, 4.

[155] "Expropriation Arbitration—Deed of Lands Taken for the Water and Lights Works," *The Daily Times* (Moncton), August 30, 1894, 1; New Brunswick County Deed (X3, 21, 37987), Easement from John Bishop & wife (Eunice) to Moncton Gas, Light & Water Company (June 17, 1878).

[156] My 2024 reconnaissance on the eastern bank of Lynch's Brook found a large, vertical, cast-iron fitting jutting out from the ground, mere metres from the pipeline crossing. Manifestly, the eastern portion of the pipeline travelled at least partially above ground. It appears that sections of it have since been removed.

[157] *Irishtown Road Reservoir—Westmorland County/Comté de Westmorland Inner Bay of Fundy Recreational Fishing Area* (Fredericton: New Brunswick Department of Energy and Resource Development, 2018).

[158] New Brunswick Cadastral Maps; Donovan Evans, *An Baile Gaelach*, 98.

[159] Ernest Tidd, in conversation with the author, July 22, 2021.

[160] Many Monctonians are familiar with the nearby springs that dot the same east–west plateau at The Gorge, a hilly rural area in Moncton's nortwestern outskirts. The once idyllic setting has become the victim of quarrying and other industrial activity. See Blakeny, *Story of a Business*, 22–23.

[161] *Census of 1881*. See John Bishop (Moncton, Westmorland, New Brunswick, C-13184, 425), 99, and Sherman Blakeny (Moncton, Westmorland, New Brunswick, C-13184, 416), 96.

[162] "Town Council," *The Daily Times* (Moncton), September 29, 1877, 4; "Town Council," *The Daily Times* (Moncton), October 11, 1879, 3; "Last Night's Meeting of the Town Council," *The Daily Times* (Moncton), November 27, 1880, 3; Provincial Archives of New Brunswick, RS159–Westmorland County Council Records: Minutes and Financial Records F144 (1834–1852), F145 (1853–1870), F14944 (1871–1894), F146 (1895–1913); William Boyd Kinnear, ed. *The Local and Private Statutes of New Brunswick*, vol. 3 (Fredericton: J. Simpson, 1855).

[163] Pincombe and Larracey, *Resurgo*, 318.

[164] New Brunswick Cadastral Maps; Donovan Evans, *An Baile Gaelach*, 57.

[165] Orr, "Moncton Area's Water Problems."

[166] Donovan Evans, *An Baile Gaelach*, 63.

[167] Alan Cochrane, "Council Approves Expanding City Boundary for Subdivision," *The Times & Transcript* (Moncton), October 19, 2022, A5.

[168] John Clarence Webster, *The Forts of Chignecto*, pub. by author, 1930.

[169] William F. Ganong, "A Monograph of Historic Sites in the Province of New Brunswick," in *Transactions of the Historical Society of Canada—Second Series—1899–1900* (Ottawa: Hope & Sons, 1899).

[170] Pincombe and Larracey, *Resurgo*; W. E. Campbell, *The Road to Canada: The Grand Communications Route From Saint John to Quebec* (Fredericton: Goose Lane Editions, 2005); Ganong, "A Monograph."

[171] Ignace-Philippe Aubert De Gaspé, *Carte du fleuve St Laurent et de Lacadi*, Bibliothèque nationale de France, c. 1753; Ganong, "A Monograph"; Campbell, *Road to Canada*.

[172] Chaussegros De Léry (fils), *Carte du fond de la Baye Française et de la Baye Verte*. Cartothèque, 1751, Archives nationales d'outre-mer; F. J. Thorpe, "Chaussegros de Léry, Gaspard-Joseph (1721–97)," in *Dictionary of Canadian Biography*, vol. 4 (University of Toronto/Université Laval), last revised 1979, biographi.ca/en/bio/chaussegros_de_lery_gaspard_joseph_1721_97_4E.html.

[173] Chaussegros De Léry (fils), *Mémoire sur le port et la rivière de Chédaïk et du chemin qui prend au refoulle de ladite rivière et va aboutir à celle de Petitcodiac à six lieues de son embouchure*, C11A, vol. 96 (f. 206-206v), October 29, 1750.

[174] Père Germain, *Mémoire touchant la situation de la rivière St-Jean et des environs de l'Acadie, dressé en 1749*, C11E, vol. 401 (f. 215-224v), July 4, 1749.

[175] Kevin Leonard, *A Survey for French Military Supply Depots Built in 1749–50 at the Port of Shediac and on the Shediac River* (Shediac, NB: Archaeoconsulting, 2001).

[176] Grenier, *Far Reaches of Empire*; Pincombe and Larracey, *Resurgo*.

Chapter 8: Ontario: Yours to Discover

[177] "Man's Skeleton Found in Woods," *The Transcript* (Moncton), October 5, 1906, 8.

[178] "Skeleton That of 'Paddy' Donahue," *The Transcript* (Moncton), October 6, 1906, 1; "Skeleton May Not Be That of Donohue," *The Transcript* (Moncton), October 8, 1906, 8; "Not Mohan's Remains," *London Advertiser* (London, ON), October 23, 1906, 1.

[179] "Identity of Human Skeleton Found Near Moncton a Mystery," *Daily Telegraph* (Saint John, NB), October 20, 1906, 2.

[180] "May Throw Some Light On Cherryfield Mystery," *The Transcript* (Moncton), October 16, 1906, 8.

[181] See, for example, Paine, *Book of Buried Treasure*; McIntee, *Fortune & Glory*; Sullivan, *Curse of Oak Island*.

[182] *Census of 1871* (McGillivray, Middlesex North, Ontario, C-9903), 6; *Census of 1881* (McGillivray, Middlesex North, Ontario, C-13269, 75), 18.

[183] *Ontario, Tax Assessment Rolls, 1827–1922*, Archives of Ontario, (Rolls for the Township of Stephen, Centralia Village, 1885–1888).

[184] "Local News—Briefs," *Exeter Advocate* (Ontario), June 13, 1889; *The London City and Middlesex County Directory, 1888–1889* (London, ON: R. K. Polk, 1888), 212; *The London City and Middlesex County Directory, 1890* (London, ON: R. K. Polk, 1890), 219.

[185] *Census of 1911* (41, London City, Ontario, 159), 14.

[186] *United States Census, 1900* (Detroit Ward 9, Wayne, Michigan, 751, 3, Enumeration District: 0104, FHL 1240751; Detroit Ward 10, Wayne, Michigan, 751, 4, 0117, FHL 1240751).

[187] "London and Environs," *London Advertiser* (Ontario), 1890, 6.

[188] *Census of 1891* (Chatham, Kent, Ontario, T-6345, 48), 10.

[189] *The Chatham Directory* (Chatham, ON: Planet, 1892), 113–15.

[190] Jim Gilbert and Lisa Gilbert, *Chatham* (Charleston, SC: Arcadia, 2002).

[191] *Census of 1891* (Chatham, Kent, Ontario, T-6345, 48), 10.

[192] "Wedding Bells—Mohan Smith," *The Catholic Record* (London, ON), 1895, 8.

[193] Ron Brown, *The Train Doesn't Stop Here Anymore: An Illustrated History of Railway Stations in Canada* (Toronto: Dundurn Press, 2008).

[194] Chatham's former GTR station still stands. It is now VIA Rail's current connection to the Chatham-Kent municipality.

[195] *Ontario, Registrations of Marriages, 1869–1928*, Archives of Ontario, 86.

[196] "Wedding Bells—Mohan Smith."

[197] "A Local Budget," *London Advertiser* (Ontario), April 9, 8, "Business Changes," *The Canadian Journal of Commerce, Finance and Insurance Review* (Montréal), May 28, 1897, 817.

[198] Gilbert and Gilbert, *Chatham*.

[199] "Writs Issued, Ontario," *The Canadian Journal of Commerce, Finance and Insurance Review*, May 27, 1898, 759; *Vernon's City of Chatham Directory, 1900–1902* (Hamilton, ON: Vernon, 1900).

[200] "Chattel Mortages, Province of Ontario," *The Canadian Journal of Commerce, Finance and Insurance Review*, June 4, 1897, 858.

[201] "A Local Budget."

[202] *Census of 1901* (Chatham, Kent, Ontario, 93), 8.

[203] *United States Census, 1910* (Detroit Ward 17, Wayne, Michigan, T624_680, 1B, 0265, FHL 1374693).

[204] Division for Vital Records and Health Statistics—Death Records, Michigan Department of Community Health, (7030, 151: Wayne).

205 "Funeral at St. Peter's," *London Advertiser* (Ontario), November 14, 1910, 10.

206 *Vernon's Chatham 1900–1902*; *Vernon's City of Chatham Directory, 1902–1904* (Hamilton, ON: Vernon, 1902).

207 *Vernon's City of Chatham Directory, 1904–1906* (Hamilton, ON: Vernon, 1904), 99; *Vernon's City of Chatham Directory, 1932* (Hamilton, ON: Vernon, 1932), 142.

208 Archives of Ontario Collection, MS 935, M023570, 685, 392, 020986.

209 Archives of Ontario Collection, MS 935, 102, 332.

210 Steven C. Levi, *Boom and Bust in the Alaska Goldfields: A Multicultural Adventure* (Westport, CT: Greenwood, 2007).

211 In his mother's 1901 obituary, John Walton is listed as living in London. This may be a reference to his 1899 whereabouts—perhaps his last known address before he left for Moncton. See "Obituary—Mrs. Mary A. Mohan, London," *The Catholic Record* (London, ON), September 14, 1901, 8.

212 Régis Brun, "La capture du London, été 1750," *La Société Historique de la Mer Rouge* 3, 4 (1994): 15–21; John Francis Bosher and Jean-Claude Dubé, "Bigot, François (d. 1778)," in *Dictionary of Canadian Biography*, vol. 4 (University of Toronto/Université Laval), last revised 1979, biographi.ca/en/bio/bigot_francois_1778_4E.html.

213 Guillaume Estèbe, *État des munitions, vivres, et marchandises qui ont été délivrés,* C11A vol. 119 (f. 3-7v), October 27, 1749; François Bigot, Lettre de Bigot au ministre, C11A, vol. 96 (f. 5-9), August 20, 1750.

214 François Bigot, Lettre de Bigot au ministre, C11A, vol. 93 (f. 253-254v), September 30, 1749.

215 Finn, "Le Loutre."

216 Brun, "La capture du London."

217 François Bigot, Lettre de Bigot au ministre, C11A, vol. 96 (f. 10-15v), September 25, 1750.

218 Brun, "La capture du London."

Chapter 9: Red Tape

219 "Barrels of Money,." *The Daily Times* (Moncton), July 4, 1908, 3.

220 Barry Barton, "The Common Law of Subsurface Activity," in *The Law of Energy Underground*, ed. D. N. Zillman et al., (Oxford: Oxford University Press, 2014), 21–36.

221 John Dobra, "Divergent Mineral Rights Regimes," Fraser Institute (2014), fraserinstitute.org/sites/default/files/divergent-mineral-rights-regimes-rev_0.pdf.

222 Provincial Archives of New Brunswick, Mineral Branch Division Record Series, RS112.

223 Sherwin Lyman, "A Conjecture on the Canadian Law of Treasure-Trove," *Manitoba Law Journal* 2 (1966): 294–7; Aly Thomson, "Looters Likely to Be Scouring Sunken Treasures off Nova Scotia, Experts Warn," *The Globe and Mail* (Toronto), April 9, 2019. The Nova Scotia Treasure Trove Act was repealed in 2010, but an exception still regulates treasure hunting on Oak Island; see Mark Denhez and Marie-Laurence Daigle, *Unearthing the Law—Archeological Legislation on Lands in Canada* (Ottawa: Parks Canada Agency, Archeological Services Branch, 2019).

224 Bob Aaron, "Finders keepers—Law Not Always Golden Ticket," *Toronto Star*, March 12, 2016; Marjun Parcasio, "Finders Keepers? A Historical Survey of Lost and Abandoned Property and the Law," *Law Now*, January 6, 2014.

225 Cecil S. Emden, "The Law of Treasure Trove, Past and Present," *The Numismatic Chronicle and Journal of the Royal Numismatic Society* 9, 34 (1929): 85–105.

226 William Martin, and Godfrey Lushington, "The Law of Treasure Trove," *Journal of the Royal Society of Arts* 56, 2883 (February 21 1908): 348–59.

227 Lyman, "Conjecture on Canadian Law."

228 Barton, "Common Law of Subsurface."

229 Emden, "Law of Treasure Trove"; Martin and Lushington, "Law of Treasure Trove."

230 Denhez and Daigle, *Unearthing the Law*.

[231] Martin and Lushington, "Law of Treasure Trove," 351.

[232] *The Canadian Encyclopedia*, "Income Tax in Canada," by Maya Bilbao, January 28, 2022, thecanadianencyclopedia.ca/en/article/income-tax; Colin Campbell, and Robert Raizenne, *A History of Canadian Income Tax. Volume I: The Income War Tax Act 1917–1948* (Toronto: Osgood Society, 2022).

[233] Chris M. Hand, *The Siege of Fort Beauséjour, 1755* (Fredericton: Goose Lane Editions, 2004), 11–12, 76.

[234] Bernard Pothier, "Du Pont Duchambon de Vergor, Louis," in *Dictionary of Canadian Biography*, vol. 4 (University of Toronto/Université Laval), last revised 1979, biographi.ca/en/bio/du_pont_duchambon_de_vergor_louis_4E.html.

[235] Étienne Taillemite, "Jacau (Jacault, Jacob) de Fiedmont, Louis-Thomas," in *Dictionary of Canadian Biography*, vol. 4 (University of Toronto/Université Laval) last revised 1979, biographi.ca/en/bio/jacau_de_fiedmont_louis_thomas_4E.html.

[236] Hand, *Siege of Fort Beauséjour*, 46, 50.

[237] Terry A. Crowley, "Pichon, Thomas (Thomas Tyrell (Thirel, Tirel))," in *Dictionary of Canadian Biography*, vol. 4 (University of Toronto/Université Laval), last revised 1979, biographi.ca/en/bio/pichon_thomas_4E.html; John Clarence Webster, *The Life of Thomas Pichon, "The Spy of Beausejour," An Account of His Career in Europe and America* (Halifax: Public Archives of Nova Scotia, 1937).

[238] Hand, *Siege of Fort Beauséjour*, 50, 66–67.

[239] Ian K. Steele, "Monckton, Robert," in *Dictionary of Canadian Biography*, vol. 4 (University of Toronto/Université Laval), last revised 1979, biographi.ca/en/bio/monckton_robert_4E.html; Barry M. Moody, "Winslow, John," in *Dictionary of Canadian Biography*, vol. 4 (University of Toronto/Université Laval), last revised 1979, biographi.ca/en/bio/winslow_john_4E.html; Charles Perry Stacey, "Scott, George," in *Dictionary of Canadian Biography*, vol. 3 (University of Toronto/Université Laval), last revised 1974, biographi.ca/en/bio/scott_george_3E.html.

[240] Hand, *Siege of Fort Beauséjour*, 50–101; Jonathan Fowler and Earle Lockerby, "Operations at Fort Beauséjour and Grand-Pré in 1755: A Soldier's Diary," *Journal of the Royal Nova Scotia Historical Society* 12 (2009): 145.

[241] The ruins of Fort Beauséjour have inspired legends of buried treasure. See "Searching for Treasure Around the Old Fort," *The Transcript* (Moncton), June 1, 1912, 4.

[242] Hand, *Siege of Fort Beauséjour*, 54.

Chapter 10: Winters of Discontent

[243] "The Hull Fire!," *The Daily Times* (Moncton), April 27, 1900, 1.

[244] Moncton authorities briefly arrested the playwright in 1882 on ill-founded charges of reneging on a lecture engagement. See "Oscar Wilde Explains," *The Daily Times* (Moncton), October 18, 1882, 2; "Oscar Wilde in Moncton," *The Daily Times* (Moncton), October 13, 1882, 3.

[245] "A Search for Buried Treasure," *The Daily Trainscript* (Moncton), September 25, 1901, 7.

[246] Pincombe and Larracey, *Resurgo*, 172–5.

[247] Bridget Murphy, Moncton Museum, personal communication.

[248] Art Clowes (the New Brunswick Railway Museum) and Mylène Bélanger (Exporail, the Canadian Railway Museum), personal communications.

[249] In France, the redemption of gold coins minted in the seventeenth and eighteenth centuries stopped at the time of the revolution. A louis d'or nominal worth of 24 livres would therefore have meant little to Simpson. In 1901, though, a louis d'or would have fetched about $4.98 (~$174.35), based solely on its gold content of 7.480 g (0.241 troy ounces). Such a coin would have weighed about 10 percent more because of metal impurities in its composition. See James Powell, and Bank of Canada, *A History of the Canadian Dollar* (2005).

[250] In 1754, France increased overseas expenditures to 2,200,000 livres (~$50M) for the entire colony of New France, or nearly 1 percent of France's entire budget. See Guy Frégault, "Essai sur les finances canadiennes (1700–1750) (suite et fin)," *Revue d'histoire de l'Amérique française* 13, 2 (1959): 157–82.

[251] William Alexander Binny Douglas, "Rous, John," in *Dictionary of Canadian Biography*, vol. 3 (University of Toronto/Université Laval), last revised 1974, biographi.ca/en/bio/rous_john_3E.html.

[252] LeBlanc, "Deschamps de Boishébert."

[253] William Odber Raymond, *The River St. John, Its Physical Features Legends and History From 1604 to 1784* (Saint John, NB: Strathmore 1910); Grenier, *Far Reaches of Empire*, 49; Hand, *Siege of Fort Beauséjour*, 25.

[254] Douglas, "Rous, John."

[255] Roger Sarty and Doug Knight, *Saint John Fortifications, 1630–1956*, (Fredericton: Goose Lane Editions, 2003).

[256] Dismasted during the fight, the damaged *Saint-François* was seized and towed to Halifax. Vergor's bravery was later disputed. He is also credited with a monumental gaffe during the fall of Quebec in 1759. On the night of the British attack, he was caught unprepared and possibly asleep at his station. See Pothier, "Du Pont Duchambon" and Louis-Léonard Aumasson de Courville, *Mémoires sur le Canada depuis 1749 jusqu'à 1760* (Québec: Société Littéraire et Historique de Québec, 1838).

[257] Phyllis R. Blakeley, "Cobb, Silvanus," in *Dictionary of Canadian Biography*, vol. 3 (University of Toronto/Université Laval), last revised 1974, biographi.ca/en/bio/cobb_silvanus_3E.html.

[258] Clos (procureur), *Mémoire pour le Sieur de Boishebert* (Paris: Moreau, 1763).

[259] Sarty and Knight, *Saint John Fortifications*; Blakeley, "Cobb, Silvanus."

[260] Raymond, *River St. John.*

[261] La Jonquière, Lettre au ministre, May 1.

[262] Campbell, *Road to Canada*; Raymond, River St. John.

[263] Raymond, *River St. John.*

[264] Jacques-Pierre de Taffanel de La Jonquière, Lettre de La Jonquière au ministre, C11A, vol. 97 (f. 16-33v), May 1, 1751.

[265] Thomas Fressin, "Convertisseur de monnaie ancienne," convertisseur-monnaie-ancienne.fr.

Chapter 11: The Trilogy of the Times

[266] Stuart Banner, *American Property: A History of How, Why, and What We Own* (Boston: Harvard University Press, 2011).

[267] "Persistent Treasure Seekers—An Ontario Man's Search for Hidden Millions," *The Daily Times* (Moncton), September 25, 1901, 1.

[268] "Improved Boring Machine," *Scientific American*, April 11, 1874, 233.

[269] "Honors for a Monctonian," *Daily Telegraph* (Saint John, NB), September 22, 1892, 3.

[270] "A Partial Eclipse of the Sun," *The Daily Transcript* (Moncton), May 28, 1900, 4; "Anniversary of Cold Friday," *The Daily Times* (Moncton), Februrary, 1904, 3; "Some Facts About the River Tides," *The Daily Times* (Moncton), October 4, 1909, 1; "The Petitcodiac Bore," *The Daily Transcript* (Moncton), April 11, 1899, 2.

[271] Isle Haute, once visited by Champlain, has inspired many legends. Edward Rowe Snow's treasure hunt there garnered much publicity; see Edward Rowe Snow, "Red-Taped Pirate Gold," *Life*, July 21, 1952, 37–40; Edward Rowe Snow, *True Tales of Pirates and Their Gold* (New York: Dodd, Mead, 1953). Snow claimed that a treasure map by famed pirate Ned Low pointed to Isle Haute, and he produced Spanish and Portuguese coins that were later impounded by Canadian authorities. Snow went on to literary success, but he never shook suspicions he had staged a hoax.

[272] "The Missing Men," *The Daily Times* (Moncton), October 30, 1879, 3. Legend also says Samuel McCready found a stone listing gold and jewels buried at a given depth. His family supposedly kept the stone in a bank vault. See Robert Grantham et al., "The Nova Scotia Museum Isle Haute Expedition July, 1997," *Curratorial Report 90* (Museum of Natural History, Nova Scotia Museum, Nova Scotia Department of Tourism and Culture, 2000).

[273] "Geo. W. McCready Has Passed Away," *The Transcript* (Moncton), June 9, 1908, 8.

[274] "Moncton Cotton Manufacturing Co.," *The Daily Times* (Moncton), November 15, 1882, 3.

[275] "Little Local Links," *The Daily Times* (Moncton), May 11, 1894, 4.

[276] Brian McCready (geart-great-great-grandson of George McCready), personal communication.

[277] "The Treasure Seeker's Dream," *The Daily Times* (Moncton), October 17, 1901, 1.

[278] Ganong, "A Monograph."

[279] Placide Gaudet, Fonds Placide Gaudet, Centre d'études acadiennes Anselme Chiasson, Université de Moncton; Placide Gaudet, "Généalogies acadiennes et documents se rattachant à l'expulsion des Acadiens," in *Rapport concernant les archives canadiennes pour l'année 1905* (Ottawa: Parmelee, 1909).

[280] "The Treasure Seekers," *The Daily Times* (Moncton), October 30, 1901, 4.

[281] Naomi E. S. Griffiths, "The Golden Age: Acadian Life, 1713–1748," *Histoire sociale/Social History* 17, 33 (1984).

[282] Ronnie-Gilles LeBlanc, "Les réfugiés acadiens au camp d'Espérance de la Miramichi en 1756–1761 : un épisode méconnu du Grand Dérangement," *Acadiensis* 41, 1 (winter/spring) (2012): 128–68.

[283] Josée Bergeron, "Migrations et contributions des Acadiens à la population québécoise," *Histoire Québec* 20, 1 (2014): 35–38.

[284] Faragher, *Great and Noble Scheme*.

[285] Naomi E. S. Griffiths, "Acadians in Exile: the Experiences of the Acadian in the British Seaports," *Acadiensis* 4, 1 (1974): 67–84.

[286] Jean-François Mouhot, *Les réfugiés acadiens en France, 1758–1785: l'impossible réintégration ?* (Québec: Septentrion, 2009).

[287] Faragher, *Great and Noble Scheme*; Christopher Hodson, *The Acadian Diaspora: An Eighteenth-Century History*, (Oxford, UK: Oxford University Press, 2012).

[288] Ronnie-Gilles LeBlanc, ed., *Du Grand Dérangement à la Déportation: nouvelles perspectives historiques* (Moncton: Chaire d'Études Acadiennes, Université de Moncton, 2005); Arsenault and Alain, *Histoire des Acadiens*.

[289] Nicolas Landry and Nicole Lang, *Histoire de l'Acadie*, 2e éd. (Québec: Septentrion, 2014).

[290] Goss, "Harbour Treasures Prove Elusive"; Soucoup, *Looking Back*.

[291] Arsenault and Alain, *Histoire des Acadiens*, 206; Jonathan Fowler, "The Archaeologist's Evangeline: Historical Archaeology in Acadia," in *The Oxford Handbook of Historical Archeology*, ed. J. Symonds and V-P. Herva (Oxford, UK: Oxford University Press, 2014).

[292] Catherine Jolicoeur, *Les plus belles légendes acadiennes*, (Montréal: Stanké, 1981); Jean-Claude Dupont, *Contes et légendes* (Sainte-Foy, QC: GID, 2002); Jean-Claude Dupont, *Les trésors cachés: Québec et Acadie* (pub. by author, 1999). For the rumour of gold and silver found near Moncton by Eustache Babin, see Placide Gaudet, "Établissements acadiens de la rivière Petcoudiac au temps de la dispersion," *l'Évangéline* (September 1, 1927), 11–12; Pincombe and Larracey, *Resurgo*, 426–7. Another rumour is the so-called *fortune des LeBlanc*, an unclaimed inheritance reportedly bequeathed by Charles LeBlanc (White) Jr. *dit* Le Riche to all the LeBlancs of Acadian descent. Deported to Philadelphia, LeBlanc prospered as a businessman. The Registrar of Wills of Philadelphia put all rumours to rest in 1934 when it wrote, "This estate has been exploited from time to time by persons fraudulently claiming there were undistributed funds without the slightest basis for such statements"; see Robert T. Ives, Re: Estate of Charles (White) LeBlanc, Registrar of Wills, Philadelphia City Hall (Philadelphia, PA: November 26, 1934). LeBlanc's money was split between his many relatives (see Hodson, *Acadian Diaspora*, 205–12).

[293] Janice Evans, "Acadian Treasure" *Land and Sea*, aired February 14, 2014, on CBC. There are exceptions. Acadians hoarded small quantities of coins; see Adam Shortt, *Documents Relating to Canadian Currency, Exchange and Finance During the French Period—II*, (Ottawa: Acland, 1925), 737. Also, Joseph-Nicolas Gautier *dit* Bellair was a wealthy farmer, merchant, and navigator; see Bernard Pothier, "Gauthier, *dit* Bellair, Joseph-Nicolas," in *Dictionary of Canadian Biography*, vol. 3 (University of Toronto/Université Laval), last revised 1974. biographi.ca/en/bio/gautier_joseph_nicolas_3E.html.

Chapter 12: The House of Weld

[294] "Death of Mr. William Weld," *The Farmer's Advocate* (London, ON), February, 1891, 1–2; W A. Irwin, "The House of Weld," *Maclean's Magazine*, July 15, 1931, 10, 44–45; Ian M. Stewart, "Weld, William," in *Dictionary of Canadian Biography*, vol. 12 (University of Toronto/Université Laval), last revised 1990, biographi.ca/en/bio/weld_william_12E.html.

[295] Irwin, "The House of Weld."

[296] "Death of Mr. William Weld."

[297] "Great Crowd at Delaware," *London Advertiser* (Ontario), October 10, 1901, 3.

[298] "Lawn Bowling," *London Advertiser* (Ontario), September 28, 1901, 7.

[299] "Official Closing of the London Club's Season," *Daily Free Press* (London, ON), October 10, 1901, 6.

[300] "The Day's Sports—Lawn Bowling," *Daily Free Press* (London, ON), September 24, 1901.

[301] "Death of Mr. T. S. Weld," *The Farmer's Advocate* (London, ON), January 7, 1909, 16.

[302] "Late Local Items," *London Advertiser* (Ontario), November 16, 1901, 8.

[303] "Death of Mr. T. S. Weld," *Farmer's Advocate*, 16.

[304] "Found Dead With Shotgun Beside Him," *The Leamington Post and News* (ON), November 9, 1933, 1.

[305] "Englishmen Win!—Lawn Bowling," *London Advertiser* (Ontario), September 9, 1901, 7.

[306] "Births, Marriages, and Deaths," *London Advertiser* (Ontario), June 29, 1900, 1; *Census of 1911* (Winnipeg City, Manitoba, 56), 8.

[307] *Foster's London City and Middlesex County Directory 1901* (London, ON: J. G. Foster, 1901), 346.

[308] William Weld's three nephews—Henry Johnson, Octavus, and Edgar—are unlikely candidates for Wheld. Henry Johnson, a veterinarian, emigrated to Wisconsin in the early 1890s. Octavus and Edgard were both farmers in Ontario. Weld's nephews do not appear in their uncle's will and do not seem to have benefitted much from his wealth.

[309] "London Letter," *Cycling* (Toronto), January 28, 1891, 37.

[310] "Englishmen Celebrate," *London Advertiser* (Ontario), April 24, 1894, 1; "The Biggest and the Best," *London Advertiser*, December 8, 1901, 1; "Joyously Celebrated—St. Georges Society's 34th Annual Reunion," *London Advertiser* (Ontario), April 24, 1901, 2.

[311] "Births, Marriages, and Deaths."

[312] "Windgold Guessing Contest," *The Farmer's Advocate and Home Journal* (Winnipeg), September 1, 1909: 1209.

[313] *Census of 1911* (Winnipeg City, Manitoba, 56), 8.

[314] *Census for Prairies 1916* (Winnipeg Centre, 07, T-21932, 47), 4.

[315] *Census of 1921* (British Columbia, South Okanagan, Kelowna City, 225), 19.

[316] Elizabeth Muriel Anderson, in conversation with the author, August 4, 2020.

[317] "Corbin Weld," *The Winnipeg Evening Tribune*, May 4, 1942, 17.

[318] "London Old Boys Are on the Green," *London Advertiser* (Ontario), July 25, 1911, 7.

[319] "Four Hundred Bowlers in Action at Opening of Americas Greatest Tourney—Snapshot at Some of the Bowlers," *London Advertiser* (Ontario), July 25, 1911, 6.

[320] "More Bowlers Than Ever Before," *London Advertiser* (Ontario), July 22, 1911, 11. Quotations marks indicated "Cobb" was a diminutive.

[321] *Census of 1901* (Delaware, Middlesex South, Ontario, 60), 6.

[322] *Census of 1901* (London City, Ontario, 143), 13.

[323] *Census of 1901* (London City, Ontario, 219), 22.

[324] *Census of 1901* (Westminster, Middlesex South, Ontario, 108), 10.

[325] *Census of 1901* (London City, Ward 2, 14), 3.

[326] *Census of 1901* (Vancouver City, Burrard, British Columbia, 38), 4.

[327] "The Late Mr. Weld's Will," *Toronto Daily Mail*, January 23, 1891.

[328] Irwin, "The House of Weld."

[329] "Death of Mr. William Weld."

[330] "Death Takes John Weld," *The Border Cities Star* (Windsor, ON), September 16, 1931; "Overcome in Hot Spell, John Weld Succumbs," *Globe* (Toronto), September 16, 1931, 3.

[331] "Death Takes John Weld."

[332] George-Louis Le Rouge, "L'isthme de l'Acadie, baye du Beaubassin, en anglois Shegnekto, environs du fort Beauséjour," Bibliothèque nationale de France, 1755.

[333] Gaudet, *Fonds Placide Gaudet*, 1.27.8.

[334] Cyril Chapman (a.k.a. Nampahc), "The Story of Fort Folly and Other Interesting Historical Notes," *Tribune-Post* (Sackville, NB), March 7, 1950; Gérald Leblanc, "La Pointe Folly—Site d'un fort militaire et d'un phare maritime," *Les cahiers de la société d'histoire de Memramcook* 28, 1 (November 2016): 8–35.

[335] Charles Henry Lincoln, *Correspondence of William Shirley, Governor of Massachusetts and Military Commander in America, 1731–1760*, vol. 2 (New York: Macmillan, 1912), 63. Shirley was a chief proponent and enabler of the Acadian deportation (see Arsenault and Alain, *Histoire des Acadiens*; Faragher, *Great and Noble Scheme*).

[336] George Alexander Rawlyk, "Eddy, Jonathan," in *Dictionary of Canadian Biography*, vol. 5 (University of Toronto/Université Laval), last revised 1983, biographi.ca/en/bio/eddy_jonathan_5E.html; Ernest Clarke, *The Siege of Fort Cumberland, 1776: An Episode in the American Revolution* (Montreal and Kingston: McGill-Queen's University Press, 1995).

[337] Charles Perry, "Labour of Love," *The Times & Transcript* (Moncton), September 3, 1988, 17; Helen Kristmanson, *A Short History of Beaumont, New Brunswick* (Fredericton: Archaeological Services, Heritage Branch, 2004).

[338] Locals have said the name "Fort Folly" referred to the lack of anything to defend; see Ganong, "A Monograph," 290. Ganong speculated the site was one of several French lookouts on the Bay of Chignecto. Only later did he learn of rumours about a French fortlet and its two bronze cannons (see Leblanc, "La Pointe Folly").

[339] Wallie Sears, "Fort Folly Indians Revive Ste. Anne Celebration," *The Times & Transcript* (Moncton), 1984, 19.

Chapter 13: The Three Simpsons

[340] "A Woman Who Talked Magistrate and Lawyers Down," *The Daily Transcript* (Moncton), May 30, 1903, 10.

[341] *Census of 1901*; automatedgenealogy.com/census/.

[342] *Census of 1901*; automatedgenealogy.com/census/.

[343] Barbora Zahradnikova, Sona Duchovicova, and Peter Schreiber, "Facial Composite Systems: Review," *Artificial Intelligence Review: An International Science and Engineering Journal* 49, 1 (2018): 131–52.

[344] *Census of 1851*, Frontenac, Canada West, C-11721, 145, 1; *Census of 1861* (C-1022).

[345] *Sutherland's General Directory for the City of Kingston* (Kingston, ON: James Sutherland, 1866), 143.

[346] "What Do Judges and Justices of the Peace Do?," Ontario Court of Justice, ontariocourts.ca/ocj/judges-and-justices-of-the-peace/.

[347] *Ontario, Deaths and Deaths Overseas, 1869–1948*, Archives of Ontario, (MS935, 47, 223).

[348] *Ontario, Registrations of Marriages* (63, 545, 003943).

[349] *Census of 1881* (Kingston, Frontenac, Ontario, C 13235, 66), 15; *Census of 1891* (Kingston, Frontenac, Ontario, T-6336, 17), 4; *Census of 1901* (Kingston, Frontenac, Ontario, 119), 14; *Foster's Kingston Directory* (Toronto: J. G. Foster, 1905), 213.

[350] *Census of 1911* (Kingston, Frontenac, Ontario, 43), 4.

[351] *Ontario, Deaths* (MS935, 207, 013366).

[352] *Census of 1921* (London, Ontario, 268), 21.

[353] *Census of 1851* (Huron, Canada West, C-11728, 28), 39; *Census of 1861* (C-1037, 48), 17.

[354] *Ontario, County Marriage Registers, 1858–1869*, Archives of Ontario, (20, MS 248, Reel 8).

[355] *Census of 1871* (Stephen, Huron South, Ontario, C-9928, 141), 44.

[356] *Census of 1881* (Parkhill, Middlesex North, Ontario, C-13270, 121), 26; *Census of 1891* (Parkhill, Middlesex North, Ontario, Canada, T-6352, 17), 4.

[357] *McAlpine's London City and County of Middlesex Directory, 1875* (McAlpine, Everett, 1875), 285; "Biddulph Briefs," *The Exeter Times* (Ontario), March 14, 1; "Corbett—Briefs," *The Exeter Times* (Ontario), April 11, 1; *North Middlesex: How It Came to Be* (Parkhill, ON: Sesquicentennial Committee, 2010), 246–51.

[358] *Census of 1881*.

[359] "Canadian—Encounter with a Burglar at Parkhill," *London Advertiser* (Ontario), October 11, 1889, 1; "In and About in the County," *Huron News-Record* (Clinton, ON), October 9, 1889, 8.

[360] *Ontario, Registration of Marriages* (72, 007675).

[361] *Ontario, Deaths* (MS935, 68); "Local Happenings," *Exeter Times* (Ontario), September 21, 1893, 7.

[362] *Ontario, Deaths* (MS935, 58, 010237); M. MacKinnon, "Death of Mrs. William Simpson," *Parkhill Gazette* (Parkhill, ON), September 21, 1893.

[363] *Historical Books*, Abstract/Parcel Registry Book, Middlesex County (LRO 33), Parkhill, Book 1 (Abstract Index A; Parkhill Survey), 367, 2955.

[364] "Exeter," *Huron Expositor* (Seaforth, ON), December 7, 1894, 4. Record of the marriage could not be found.

[365] "Local Happenings," *Exeter Times* (Ontario), December 6, 1894, 8.; "Local Happenings," *Exeter Times* (Ontario), July 4, 1895, 8; "Local Jottings," *Exeter Advocate* (Ontario), April 23, 1896, 16; "Local Jottings," *Exeter Advocate* (Ontario), June 24, 1897, 8.

[366] *Historical Books*, Abstract/Parcel Registry Book, Middlesex County (LRO 33), Parkhill, Book 1 (Abstract Index A; Parkhill Survey), 367, 3133 (September 14, 1895) and 3153 (November 15, 1895). The British Mortgage Loan Company issued two writs against William and Page for payment default: "Writs Issued, Ontario," *The Canadian Journal of Commerce, Finance and Insurance Review* (April 3, 1896), 657; and "Writs Issued, Ontario," *The Canadian Journal of Commerce, Finance and Insurance Review* (November 6, 1896), 803.

[367] *Historical Books*, Abstract/Parcel Registry Book, Middlesex County (LRO 33)—Parkhill, Book 1 (Abstract Index A; Parkhill Survey), 367, 3504 1/2 (December 1, 1897).

[368] *Foster's London City and Middlesex County Directory, 1897–8* (Toronto: J. G. Foster, 1897), 447; "Hensall—Briefs," *Exeter Times* (Ontario), October 13, 1898, 1; *North Middlesex*, 251.

[369] M. MacKinnon, "The Gazette-Review," *Parkhill Gazette* (Ontario), September 22, 1898; *Census of 1901*, London City, Ward 1, Ontario, 12, 122.

[370] "Exeter," *Huron Expositor* (Seaforth, ON), April 8, 1898, 16.

[371] "Hensall—Briefs."

[372] *Ontario, Tax Assessment Rolls* (Collector Rolls for Village of Exeter).

[373] *Census of 1901* (Hibbert, Perth South, Ontario, 133), 13.

[374] "Late Local Items," *London Advertiser* (Ontario), October 25, 1900, 6.

[375] *Foster's London Directory 1901*, 317.

[376] *Census of 1901* (Hibbert, Perth South, Ontario, 133), 13. William's census entry was recorded on April 13.

[377] "Death of William Simpson," *Exeter Advocate* (Ontario), December 13, 1906, 8; *Ontario, Deaths* (MS935, 126, 018534).

[378] *Census for 1861* (C-1065); Bill Martin, "Wesleyan Methodist Baptismal Register," (collection held by United Church of Canda), vol. 2, 857, freepages.rootsweb.com/~wjmartin/genealogy/wm-s_66.htm; *Ontario, County Marriage* (1030063).

[379] *Toronto Trust Cemeteries, 1826–1989*, Mount Pleasant Cemetery (Toronto), 4, 191; *Forty-Fifth Annual Catalogue of the Officers and Students of the Maine Wesleyan Seminary* (Readfield, ME: Gardiner Morrell, 1868), 13.

[380] "Prohibition—Lecture by J. W. Simpson," *The Listowel Banner* (ON), November 17, 1876, 8.

[381] "Temperance Lecture," *Free Press* (Acton, ON), March 8, 1877.

[382] "Wallace," *The Listowel Banner* (ON), October 20, 1876, 8.

[383] "Cardinal Manning a Dunkinite," *Guelph Daily Mercury* (Ontario), November 21, 1877, 1.

[384] "Temperance Lecture."

[385] "Local News," *Guelph Daily Mercury and Advertiser* (Ontario), October 10, 1878, 1.

[386] "This Afternoon's Dispatches," *Guelph Mercury and Advertiser* (Ontario), Februrary 9, 1880, 1.

[387] "Miscellaneous," *The Grey Review* (Durham, ON), September 2, 1880, 3.

[388] *Ontario, Registrations of Births and Stillbirths, 1869–1913*, Archives of Ontario, (69, 80–82).

[389] *The Toronto City Directory for 1885* (Toronto: Polk, 1885), 698.

[390] *The Toronto City Directory for 1886* (Toronto: Polk, 1886), 739.

[391] *The Toronto City Directory for 1887* (Toronto: Polk, 1887), 642.

[392] *The Toronto City Directory for 1888* (Toronto: Polk, 1888), 950.

[393] *The Toronto City Directory for 1889* (Toronto: Polk, 1889), 1055.

[394] *The Toronto City Directory for 1890* (Toronto: Polk, 1890), 793.

[395] A. Wilford Hall, *Dr. A. Wilford Hall's Hygenic Treatment for the Cure of Disease, Preservation of Health and the Promotion of Longevity Without Medicine* (Toronto: Simpson Publishing, 1890).

[396] J. J. Wesley Simpson, *The Microcosmic Health Pamphlet; Or the Wilford Hall Revolution With a Supplement by J. J. Wesley Simpson, Esq.* (Toronto: Simpson Publishing, 1890).

[397] "A $30,000 Writ," *Toronto World*, January 3, 1891, 4.

[398] "Gossip From Toronto," *The Montreal Gazette*, June 19, 1891, 1.

[399] *The Toronto City Directory for 1893*, vol. 17 (Toronto: Might, 1893), 1241; *The Toronto City Directory for 1896*, vol. 20 (Toronto: Might, 1896), 1252; *The Toronto City Directory for 1897*, vol. 22 (Toronto: Might, 1897), 1231.

[400] "The Election," *The Fenelon Falls Gazette* (Ontario), June 22, 1894, 2.

[401] *Western Ontario Gazeteer and Directory, 1898–99* (Ingersoll, ON: Ontario Publishing & Advertising, 1898), 689.

[402] *Census of 1901* (Woodstock City, Oxford North, Ontario, 36), 4.

[403] *Census of 1911* (Ward 5, Toronto West, Ontario, 67), 6; "Returns to Woodstock," *Toronto World*, April 24, 1918, 2.

[404] *Ontario, Deaths* (MS935, 252).

[405] Maurice Basque, "Atlantic Realities, Acadian Identities, Arcadian Dreams," in *Shaping an Agenda for Atlantic Canada*, ed. J. G. Reid and D. J. Savoie (Halifax: Fernwood Publishing, 2011).

[406] Johnston, "Borderland Worries"; Arsenault and Alain, *Histoire des Acadiens*; Landry and Lang, *Histoire de l'Acadie*.

[407] Clarence Joseph d'Entremont, "Brossard (Broussard), *dit* Beausoleil, Joseph," in *Dictionary of Canadian Biography*, vol. 3 (University of Toronto/Université Laval), last revised 1974, biographi.ca/en/bio/brossard_joseph_3E.html.

[408] A British squadron intercepted the French *Alcide* and *Lys* off Cape Race, Newfoundland. The boats were brought into Halifax's harbour; see Thomas Pichon, *Lettres et mémoires pour servir à l'histoire naturelle, civile et politique du Cap Breton* (The Haugue: Gosse, 1760), 248–56. Reportedly, twenty leather cases containing ten thousand scalping knives were found earmarked for Beausoleil Broussard and Abbé Le Loutre's guerillas; see Dianne Marshall, *Heroes of the Acadian Resistance: The Story of Joseph Beausoleil Broussard and Pierre II Surette 1702–1765* (Halifax: Formac Publishing, 2011), 126; Raddall, *Halifax, Warden*, 45). Whether accurate or not, the rumour would only have spurred further British action.

[409] Warren A. Perrin, *Acadian Redemption: From Beausoleil Broussard to the Queen's Royal Proclamation* (Opelousas, LA: Andrepont Publishing, 2005).

[410] D'Entremont, "Brossard, Beausoleil."

[411] D'Entremont, "Brossard, Beausoleil."

[412] John Knox, "An Extract of a Letter From Fort Cumberland, to Another Gentleman of This Garrison (1758)," in *An Historical Journal of the Campaigns in North America: For the Years 1757, 1758, 1759, and 1760* (London: W. Johnston and J. Dodsley, 1769), 85; Paul Delaney, "La reconstitution d'un rôle des passagers du Pembroke," *Les Cahiers de la Société historique acadienne* 35, 12 (2004): 4–75.

[413] Faragher, *Great and Noble Scheme*, 351.

[414] Boishébert set up his Camp de l'Espérance on Beaubears Island near the mouth of the Miramichi. The island's name recalls Boishébert's surname in corrupted form.

[415] LeBlanc, "Les réfugiés acadiens."

[416] Grenier, *Far Reaches of Empire*, 198; Faragher, *Great and Noble Scheme*, 402. Evidence favours Le Coude as the probable location of the battle. See Pincombe and Larracey, *Resurgo*, 33–38; Larracey, *Chocolate River*.

[417] Boishébert likely participated in the skirmish. The date of the battle coincides with his return from Louisbourg in the summer of 1758, during which time he recalled travelling from Shediac to the Petitcodiac River. There, he claimed, he and a hundred men engaged a British detachment and lost fifteen men in the battle. See Charles Deschamps de Boishébert, "Journal de ma campagne de Louisbourg," in *Recherches historiques* (Lévis: Pierre-Georges Roy, 1758), 51–52.

[418] John Knox, "An Extract of a Letter," 139.

[419] Phyllis R. Blakeley, "Danks, Benoni," in *Dictionary of Canadian Biography*, vol. 4 (University of Toronto/Université Laval), last revised 1979, biographi.ca/en/bio/danks_benoni_4E.html; David A. Charters and Stuart R. J. Sutherland, "Goreham (Gorham), Joseph," in *Dictionary of Canadian Biography*, vol. 4 (University of Toronto/Université Laval), last revised 1979, biographi.ca/en/bio/goreham_joseph_4E.html.

[420] William F. Ganong, "The Report and Map of Major George Scott's Expedition to Remove the French From the Petitcodiac in 1758," in *Historical-Geographical Documents Relating to New Brunswick* (Saint John, NB: Barnes, 1914), 98.

[421] Pothier, "Gautier, Bellair"; George MacBeath, "Godin, *dit* Bellefontaine, *dit* Beauséjour, Joseph," in *Dictionary of Canadian Biography*, vol. 4 (University of Toronto/Université Laval), last revised 1979, biographi.ca/en/bio/godin_joseph_4E.html; Bernard Pothier, "Leblanc, *dit* Le Maigre, Joseph," in *Dictionary of Canadian Biography*, vol. 3 (University of Toronto/Université Laval), last revised 1974, biographi.ca/en/bio/leblanc_joseph_3E.html; Marshall, *Heroes of the Acadian Resistance*; Hodson, *Acadian Diaspora*.

422 Blakeny presumed that the old skeletons he saw unearthed during the construction of the Moncton Sugar Refinery in 1880 belonged to mid-eighteenth-century French troops who had fought at The Bend. The graves were more probably those of Acadian settlers buried in Le Coude's cemetery (see Pincombe and Larracey, *Resurgo*, 38). Similarly, a Moncton blacksmith unearthed sixteen bodies in 1835 while digging for foundations. In his book *Chocolate River*, Larracey entertains the possibility that the remnants could be those of Acadian militiamen killed during what he called the Battle of Moncton (see page 29). He offers no evidence to support his claim.

Chapter 14: Simpson's Sketch

423 Ian M. Drummond, *Progress Without Planning: The Economic History of Ontario From Confederation to the Second World War* (Toronto: University of Toronto Press, 1987).

424 Robert Bourbeau and Nadine Ouellette, "Trends, Patterns, and Differentials in Canadian Mortality Over Nearly a Century, 1921–2011," *Canadian Studies in Population* 43, 1–2 (2016): 48–77.

425 *Historical Statistics, Urban and Rural Population* (17-10-0068-01, formerly CANSIM 075-0010), Ottawa: Statistics Canada, 2015, doi.org/10.25318/1710006801-eng.

426 Drummond, *Progress Without Planning*.

427 "Mortgage Sale," *London Advertiser* (Ontario), September 28, 1901, 1; *Foster's London Directory 1901*, 107.

428 Others named "William Simpson" appear in city directories, but we can rule them out by cross-referencing with other sources, including matching civic addresses from previous editions.

429 We transformed barcodes into probabilistic Gaussian priors embodying both our knowledge (μ) and degree of uncertainty (σ) regarding Simpson. Parameters went as follows: age ($\mu = 63.0$ years, a "best guess" of Simpson's age, and $\sigma = 10.0$ years), distance from London ($\mu = 0.0$ km, $\sigma = 15.0$ km), income ($\mu = \$200$, $\sigma = \$500$), lifestyle ($\mu = 100$ percent, $\sigma = 100$ percent), and freedom ($\mu = 100$ percent, $\sigma = 100$ percent). Expressing prior knowledge and uncertainty in this way enables variously reliable data to be combined (i.e., multiplied) into a single, goodness-of-fit measure or likelihood score; see Taroni et al., *Data Analysis in Forensic Science: A Bayesian Decision Perspective* (Hoboken, NJ: John Wiley & Sons, 2010).

430 The 1901 Canada census lists William's putative birth date as October 11, 1941. In contrast, other sources state his age only to the nearest year. The more fleshed-out 1901 census entry may appear more reliable at first blush, but it underestimates William's age relative to other sources. A linear regression (fixed unit slope) across all available data puts William's birth year at 1839. Removing the 1901 census outlier from the analysis pushes back his estimated birth year to 1838. In other words, in 1901, William was probably closer to sixty-three than to fifty-nine. Had we used his estimated age instead of his listed one, the retired Parkhill hotelkeeper would have scored a likelihood of 98.0 percent—a virtually perfect match to our idealized Simpson.

431 Parameter values matter little for ranking outcomes provided they agree reasonably well with Simpson's composite sketch. We remained conservative in estimating missing data for income and freedom. If anything, then, top candidates are more probable stand-ins than their likelihood scores suggest.

432 William John Eccles, "Meulles, Jacques de," in *Dictionary of Canadian Biography*, vol. 2 (University of Toronto/Université Laval), last revised 1982, biographi.ca/en/bio/meulles_jacques_de_2E.html.

433 James S. Pritchard, *In Search of Empire: The French in the Americas, 1670–1730* (Cambridge: Cambridge University Press, 2004), 189–229.

434 Eccles, "Meulles, Jacques de."

435 James Powell and Bank of Canada, *A History of the Canadian*, 4–5.

436 Kenneth S. Rogoff, "The Curse of Cash," in *The Curse of Cash* (Princeton, NJ: Princeton University Press, 2017), 15–30; James Powell and Bank of Canada, *A History of the Canadian*, 8.

437 "Considerations on the Present State of Canada," in Shortt, *Documents Relating*, vol. 2, 873.

438 Pritchard, *In Search of Empire*, 225–6.

439 James Powell and Bank of Canada, *A History of the Canadian*, 8.

[440] Clos (procureur), *Mémoire pour le Sieur*, 37.

[441] Rénald Lessard, "L'établissement d'une nouvelle Acadie: L'apport des billets de l'Acadie," *Nouvelle-France: histoire et patrimoine n° 4—Le grand dérangement des Acadiens: 1755*, 4 (2021): 41–48.

[442] Rénald Lessard (coordinating archivist at the Archives nationales du Québec), personal communication, August 25, 2021. See also, for instance, "*État des paiements à faire aux capitaines et commandants*," C11A, vol. 53 (f. 290-292v), January 31, 1730.

[443] Archeological investigations on old Acadian sites have found the occasional cache. But so far, the concealed artifacts tend to be personal rather than monetary in nature (see Fowler, "Archaeologist's Evangeline").

Chapter 15: Two Birds, One Stone

[444] Jane Regent, in conversation with the author, November 9, 2020. Jane Regent is a pseudonym to protect Brian Holland's widow from casual inquiries.

[445] I have been careful throughout my interviews to ask mostly open-ended questions and to avoid leading interviewees or offering information they could later come to regard as their own. In Jane's case, I introduced myself as someone doing research for a book and explained that I was seeking to identify someone by the name of Simpson, who had conducted a treasure hunt near Moncton in the late 1800s. Only in my debrief—that is, only after Jane's extraordinary comment—did I mention Simpson's document. Her mention of a treasure map in her possession was therefore spontaneous, unprompted, and unexpected, all the more so that, at that point in time, I had not identified Simpson nor had I begun searching for his map in earnest.

[446] Brian and Jane were unsure how they inherited the document. The letter's allusion to the general Moncton area led the pair to suspect it could have come from Jane's side of the family. As it turns out, her adoptive father hailed from the region.

[447] In August 2025, I reached out to Brian and Jane's daughter, Jennifer Mackintosh. When I told her of her ancestor's treasure hunt in Moncton, she spontaneously said that she had overheard her parents speak of a "treasure map" in their possession. In her view, the chart had been handed down from her father's side of the family. Since then, Jennifer has taken on the task of helping her mother search for the elusive document in her father's vast posthumous stash of material.

[448] "Mrs. Jas. Horney Celebrates Her 93rd Birthday," *Exeter-Times Advocate* (Ontario), September 19, 1935, 7.

[449] "Mrs. Jas. Horney."

[450] "Death of William Simpson."

[451] *Ontario, Surrogate Court (Huron County)*, Archives of Ontario; *Ontario, Surrogate Court (Middlesex County)*, Archives of Ontario.

[452] William G. Godfrey, "Bradstreet, John (baptized Jean-Baptiste)," in *Dictionary of Canadian Biography*, vol. 4 (University of Toronto/Université Laval), last revised 1979, biographi.ca/en/bio/bradstreet_john_4E.html. Surprisingly, Bradstreet had an Acadian lineage.

[453] Donald Chaput, "Payen de Noyan et de Chavoy, Pierre-Jacques," in *Dictionary of Canadian Biography*, vol. 3 (University of Toronto/Université Laval), last revised 1974, biographi.ca/en/bio/payen_de_noyan_pierre_benoit_3E.html.

[454] Charles Howard Widdifield, "A Barrel of Gold," in *Picturesque Prince Edward County*, ed. Helen M. Merrill (Picton, ON: Gazette Book and Job Printing House, 1892).

[455] John Bradstreet, *An Impartial Account of Lieut. Col. Bradstreet's Expedition to Fort Frontenac* (London: Wilcox, Owen, Cooper & Cooke, 1759).

Chapter 16: Rocks of Ages

[456] "The History of a Stone," *The Daily Times* (Moncton), May 17, 1894, 4.

[457] "The History of a Stone."

[458] "Treasure Hunt On Near City—Boulders Bearing Inscription Lead to Search for Buried Gold," *The Transcript* (Moncton), May 23, 1924, 1.

[459] Moncton city limits proceeded mostly westward for decades. Sunny Brae was only annexed to Moncton in 1955. See Braesiders, *Sunny Brae.*

[460] Donovan Evans, *An Baile Gaelach.*

[461] Donovan Evans, *An Baile Gaelach.*

[462] "John Bishop," *The Transcript* (Moncton), October 3, 3.

[463] "McDonald vs. Bishop," *The Daily Times* (Moncton), September 2, 1896, 4; "Stray Gossip From Both City and Country," *The Daily Transcript* (Moncton), October 10, 1896, 4.

[464] "West. County Court—Bishop Junior Sentenced to a Month in Jail," *The Daily Transcript* (Moncton), March 6, 1897, 4; "Westmorland County Court," *Daily Telegraph* (Saint John, NB), December 4, 1899, 1.

[465] Alma Margaret Stiles, in coversation with Norman Weir, July 11, 2020.

[466] Jackie Tilton (née Richards), in conversation with the author, May 7, 2020.

[467] Donovan Evans, *An Baile Gaelach.*

[468] In my interview with Ernest Tidd on October 12, 2019, he informed me that the Anketell farm remained in the family until a gale blew down the barn.

[469] Belliveau, *Monctonians: Citizens.*

[470] Machum, *History of Moncton*; Larracey, *First Hundred.*

[471] Linda Donovan Evans in conversation with the author, November 10, 2019.

[472] Shirley Landry Cail, personal communication, March 26, 2024.

[473] Ernest Tidd, in coversation with the author, October 18, 2018.

[474] Ernest Tidd, in coversation with the author, October 12, 2019.

[475] Ernest Tidd, October 18, 2018; *New Brunswick County Deed* (179346, R14, 313, 1948).

[476] Ernest Tidd, October 18, 2018.

[477] *New Brunswick County Deed* (S13, 342); Ernest Tidd, October 18, 2018.

[478] Ernest Tidd, October 18, 2018.

[479] "National Radiation Instrument Catalog," national-radiation-instrument-catalog.com.

[480] firsttexasproducts.com/pages/aboutus.

[481] Patrick Bishop, *Operation Jubilee: Dieppe, 1942: The Folly and the Sacrifice* (Toronto: McClelland & Stewart, 2021). Between 1939 and 1941, Moncton also became an inevitable waypoint for the wholesale shipping of British gold reserves to the safety of the Bank of Canada's vaults in Ottawa. Fearful of a German invasion, London put about 1,000 tons of gold (~$68 billion) onboard dozens of vessels bound for Halifax. There, the gold was loaded onto special trains that then made their way to the nation's capital under heavy guard. The top-secret operation represents the largest single physical transfer of wealth in history. See Alfred Draper, *Operation Fish: The Race to Save Europe's Wealth, 1939–1945* (London: Cassell, 1979).

[482] Larracey, *Resurgo*, 327–59; Machum, *History of Moncton*, 341–60.

[483] Ernest Tidd, October 18, 2018.

[484] McLennan, *Louisbourg*; B. A. Balcom, *The Cod Fishery of Isle Royale, 1713–58* (Ottawa: Parks Canada, National Historic Parks and Sites Branch, 1984).

[485] Frégault, "Essai sur les finances."

[486] Christopher Moore, "The Other Louisbourg: Trade and Merchant Enterprise in Ile Royale 1713–58," *Histoire sociale/Social History* 12, 23 (1979).

[487] Moogk, "When Money Talks," 90; McCullough, *Money and Exchange*, 125–6; McLennan, *Louisbourg*, 228.

[488] Moore, "The Other Louisbourg," 84–85.

[489] Moore, "The Other Louisbourg," 86.

[490] McCullough, *Money and Exchange*, 126.

[491] Shortt, *Documents Relating*, vol. 2, 811n.

[492] *État de la répartition sur les vaisseaux allant au Canada et à l'île Royale des espèces d'or et d'argent*, C11A, vol. 100 (f. 296), 1755, Archives nationales d'outre-mer. Soldiers from the *compagnies franches de la Marine* stationed at Louisbourg continued earning their salaries through redeemable certificates.

[493] McCullough, *Money and Exchange*, 125.

[494] Peter N. Moogk, "A Pocketful of Change at Louisbourg," *Canadian Numismatic Journal* 21, 3 (March 1976); Moogk, "When Money Talks."

[495] Storm, *Seaweed and Gold*; "N.S. Search for Buried Treasure," *Daily Gleaner* (Fredericton), July 20, 1926, 7; "Relic Hunt at Louisbourg Cape Breton," *The Transcript* (Moncton), March 1, 1912, 3.

[496] Frégault, "Essai sur les finances"; Bosher and Dubé, "Bigot, François"; Terry A. Crowley, "Prevost de La Croix, Jacques," in *Dictionary of Canadian Biography*, vol. 4 (University of Toronto/Université Laval), last revised 1979, biographi.ca/en/bio/prevost_de_la_croix_jacques_4E.html; John Francis Bosher, "Laborde (La Borde), Jean," in *Dictionary of Canadian Biography*, vol. 4 (University of Toronto/
Université Laval), last revised 1979, biographi.ca/en/bio/laborde_jean_4E.html.

[497] Bosher, "Laborde (La Borde)."

[498] Laborde, while never formally charged, deserves mention as part of *l'Affaire du Canada*. The Paris trial investigated corruption under New France's defunct regime; see André Côté, "L'affaire du Canada (1761–1763)," *Cap-aux-Diamants*, 83 (2005): 10–14. Though some New France officials were far from blameless, the proceedings engaged in scapegoating to divert blame for the loss of the colony away from the King and his entourage. The hearing also provided France with a fig leaf to devalue New France's remaining paper money and shield itself from creditors.

[499] Johnston, *Endgame 1758*.

[500] In 1758, Boishébert travelled from Quebec to Louisbourg and raised a war party of Acadian and Indigenous irregulars. His itinerary included journeys along the North Shore and various portages in continental Acadie. As part of his return trip, he travelled from Shediac to the Petitcodiac, where he skirmished with British troops (see Boishébert, "Journal de ma campagne," 48–53).

[501] For French troops, breaking through Louisbourg's siege was virtually impossible. Yet one French courier accomplished just that to deliver, of all things, a bit of French gold in the form of a *Croix de Saint-Louis* decoration. Louisbourg's governor awarded the distinction to Boishébert who camped just beyond enemy lines (see Johnston, *Endgame 1758*, 241–2).

[502] Bosher and Dubé, "Bigot, François."

[503] The lack of gold and silver coins found at Louisbourg is not surprising, as these are normally guarded more closely (see Moogk, "When Money Talks," 71–72). But while never dire, Louisbourg's currency supply did decline in the two decades preceding the 1758 siege (see Balcom, *Cod Fishery*, [9]).

Chapter 17: A Stone Left Unturned

[504] Ernest Tidd, October 18, 2018.

[505] Soucoup, "Search for Buried Gold."

[506] Ernest Tidd, October 12, 2019.

[507] Ernest Tidd, in conversation with the author, July 22, 2021.

[508] Ernest Tidd, October 12, 2019. Perhaps Thomas had heard about Dr. Amos Chandler's late-nineteenth-century treasure hunt on Joseph Gueguen (Goguen)'s former property in Cocagne (Kent County, NB). By the late 1700s, Gueguen had become Acadie's most prosperous merchant as well as a noted translator, Justice of the Peace, scholar, notary, and elder statesman. His neutral stance on the American War of Independence attracted reprisals from irate revolutionary

rebels. In 1778, Yankee privateers raided his Cocagne farm and stole goods and money, as well as his schooner. Chandler believed Gueguen anticipated the attack and concealed a stash of gold somewhere on his land. His search proved futile; see Régis Brun, "Gueguen (Goguen), Joseph," in *Dictionary of Canadian Biography*, vol. 6 (University of Toronto/Université Laval), last revised 1987, biographi.ca/en/bio/gueguen_joseph_6E.html; Belliveau, *Monctonians: Citizens*, 220).

509 "A Search for Buried Treasure."

510 Ernest Tidd, October 12, 2019.

511 Donovan Evans, *An Baile Gaelach.*

512 Ernest Tidd, July 22, 2021.

513 An unrelated lawsuit launched by Jack Bishop in 1899 proves that he was of sound mind at the time—see "Irishtown Jottings," *The Daily Times* (Moncton), April 1, 1899, 2.

514 Garfield, *On the Map*, 240–54.

515 John Knox, *An Historical Journal of the Campaigns in North America: For the Years 1757, 1758, 1759, and 1760*, vol. 1 (London: W. Johnston and J. Dodsley, 1769), 238.

516 Charles Perry Stacey, "Knox, John," in *Dictionary of Canadian Biography*, vol. 4 (University of Toronto/Université Laval), last revised 1979, biographi.ca/en/bio/knox_john_4E.html.

517 Faragher, *Great and Noble Scheme.*

518 Edward A. Whitcomb, *A Short History of New Brunswick* (Ottawa: From Sea to Sea, 2010).

519 Ray Howard Blakeny, *My Help Comes From Above—The Blakeney/Blakeley Family History* (Windsor, NS: Ed Martin, 2004).

520 Blakeny, *Story of a Business.*

Chapter 18: The Riddle of Skull Island

521 Procès-verbal; Deux lettres; Mémoire annoté sur le naufrage.

522 For Acadian legends, see Jolicoeur, *Les plus belles légendes*; Dupont, *Contes et légendes*; Dupont, *Les trésors cachés.*

523 De Léry (fils), Mémoire sur le port; De Léry (fils), *Carte du fond de la Baye.*

524 Ganong, "A Monograph"; Kevin Leonard, *Mi'kmaq Culture During the Late Woodland and Early Historic Periods* (Toronto: University of Toronto Press, 1996); Leonard, *Survey for French*; "L'nu Place Names," migmawel.org/lnu-place-names/; Kevin Leonard, *Jedaick (Shediac, NB): A Nexus Through Time* (Shediac Bridge, NB: Shediac Bay Watershed Association, 2002).

525 Ganong, "The Report and Map," 104–14; John Clarence Webster, *A History of Shediac, New Brunswick* (pub. by author, 1928), 5; Larracey, *Chocolate River*, 34. In 1749, the Jesuit Père Germain wrote of the Le Coude–Shediac portage, "From the river called Chedaïque [Shediac], by a portage of about four leagues, one can travel to the French dwellings of Petkoudiak [Petitcodiac] and Mememramcouck [Memramcook]. The portage, from what is commonly asserted, is very good and very easy, all tall hardwoods without quagmires." In Germain, *Mémoire touchant.*

526 Ganong, "A Monograph," 250.

527 *Voyage en hyver, et sur les glaces du sieur Gauthier*, C11E, vol. 4 (f. 134-137v), 1756.

528 William Francis Ganong, *Map to Show the Connections Between the Waters of Shediac, Petitcodiac & Memramcook, as a Basis for the Determination of the Ancient Portages* (Saint John, NB: New Brunswick Museum Archives and Research Library, January 1928).

529 In 1750, De Léry reported touching the bottom of the Shediac River with his canoe on more than one occasion.

530 Leonard, *Survey for French.*

531 Webster, *History of Shediac*, 9; Francis Gillman Stanley George, "John Clarence Webster: The Laird of Shediac," *Acadiensis* 3, 1 (1973).

532 Robert Doyle, *Ancient First Nation Portages, Canoe Carrying Places in What is Now the Province of New Brunswick*, unpublished manuscript.

[533] Walling's map from 1862 mistakenly links Lynch's Brook to Humphreys Brook to the south. In fact, Lynch's Brook is a tributary of Ogilvie Brook to the west.

[534] Caledonia Road follows a path of least resistance through hilly terrain toward the Shediac River. It could correspond to the portage section of the old French road to Shediac. Today, an abandoned bit of Caledonia Road cuts across now submerged land on the southeastern end of the Moncton reservoir. According to the first aerial photographs taken of the area, the same held true in 1944. Potentially, then, the roadway could predate the reservoir's construction in 1878.

[535] Webster, *History of Shediac*, 1–3.

[536] Louis Chevalier de La Corne, Lettre de Louis de La Corne au ministre, C11A, vol. 96 (f. 190-191v), March 31, 1750.

[537] Estèbe, *État des munitions.*

[538] Régis Brun, "Le fort de Chédaïque," *La Société Historique de la Mer Rouge* 3, 5 (1995): 4–10.

[539] La Corne, Lettre, Mar. 31; François Bigot, Lettre de Bigot au ministre, C11A, vol. 96 (f. 77), October 24, 1750.

[540] De Léry (fils), *Mémoire sur le port.*

[541] De Léry was incorrect in stating that ships could not reach Shediac Bay's coastline. A pier, Queen's Wharf, was built on the mainland's western shore in 1839 (see Webster, *History of Shediac*, 11).

[542] The outpost's buildings consisted of five structures built in 1749 and of two more erected in 1750. De Léry lists two other buildings at the Shediac River's head of tide. The report includes dimensions for each, but it fails to specify their exact location.

[543] De Léry (fils), *Carte du fond de la Baye.*

[544] Jean-Baptiste Bourguignon d'Anville, "Canada, Louisiane et terres angloises," Bibliothèque nationale de France, 1755. The map served as the basis for others, including Montresor's map of 1768.

[545] Ganong, "A Monograph," 291–3. The name "Skull Island" refers to the island's former Mi'kmaw cemetery; see "Le cimetière de la réserve Mi'kmaq (Fort Folly) de Beaumont," Société d'histoire de Memramcook, histoirememramcook.ca/.

[546] Leonard, *Survey for French.*

[547] Ganong, "A Monograph," 291–3.

[548] Leonard, *Survey for French*. Unfounded rumour has it that the fort was a redoubt erected by the crew of a French frigate that wintered in Shediac Bay in 1759 (see Webster, *History of Shediac*, 5).

[549] Joseph Frederick Wallet DesBarres, *Port Shediack (Plate 35, surveyed in 1781)*, (London: The Atlantic Neptune, 1800).

[550] DesBarres's 1781 map shows Acadian homes on the coast of Shediac Bay. Some have speculated the dwellings could have been built on the site of France's abandoned Shediac outpost (see Brun, "Le fort de Chédaïque"; Leonard, *Survey for French*). However, the homes are located nowhere near the Shediac River and would have been impractically far from the portage road to Le Coude.

[551] Leonard, *Survey for French*, 32.

[552] In 1923, Shediac local Samuel Teed brought Webster and Ganong to a rumoured old French fort near the Shediac River's head of tide (see Webster, *History of Shediac*, 4). The stone ruins are more likely the remains from an abandoned nineteenth-century farmhouse (see Leonard, *Survey for French*, 22).

[553] Louis Franquet, "Le voyage de Franquet aux îles Royale et Saint-Jean et en Acadie 1751," *Rapport de l'Archiviste de la province de Québec* (1923–1924): 111–40.

[554] Skull Island has inspired rumours as well as published fiction. Treasure hunts on the island go back at least to 1920; see Denis Boucher and Paul Roux, *L'Île-au-crâne de Shédiac* (Moncton: Bouton d'or Acadie, 2016) and Gordon M. MacDonald, *The Secret About Skull Island and the Hidden History of Shediac* (pub. by author, 2015).

[555] Robert Doyle, personal communication, 2021.

[556] Robert Doyle has expressed similar ideas in his unpublished manuscript, *Ancient First Nation Portages, Canoe Carrying Places in What is Now the Province of New Brunswick*, vol. 2.

[557] Simon Singh, *The Code Book* (New York: Doubleday, 1999); Joseph Gagné, "Voix de Guerre: Le renseignement au sein de l'armée française lors de la guerre de Sept Ans en Amérique du Nord" (PhD diss., Université Laval, 2020).

Chapter 19: A Last Hurrah

[558] Jacques-Pierre de Taffanel de La Jonquière, Lettre de La Jonquière au ministre, C11A, vol. 97 (f. 16-33v), May 1, 1751.

[559] Feuille au net basée sur les rapports de La Jonquière, Des Herbiers et Bigot en Acadie, C11A, vol. 96 (f. 242-245), November, 1750.

[560] La Jonquière, Lettre, May 1.

[561] Faragher, *Great and Noble Scheme*, 265–8.

[562] De Léry (fils), *Mémoire sur le port.*

[563] In 1751, on Saint-Ours's orders, the *Aimable Jeanne* made a pit stop in Shediac to pick up biscuits for its return trip to Quebec. See Pierre-Roch de Saint-Ours Deschaillons, Instructions de Pierre-Roch de Saint-Ours Deschaillons à Charles Lefebvre, C11A, vol. 98 (f. 199-199v), April 30, 1751.

[564] On March 6, 1751, Saint-Ours wrote to Louisbourg's governor, "there is no longer mention today of the port of Jaidaique [Shediac]." See Pierre-Roch de Saint-Ours Deschaillons, Monsieur de Saint-Ours Dechaillon, commandant les postes de l'Acadie, Lettre à monsieur Desherbiers, C11B, vol. 30 (f. 96-98v), March 6, 1751.

[565] Jacques-Pierre de Taffanel de La Jonquière, Lettre de La Jonquière au ministre, C11A, vol. 95 (f. 267-273), October 3, 1750; François Bigot, Lettre de Bigot au ministre, C11A, vol. 96 (f. 10-15v), September 25, 1750.

[566] Rénald Lessard, "Les archives publiques au Québec: La difficile construction d'une mémoire collective," *Archives* 36, 2 (2004–2005): 173–98. New France's notarial and judicial archives have stayed largely intact.

[567] Jacques-Pierre de Taffanel de La Jonquière, Lettre de La Jonquière au ministre, C11A, vol. 95 (f. 361-363), November 6, 1750.

[568] Couriers travelling from Shediac to Quebec took between ten and twelve days; see François Bigot, Lettre de Bigot au ministre, C11A, vol. 96 (f. 63-68v), October 22, 1750, and Louis Leneuf de La Vallière, *Journal de ce qui s'est passé à Chignectou*, C11A, vol. 87 (f. 376-386v), 1751.

[569] Hand, *Siege of Fort Beauséjour*, 16–22. Also see Résumé d'une lettre de Le Loutre au ministre (July 29th), C11C, vol. 9 (f. 130-131v), July 29, 1749.

[570] François Bigot, Mémoire d'instructions de l'intendant Bigot pour le sieur Brassard, Fond Intendants (E1), Ordonnances (S1), Cahier 38: Registre des Commissions, f. 64-68, P4030, Bibliothèque et Archives nationales du Québec (henceforth BAnQ), May 1, 1751.

[571] Louis Leneuf de La Vallière, *Journal de ce qui s'est passé* . See also Jacques-Pierre de Taffanel de La Jonquière, Ordre de La Jonquière à Chaussegros De Léry, Fonds Famille Chaussegros De Léry (P386, D297), BAnQ, April 12, 1751.

[572] Druillet, the Shediac storekeeper, was reassigned to Fort Gaspareaux in September 1751; see François Bigot, Mémoire d'instructions de l'intendant Bigot au sieur Almain, Fond Intendants (E1), Ordonnances (S1), Cahier 38: Registre des Commissions, f. 78v-82, P4050, BAnQ, September 14, 1751. The reassignment may well mark the official end of France's Shediac outpost.

[573] In 1751, Le Mercier oversaw the casting of cannons and mortars in the Forges du Saint-Maurice at Trois-Rivières, Québec; see Jean Pariseau, "Le Mercier (Mercier), François-Marc-Antoine," in *Dictionary of Canadian Biography*, vol. 4 (University of Toronto/Université Laval), last revised 1979, biographi.ca/en/bio/le_mercier_francois_marc_antoine_4E.html.

[574] François-Marc-Antoine Le Mercier, *État des ustensiles d'artillerie qui ont été envoyés à Chedaïk par la goélette la Louise le 12 mai 1751*, November 4, 1751.

[575] La Jonquière, Lettre, May 1.

[576] Leneuf de La Vallière, *Journal de ce qui s'est passé*. La Vallière's report is six cannons shy of *La Louise*'s twelve, but it may not have counted the four four-pounders sent to Fort Gaspareaux. As for the two missing six-pounders, *La Louise*'s cannons may have journeyed separately overland and arrived at Beauséjour in staggered fashion.

[577] The *Aimable Catherine* probably left Quebec for Baie Verte shortly after September 14, 1751. On that date, the Sieur Almain was to board the *Aimable Catherine* "chartered by the King and destined for Fort Gaspareaux"" (see Bigot, *Mémoire d'instructions au sieur Almain*).

[578] François-Marc-Antoine Le Mercier, *État des pièces et munitions d'artillerie qui sont dans les forts*, October 20, 1752C11A, vol. 98 (f. 47-49).

[579] Ernest Picard and Louis Jouan, *L'artillerie française au XVIIIe siècle*, (Paris: Berger-Levrault, 1906).

[580] Around May 1751, only six cannons—presumably half of *La Louise*'s cargo—had arrived at Fort Beauséjour (see Leneuf De La Vallière, *Journal de ce qui s'est passé*).

[581] Louis Chevalier de La Corne, Instructions du Chevalier de la Corne, commandant de l'Acadie, pour De Léry, Fonds Famille Chaussegros De Léry (P386, D93), BAnQ, 1750.

[582] De Léry kept two more letters from La Corne; see Louis Chevalier de La Corne, Lettre du Chevalier à De Léry, Fonds Famille Chaussegros De Léry (P386, D95), BAnQ, September 12, 1750, and Louis Chevalier de La Corne, Lettre du Chevalier, à Memramcook, Fonds Famille Chaussegros De Léry (P386, D94), BAnQ, September 7, 1750.

[583] Fonds Famille Chaussegros De Léry (1682–1945), fond number P386, BAnQ.

[584] Jane Regent, in conversation with the author, Jan. 24, 2022.

Chapter 20: The Peter Pan Within

[585] Blakeny, *Story of a Business*, 30.

[586] The "old planking" could be the remnants of a bridge "laid across Hall's Creek opposite Crow's Island" in 1878 as part of the construction of the Moncton reservoir's pipeline. See "A Bridge Has Been Completed," *The Daily Times* (Moncton), September 23, 1878, 4.

[587] Blakeny, *Story of a Business*, 30.

[588] "Local Scraps," *The Daily Times* (Moncton), May 27, 1878, 4.

[589] "Looking for Kidd's Gold," *The Daily Times* (Moncton), September 22, 1888, 3.

[590] Despite its name, Crow's Island was in fact a peninsula that extended westward from the eastern bank of Halls Creek.

[591] Ronnie-Gilles LeBlanc, "Les archives en Acadie," *Archives* 36, 2 (2004–2005): 9–22.

[592] Mark Twain, *The Adventures of Tom Sawyer* (Hartford, CT: American, 1876).

[593] The prevailing view in neuroscience is that emotion guides reason, not vice versa; see Antonio R. Damasio, *Descartes' Error: Emotion, Reason, and the Human Brain* (New York: Putnam, 1994). Similar ideas exist in behavioural economics; see Daniel Kahneman, *Thinking, Fast and Slow* (New York: Farrar, Straus and Giroux, 2013).

[594] Blakeny, *Story of a Business*, 149.

Epilogue

[595] "In Search of Treasure Said to Have Been Buried Near Moncton," *The Daily Times* (Moncton), May 5, 1899, 1.

[596] Pincombe and Larracey, *Resurgo*, 38.

[597] Charles Alexander Pincombe, "The History of Monckton Township (CA. 1700–1875)," master's thesis, University of New Brunswick, 1970, footnote 122, 142.

[598] Pincombe and Larracey, *Resurgo*, 68; Larracey, *First Hundred*, 72–75; Les Bowser, *The Settlers of Monckton Township* (Omemee, ON: 250th Productions, 2016); Larracey, *Chocolate River*.

Bibliography

This section testifies to the extensive research I carried out to tell the story in Nine Bags of Gold. Despite its length, the partial listing below can do justice neither to the many archival dead ends I encountered nor to the many sources I surely failed to uncover. Fundamental questions remain about Simpson's enigmatic "treasure map," and there is every reason to believe that further efforts will unlock more answers. Rather than represent an exhaustive or definitive collection of facts, the bibliography is meant to inspire those interested in venturing even deeper into an engrossing mystery in Acadian and New Brunswick history.

Archival Sources

Archives nationales d'outre-mer, Aix-en-Provence, France

C11A : Correspondance générale, Canada

C11B : Correspondance générale, Île Royale

C11C : Correspondance générale, Amérique du Nord

C11 : Correspondance générale, des limites et des postes

Archives of Ontario, Toronto, ON

RG 80-2: Registration of births

RG 80-5: Registrations of marriages

RG 80-8: Registrations of deaths

Various: Tax assessment rolls

Bibliothèque et Archives nationales du Québec, Québec City, QC

E1, S1 : Fonds Intendants, Ordonnances

P386 : Fonds Famille Chaussegros de Léry

Library and Archives Canada, Ottawa, ON

RG31: Statististics Canada fonds (national and prairie censuses)

National Archives and Records Administration, Washington, DC

RG29: National Census

Ontario Land Registry Office (onland.ca)

LRO 33: Middlesex County

Provincial Archives of New Brunswick, Fredericton, NB
RS97: County Deed Registry Books (Westmorland County)
RS112: Mineral Branch Division Record Series
RS141: Vital Statistics from Government Records; Births, Marriages, and Deaths
RS159: County Council Records (Westmorland County)
RS656: Crown Lands Maps and Plans
RS686: Land Grants

City Directories

The Chatham Directory. Chatham, ON: Planet, 1892.

Foster's Kingston Directory. Toronto: J. G. Foster, 1905.

Foster's London City and Middlesex County Directory 1901. London, ON: J. G. Foster, 1901.

Foster's London City and Middlesex County Directory, 1897–8. Toronto: J. G. Foster, 1897.

The London City and Middlesex County Directory, 1888–1889. London, ON: R. K. Polk, 1888.

The London City and Middlesex County Directory, 1890. London, ON: R. K. Polk, 1890.

McAlpine's Halifax City Directory for 1874–75. Halifax: McAlpine, Everett, 1874.

*McAlpine's London City and County of Middlesex Directory, 1875.*London, ON: McAlpine, Everett, 1875.

McAlpine's Moncton City and Westmorland County Directory. Saint John, NB: McAlpine, 1903.

McAlpine's Moncton City Directory, 1899. Saint John, NB: McAlpine, 1899.

McAlpine's New Brunswick Directory for 1889–1896. Saint John, NB: McAlpine & Son, 1889.

McAlpine's New Brunswick Directory for 1896. Saint John, NB: McAlpine, 1896.

Sutherland's General Directory for the City of Kingston. Kingston, ON: James Sutherland, 1866.

The Toronto City Directory. Toronto: Polk (for 1885 to 1890).

The Toronto City Directory. Toronto: Might (for 1893, 1896, and 1897).

Vernon's City of Chatham Directory (for *1900–1902, 1902–1904, 1904–1906*, and *1932*). Hamilton, ON: Vernon.

Western Ontario Gazeteer and Directory, 1898–99. Ingersoll, ON: Ontario Publishing & Advertising, 1898.

Other Secondary Sources

Note: The bibliography makes use of the following abbreviations for Moncton newspapers: *MDTi* (*The Daily Times*); *MDTr* (*The Daily Transcript*); *MTr* (*The Transcript*); and *MT&T* (*The Times & Transcript*).

"$2,528 Damage Suit Begun at Dorchester." *Telegraph Journal* (Saint John, NB), October 31, 1934, 3.

"A $30,000 Writ." *Toronto World*, January 3, 1891, 4.

Aaron, Bob. "Finders keepers—Law Not Always Golden Ticket." *Toronto Star*, March 12, 2016.

Allen, I. *Biographical Review.* Boston: Biographical Review, 1900.

"Anniversary of Cold Friday." *MDTi*, Februrary, 1904, 3.

"Appeal Court Decides for Defendants." *MDTi*, June 15, 1935, 10.

Arsenault, Bona, and Pascal Alain. *Histoire des Acadiens.* Montréal: Fides, 2004.

"Auction Sales." *MDTi*, October 28, 1904, 5.

Aumasson de Courville, Louis-Léonard. *Mémoires sur le Canada depuis 1749 jusqu'à 1760.* Québec: Société Littéraire et Historique de Québec, 1838.

"Autour et Alentours—Les chasses aux trésors hier et aujourd'hui." *Le Canada* (Montréal), October 5, 1949, 4.

Balcom, B. A. *The Cod Fishery of Isle Royale, 1713–58.* Ottawa: Parks Canada, National Historic Parks and Sites Branch, 1984.

Balcom, B. A. "For King and Profit: Louisbourg Privateers, 1744," in *Canadian Military History Since the 17th Century*, edited by Y. Tremblay. Ottawa: National Defense, 2001.

Banner, Stuart. *American Property: A History of How, Why, and What We Own.* Boston: Harvard University Press, 2011.

"Barrels of Money." *MDTi*, July 4, 1908, 3.

Barton, Barry. "The Common Law of Subsurface Activity," in *The Law of Energy Underground*, edited by D. N. Zillman, A. McHarg, A. Bradbrook, and L. Barrera-Hernandez. Oxford: Oxford University Press, 2014.

Basque, Garnet. "French Gold Near Moncton," in *Canadian Treasure* 1, 2 (1973): 29–31.

Basque, Maurice. "Atlantic Realities, Acadian Identities, Arcadian Dreams," in *Shaping an Agenda for Atlantic Canada*, edited by J. G. Reid and D. J. Savoie. Halifax: Fernwood Publishing, 2011.

Belliveau, John Edward. *The Monctonians: Citizens, Saints, and Scoundrels.* Vol. 1. Hansport, NS: Lancelot Press, 1981.

Belliveau, John Edward. *The Monctonians: Scamps, Scholars, and Politicians.* Vol. 2. Hansport, NS: Lancelot Press, 1981.

Belshaw, J. D. *Canadian History: Pre-Confederation (2nd ed.).* Victoria, BC: BCampus, 2020.

Bergeron, Josée. "Migrations et contributions des Acadiens à la population québécoise." *Histoire Québec* 20, 1 (2014): 35–38.

"Biddulph Briefs." *The Exeter Times* (Ontario), March 14, 1.

"The Biggest and the Best." *London Advertiser*, December 8, 1901, 1.

"Births, Marriages, and Deaths." *London Advertiser* (Ontario), June 29, 1900, 1.

Bishop, Patrick. *Operation Jubilee: Dieppe, 1942: The Folly and the Sacrifice.* Toronto: McClelland & Stewart, 2021.

Blakeny, Charles Hanford. *Bits and Pieces: Rambling Through Britain, France, Italy and Switzerland.* Published by the author, 1954.

Blakeny, Charles Hanford. *Fragments: Impressions of Holland, Belgium, Germany, Austria, Luxembourg, France, Italy, Scotland, and England.* Published by the author, 1956.

Blakeny, Charles Hanford. *The Story of a Business And Its Founders.* Published by the author, 1960.

Blakeny, Ray Howard. *My Help Comes From Above—The Blakeney/Blakeley Family History.* Windsor, NS: Ed Martin, 2004.

Bobis, Laurence, Michel Combes, Suzanne Débarbat, et al. *L'Observatoire de Paris, 350 ans de science.* Paris: Gallimard, 2012.

Boishébert, Charles Deschamps de. "Journal de ma campagne de Louisbourg," in *Recherches historiques.* Lévis: Pierre-Georges Roy, 1758.

Bonner, Willard Hallam. "The Ballad of Captain Kidd." *American Literature* 15, 4 (1944): 362–80.

Boucher, Denis, and Paul Roux. *L'Île-au-crâne de Shédiac.* Moncton: Bouton d'or Acadie, 2016.

Bourbeau, Robert, and Nadine Ouellette. "Trends, Patterns, and Differentials in Canadian Mortality Over Nearly a Century, 1921–2011." *Canadian Studies in Population* 43, 1–2 (2016): 48–77.

"Bourque Sentenced to Seven Years." *MDTr*, September 5, 1900, 1.

Bowser, Les. *The Settlers of Monckton Township.* Omemee, ON: 250th Productions, 2016.

Bradstreet, John. *An Impartial Account of Lieut. Col. Bradstreet's Expedition to Fort Frontenac.* London: Wilcox, Owen, Cooper & Cooke, 1759.

Braesiders. *Sunny Brae: The Town That Was.* Sackville, NB: Tribune, 1985.

"A Bridge Has Been Completed." *MDTi*, September 23, 1878, 4.

Brown, Ron. *The Train Doesn't Stop Here Anymore: An Illustrated History of Railway Stations in Canada.* Toronto: Dundurn Press, 2008.

Brun, Régis. "La capture du London, été 1750." *La Société Historique de la Mer Rouge* 3, 4 (1994): 15–21.

Brun, Régis. "Le fort de Chédaïque." *La Société Historique de la Mer Rouge* 3, 5 (1995): 4–10.

Brun, Régis. *Les Acadiens à Moncton: un siècle et demi de présence française au Coude.* Published by the author, 1999.

Brun, Régis. "L'or du Klondike et les Acadiens: Dr Philippe LeBlanc." *Les Cahiers de la Société historique acadienne* 34, no. 3 (October 2003): 121–45.

Burns, Kevin. *The Curse of Oak Island.* History, 2014 and onwards.

"Business Changes." *The Canadian Journal of Commerce, Finance and Insurance Review* (Montréal), May 28, 1897, 817.

Campbell, Colin, and Robert Raizenne. *A History of Canadian Income Tax. Volume I: The Income War Tax Act 1917–1948.* Toronto: Osgood Society, 2022.

Campbell, W. E. *The Road to Canada: The Grand Communications Route From Saint John to Quebec.* Fredericton: Goose Lane Editions, 2005.

"Canadian—Encounter with a Burglar at Parkhill." *London Advertiser* (Ontario), October 11, 1889, 1.

"Cardinal Manning a Dunkinite." *Guelph Daily Mercury* (Ontario), November 21, 1877, 1.

Chapman (a.k.a. Nampahc), Cyril. "The Story of Fort Folly and Other Interesting Historical Notes." *Tribune-Post* (Sackville, NB), March 7, 1950.

"Chattel Mortages, Province of Ontario." *The Canadian Journal of Commerce, Finance and Insurance Review* (Montréal), June 4, 1897, 858.

"City and County Newsy Items." *MDTr*, May 4, 1901, 6.

"City and District Newsy Items." *MTr*, July 21, 1915, 8.

"City Directory for Moncton." *MDTi*, October 19, 1898, 4.

Clarke, Ernest. *The Siege of Fort Cumberland, 1776: An Episode in the American Revolution.* Montreal-Kingston: McGill-Queen's University Press, 1995.

Clos (procureur). *Mémoire pour le Sieur de Boishebert.* Paris: Moreau, 1763.

Cochrane, Alan. "Ghosts and Mysteries Around 'the Bend'—Spooky Stories Are Part of Moncton's History." *MT&T*, October 28, 1995, 31.

Cochrane, Alan. "Council Approves Expanding City Boundary for Subdivision." *MT&T*, October 19, 2022, A5.

"Collar Bone Fractured." *MDTi*, February 29, 1904, 7.

"Collection of Rare Coins." *MDTi*, April 6, 1898, 1.

"Coming Building Operations in Moncton." *The Daily Trascript* (Moncton), May 17, 1901, 4.

Cooper, James Fenimore. *The Sea Lions; Or, the Lost Sealers*. New York: Stringer & Townsend, 1856.

"Corbett—Briefs." *The Exeter Times* (Ontario), April 11, 1.

"Corbin Weld." *The Winnipeg Evening Tribune* (Winnipeg), May 4, 1942, 17.

Côté, André. "L'affaire du Canada (1761–1763)." *Cap-aux-Diamants*, 83 (2005): 10–14.

"County Court." *MDTi*, December 6, 1899, 1.

Couturier, Jacques. "Prohiber ou contrôler ? L'application de l'Acte de tempérance du Canada à Moncton, N.-B., 1881–1896." *Acadiensis* 17, 2 (1988): 3–26.

Damasio, Antonio R. *Descartes' Error: Emotion, Reason, and the Human Brain*. New York: Putnam, 1994.

"The Day's Sports—Lawn Bowling." *Daily Free Press* (London, ON), September 24, 1901.

De La Roncière, Charles. *Le flibustier mystérieux: histoire d'un trésor caché*. Paris: Le Masque, 1934.

De Peyster, Frederick. *The Life and Administration of Richard, Earl of Bellomont, Governor of the Provinces of New York*. New York Historical Society, 1879.

"The Death of Mr. T. B. LeBlanc." *MDTr*, July 5, 1904, 8.

"Death of Mr. T. S. Weld." *The Farmer's Advocate* (London, ON), January 7, 1909, 16.

"Death of Mr. William Weld." *The Farmer's Advocate* (London, ON), February, 1891, 1–2.

"Death of Peter McSweeney, Sr." *MDTi*, December 2, 1884, 3.

"Death of William Simpson." *Exeter Advocate* (Ontario), December 13, 1906, 8.

"Death Takes John Weld." *The Border Cities Star* (Windsor, ON), September 16, 1931.

Delaney, Paul. "La reconstitution d'un rôle des passagers du Pembroke." *Les Cahiers de la Société historique acadienne* 35, 12 (2004): 4–75.

Denhez, M., and M-L. Daigle. *Unearthing the Law—Archeological Legislation on Lands in Canada*. Ottawa: Parks Canada Agency, Archeological Services Branch, 2019.

Devlin, Sandra. "Open Hearts and Buried Treasure. " *MT&T*, June 13, 1998, F3, F8.

Dionne, Raoul. "L'origine acadienne de Moncton: Le Coude. " *Revue d'histoire de l'Amérique française* 37, 3 (1983): 399–416.

Donovan Evans, Linda. *An Baile Gaelach—An Historical Geography and Genealogical Study of Irishtown, NB.* Published by the author, 2016.

Draper, Alfred. *Operation Fish : The Race to Save Europe's Wealth, 1939–1945.* London: Cassell, 1979.

"Dr. C. H. Blakeny Dies Here, Age 72." *MTr*, May 24, 1961, 1–2.

Drummond, Ian M. *Progress Without Planning: The Economic History of Ontario From Confederation to the Second World War.* Toronto: University of Toronto Press, 1987.

Dupont, Jean-Claude. *Les trésors cachés: Québec et Acadie.* Published by the author, 1999.

Dupont, Jean-Claude. *Contes et légendes.* Sainte-Foy, QC: GID, 2002.

"Economy in All Civic Departments." *MDTi*, February 4, 1931, 1, 3.

Edmonds, Alan. "Treasure! How the Chameau Gave up Its Fortune." *Maclean's*, June 18, 1966.

"The Election." *The Fenelon Falls Gazette* (Ontario), June 22, 1894, 2.

"Elks Honor Mr. H. H. Warman on His 66th Birthday." *MDTi*, November 26, 1929, 5.

Emden, Cecil S. "The Law of Treasure Trove, Past and Present." *The Numismatic Chronicle and Journal of the Royal Numismatic Society* 9, 34 (1929): 85–105.

"Englishmen Celebrate." *London Advertiser* (Ontario), April 24, 1894, 1.

"Englishmen Win!—Lawn Bowling." *London Advertiser* (Ontario), September 9, 1901, 7.

"Epidemic of Fire—A Disastrous Conflagration on Steadman St." *MDTr*, September 7, 1899, 1.

Evans, Janice. "Acadian Treasure." Segment for *Land and Sea.* Aired February 14, 2014, on CBC. cbc.ca/player/play/video/1.4337003.

"Exeter." *Huron Expositor* (Seaforth, ON), December 7, 1894, 4.

"Exeter." *Huron Expositor* (Seaforth, ON), April 8, 1898, 16.

"Expression of Thanks." *MDTi*, April 13, 1939, 10.

"Expropriation Arbitration—Deed of Lands Taken for the Water and Lights Works." *MDTi*, August 30, 1894, 1.

"Expropriation Arbitration—Expert Testimony as to the Value of Machinery." *MDTi*, September 11, 1894, 1.

Fanthorpe, R. Lionel, and Patricia Fanthorpe. *The Oak Island Mystery: The World's Greatest Treasure Hunt.* 2nd ed. Toronto: Dundurn, 2012.

Faragher, John Mack. *A Great and Noble Scheme—The Tragic Story of the Expulsion of the French Acadians From Their American Homeland.* New York: W. W. Norton, 2005.

Feder, Kenneth L. "Irrationality and Popular Archaeology." *American Antiquity* 49, 3 (1984): 525–41.

Fenn, Elizabeth A. "Biological Warfare in Eighteenth-Century North America: Beyond Jeffery Amherst." *The Journal of American History* 86, 4 (2000): 1552–80.

"Forgotten New Brunswick: A Tale of Lost Treasure." *Daily Gleaner* (Fredericton), November 26, 2018, 7.

"Found Dead With Shotgun Beside Him." *The Leamington Post and News* (ON), November 9, 1933, 1.

"Four Hundred Bowlers in Action at Opening of Americas Greatest Tourney—Snapshot at Some of the Bowlers." *London Advertiser* (Ontario), July 25, 1911, 6.

Fowler, Jonathan. "The Archaeologist's Evangeline: Historical Archaeology in Acadia," in *The Oxford Handbook of Historical Archeology*, edited by J. Symonds and V-P. Herva. Oxford, UK: Oxford University Press, 2014.

Fowler, Jonathan, and Earle Lockerby. "Operations at Fort Beauséjour and Grand-Pré in 1755: A Soldier's Diary." *Journal of the Royal Nova Scotia Historical Society* 12 (2009): 145.

Franquet, Louis. "Le voyage de Franquet aux îles Royale et Saint-Jean et en Acadie 1751." *Rapport de l'Archiviste de la province de Québec* (1923–1924): 111–40.

Frégault, Guy. "L'expédition du duc d'Anville." *Revue d'histoire de l'Amérique française* 2, 1 (1948): 27–52.

Frégault, Guy. "Essai sur les finances canadiennes (1700–1750) (suite et fin)." *Revue d'histoire de l'Amérique française* 13, 2 (1959): 157–82.

Frenette, Rémi. *La résistance acadienne à la prohibition de l'alcool, 1879–1939.* Master's thesis, Université de Moncton, 2020.

"Funeral at St. Peter's." *London Advertiser* (Ontario), November 14, 1910, 10.

Gagné, Joseph. "Voix de Guerre: Le renseignement au sein de l'armée française lors de la guerre de Sept Ans en Amérique du Nord." PhD diss., Université Laval, 2020.

Ganong, William F. "A Monograph of Historic Sites in the Province of New Brunswick," in *Transactions of the Historical Society of Canada, Second Series, 1899–1900.* Ottawa: Hope & Sons, 1899.

Ganong, William F. "The Report and Map of Major George Scott's Expedition to Remove the French From the Petitcodiac in 1758." In *Historical-Geographical Documents Relating to New Brunswick.* Collections of the New Brunswick Historical Society. Saint John, NB: Barnes, 1914.

Garfield, Simon. *On the Map—Why the World Looks the Way it Does.* London: Profile Books, 2013.

Gaudet, Placide. "Généalogies acadiennes et documents se rattachant à l'expulsion des Acadiens," in *Rapport concernant les archives canadiennes pour l'année 1905*. Ottawa: Parmelee, 1909.

Gaudet, Placide. "Établissements acadiens de la rivière Petcoudiac au temps de la dispersion." *l'Évangéline*, September 1, 1927, 11–12.

Genzlinger, Neil. "Alex Storm, Finder of Sunken Treasure, Dies at 80." *The New York Times*, August 24, 2018, A, 21.

"Geo. W. McCready Has Passed Away." *MTr*, June 9, 1908, 8.

George, F. G. Stanley. "John Clarence Webster: The Laird of Shediac." *Acadiensis* 3, 1 (1973).

Gilbert, Jim, and Lisa Gilbert. *Chatham*. Charleston, SC: Arcadia, 2002.

Glenn, Daniel K. *Parc Nature—Irishtown—Nature Park: Master Plan. Final Report.* Moncton: Daniel K. Glenn, 1996.

Goss, David. "Buried Treasure Under Reservoir?" *MT&T*, October 21, 2000, G2.

Goss, David. "Harbour Treasures Prove Elusive." *MT&T*, July 29, 2000, 68.

"Gossip From Toronto." *The Montreal Gazette*, June 19, 1891, 1.

Grantham, Robert G., Dan Conlin, David Christianson, et al. "The Nova Scotia Museum Isle Haute Expedition July, 1997." Curratorial Report 90. Museum of Natural History, Nova Scotia Museum, Nova Scotia Department of Tourism and Culture, 2000.

"Great Crowd at Delaware." *London Advertiser* (Ontario), October 10, 1901, 3.

Grenier, John. *The Far Reaches of Empire: War in Nova Scotia, 1710–1760*. Norman, OK: University of Oklahoma, 2008.

Griffiths, Naomi E. S. "Acadians in Exile: the Experiences of the Acadian in the British Seaports." *Acadiensis* 4, 1 (1974): 67–84.

Griffiths, Naomi E. S. "The Golden Age: Acadian Life, 1713–1748." *Histoire sociale/ Social History* 17, 33 (1984).

Griffiths, Naomi E. S. *From Migrant to Acadian: A North American Border People, 1604–1755*. Montreal-Kingston: McGill-Queen's University Press, 2004.

Hall, A. Wilford. *Dr. A. Wilford Hall's Hygenic Treatment for the Cure of Disease, Preservation of Health and the Promotion of Longevity Without Medicine*. Toronto: Simpson Publishing, 1890.

Hand, Chris M. *The Siege of Fort Beauséjour, 1755*. Fredericton: Goose Lane Editions, 2004.

"Heart Attack is Fatal to H. H. Warman." *MTr*, May 8, 1934, 8.

"Heavy Crop of Candidates." *MDTr*, October 1, 1888, 3.

"Hensall—Briefs." *Exeter Times* (Ontario), October 13, 1898, 1.

Hergé. *Le Trésor de Rackham le Rouge*. Brussels: Casterman, 1945.

"The History of a Stone." *MDTi*, May 17, 1894, 4.

Hodson, Christopher. *The Acadian Diaspora: An Eighteenth-Century History*. Oxford, UK: Oxford University Press, 2012.

"Honors for a Monctonian." *Daily Telegraph* (Saint John, NB), September 22, 1892, 3.

"Horse Race on Saturday." *MDTr*, September 11, 1899, 4.

"The Hull Fire!" *MDTi*, April 27, 1900, 1.

"Identity of Human Skeleton Found Near Moncton a Mystery." *Daily Telegraph* (Saint John, NB), October 20, 1906, 2.

"Improved Boring Machine." *Scientific American* (New York), April 11, 1874, 233.

"In and About in the County." *Huron News-Record* (Clinton, ON), October 9, 1889, 8.

"In Klondike." *MDTi*, September 27, 1899, 4.

"In Search of Treasure Said to Have Been Buried Near Moncton." *MDTi*, May 5, 1899, 1.

"Irishtown Jottings." *MDTi*, April 1, 1899, 2.

Irishtown Road Reservoir—Westmorland County/Comté de Westmorland Inner Bay of Fundy Recreational Fishing Area. Fredericton: New Brunswick Department of Energy and Resource Development, 2018.

Irving, Washington. "Wolfert Webber, or Golden Dreams," in *Tales of a Traveller*. New York: George P. Putnam, 1852.

Irving, William Henry. *Fundy Family*. Durham, NC: Seeman, 1972.

Irwin, W A. "The House of Weld." *Maclean's*, July 15, 1931, 10, 44–45.

"John Bishop." *MTr*, October 3, 3.

Johnston, Andrew John Bayly. "Borderland Worries: Loyalty Oaths in Acadie/Nova Scotia, 1654–1755." *French Colonial History* 4, 1 (2003): 31–48.

Johnston, Andrew John Bayly. "Défricheurs d'eau: An Introduction to Acadian Land Reclamation in a Comparative Context." *Material Culture Review* 66 (2007), 32–41.

Johnston, Andrew John Bayly. *Endgame 1758: The Promise, the Glory, and the Despair of Louisbourg's Last Decade*. Lincoln, NE: University of Nebraska, 2007.

Jolicoeur, Catherine. *Les plus belles légendes acadiennes*. Montréal: Stanké, 1981.

Jonkers, Art Roeland Theo. "Parallel Meridians: Diffusion and Change in Early-Modern Oceanic Reckoning," in *Noord-Zuid in Oostindisch perspectief*, edited by J. Parmentier. The Hague: Walburg, 2005.

"Joyously Celebrated—St. Georges Society's 34th Annual Reunion." *London Advertiser* (Ontario), April 24, 1901, 2.

Kahneman, Daniel. *Thinking, Fast and Slow.* New York: Farrar, Straus and Giroux, 2013.

Kinnear, William Boyd, ed. *The Local and Private Statutes of New Brunswick.* Vol. 3. Fredericton: J. Simpson, 1855.

Knox, John. *An Historical Journal of the Campaigns in North America: For the Years 1757, 1758, 1759, and 1760.* Vol. 1. London: W. Johnston and J. Dodsley, 1769.

Kristmanson, Helen. *A Short History of Beaumont, New Brunswick.* Fredericton: Archaeological Services, Heritage Branch, 2004.

Landry Cail, Shirley. *Village of Tankville.* Published by the author, 2004.

Landry, Nicolas, and Nicole Lang. *Histoire de l'Acadie.* 2e éd. Québec: Septentrion, 2014.

Larracey, Edward W. *The First Hundred; A Story of the First 100 Years of Moncton's Existence.* Moncton: Moncton Publishing Company Ltd., 1970.

Larracey, Edward W. *Chocolate River: A Story of the Petitcodiac River From the Beginning of Habitation in the Late 1600s.* Hantsport, NS: Lancelot Press, 1985.

Larracey, Edward W. "Flashback on the Petitcodiac—Remembering the River Scows." *MT&T,* June 20, 1987, 17, 37.

Larracey, Edward W. *Resurgo: The History of Moncton.* Vol. 2. Moncton: City of Moncton, 1990.

"Last Night's Meeting of the Town Council." *MDTi,* November 27, 1880, 3.

"Late Local Items." *London Advertiser* (Ontario), October 25, 1900, 6.

"Late Local Items." *London Advertiser* (Ontario), November 16, 1901, 8.

"The Late Mr. Sherman Blakeny." *MDTi,* July 26, 1949, 4.

"The Late Mr. Weld's Will." *Toronto Daily Mail,* January 23, 1891.

Lawlor, Allison. "Treasure Hunter Alex Storm Struck Gold Off Cape Breton Island." *The Globe and Mail* (Toronto), August 28, 2018.

"Lawn Bowling." *London Advertiser* (Ontario), September 28, 1901, 7.

Leblanc, Gérald. "La Pointe Folly—Site d'un fort militaire et d'un phare maritime." *Les cahiers de la société d'histoire de Memramcook* 28, 1 (November 2016): 8–35.

LeBlanc, Ronnie-Gilles. "Les archives en Acadie." *Archives* 36, 2 (2004–2005): 9–22.

LeBlanc, Ronnie-Gilles, ed. *Du Grand Dérangement à la Déportation: nouvelles perspectives historiques.* Moncton: Chaire d'Études Acadiennes, Université de Moncton, 2005.

LeBlanc, Ronnie-Gilles. "Les réfugiés acadiens au camp d'Espérance de la Miramichi en 1756–1761 : un épisode méconnu du Grand Dérangement." *Acadiensis* 41, 1 (winter/spring) (2012): 128–68.

Leonard, Kevin. *Mi'kmaq Culture During the Late Woodland and Early Historic Periods.* Toronto: University of Toronto Press, 1996.

Leonard, Kevin. *A Survey for French Military Supply Depots Built in 1749–50 at the Port of Shediac and on the Shediac River.* Shediac Bay Watershed Association (Shediac, NB: Archaeoconsulting, 2001).

Leonard, Kevin. *Jedaick (Shediac, NB): A Nexus Through Time.* Shediac Bridge, NB: Shediac Bay Watershed Association, 2002.

Lescarbot, Marc. *The History of New France.* Translated by W. L. Grant. Toronto: Champlain Society, 1907.

Lessard, Rénald. "Les archives publiques au Québec: La difficile construction d'une mémoire collective." *Archives* 36, 2 (2004–2005): 173–98.

Lessard, Rénald. "L'établissement d'une nouvelle Acadie: L'apport des billets de l'Acadie." *Nouvelle-France, histoire et patrimoine* 4 (2021): 41–48.

"Letter from the Klondike." *MDTi*, January 29, 1898, 1.

Levi, Steven C. *Boom and Bust in the Alaska Goldfields: A Multicultural Adventure.* Westport, CT: Greenwood, 2007.

Lincoln, Charles Henry. *Correspondence of William Shirley, Governor of Massachusetts and Military Commander in America, 1731–1760.* Vol. 2. New York: Macmillan, 1912.

"List of Taxpayers." *MDTi*, July 19, 1884, 2.

"Little Local Links." *MDTi*, May 11, 1894, 4.

"A Local Budget." *London Advertiser* (Ontario), April 9, 8.

"Local Happenings." *Exeter Times* (Ontario), September 21, 1893, 7.

"Local Happenings." *Exeter Times* (Ontario), December 6, 1894, 8.

"Local Happenings." *Exeter Times* (Ontario), July 4, 1895, 8.

"Local Jottings." *Exeter Advocate* (Ontario), April 23, 1896, 16.

"Local Jottings." *Exeter Advocate* (Ontario), June 24, 1897, 8.

"Local Miscellany." *MDTr*, September 20, 1900, 4.

"Local News." *Guelph Daily Mercury and Advertiser* (Ontario), October 10, 1878, 1.

"Local News—Briefs." *Exeter Advocate* (Ontario), June 13, 1889.

"Local Scraps." *MDTi*, May 27, 1878, 4.

"London and Environs." *London Advertiser* (Ontario), 1890, 6.

"London Letter." *Cycling* (Toronto), January 28, 1891, 37.

"London Old Boys Are on the Green." *London Advertiser* (Ontario), July 25, 1911, 7.

"Looking for Kidd's Gold." *MDTi*, September 22, 1888, 3.

"Lounsbury a Long-Time Resident of Moncton." *MT&T*, June 15, 72.

Lyman, Sherwin. "A Conjecture on the Canadian Law of Treasure-Trove." *Manitoba Law Journal* 2 (1966): 294–97.

MacDonald, Gordon M. *The Secret About Skull Island and the Hidden History of Shediac*. Holisticwebs.com, 2015.

Machum, Lloyd Alexander. *A History of Moncton Town and City, 1855–1965*. Moncton: City of Moncton, 1965.

MacKinnon, M. "Death of Mrs. William Simpson." *Parkhill Gazette* (Parkhill, ON), September 21, 1893.

MacKinnon, M. "The Gazette-Review." *Parkhill Gazette* (Parkhill, ON), September 22, 1898.

"Making River a Highway for Traffic Again." *MTr*, May 27, 1930, 10.

"Man's Skeleton Found in Woods." *MTr*, October 5, 1906, 8.

Mann, Barbara Alice. *The Tainted Gift: The Disease Method of Frontier Expansion*. Santa Barbara, CA: ABC-CLIO, 2009.

Marquis, Greg. "The History of Policing in the Maritime Provinces: Themes and Prospects." *Urban History Review/Revue d'histoire urbaine* 19, 2 (1990): 84–99.

Marshall, Dianne. *Heroes of the Acadian Resistance: The Story of Joseph Beausoleil Broussard and Pierre II Surette 1702–1765*. Halifax: Formac Publishing, 2011.

Martin, William, and Godfrey Lushington. "The Law of Treasure Trove." *Journal of the Royal Society of Arts* 56, 2883 (February 21 1908): 348–59.

"May Throw Some Light On Cherryfield Mystery." *MTr*, October 16, 1906, 8.

Mazerolle, Brent. "Sign Recalls Moncton's First Waterworks." *MT&T*, October 22, 2007, A4.

McCullough, Alan Bruce. *Money and Exchange in Canada to 1900*. Toronto: Dundurn, 1996.

"McDonald vs. Bishop." *MDTi*, September 2, 1896, 4.

McIntee, David. *Fortune & Glory—A Treasure Hunter's Handbook*. Oxford: Osprey, 2016.

McLennan, J. S. *Louisbourg: From Its Foundation to Its Fall, 1713–1758*. London: Macmillan, 1918.

"Miscellaneous." *The Grey Review* (Durham, ON), September 2, 1890, 3.

"The Missing Men." *MDTi*, October 30, 1879, 3.

"Moncton Cotton Manufacturing Co." *MDTi*, November 15, 1882, 3.

"Moncton's Three Hundred Million Gallon Reservoir About Completed." *MTr*, July 8, 1914, 1.

"Monday's Race on the Driving Park." *MDTi*, May 23, 1885, 3.

Moogk, Peter N. "A Pocketful of Change at Louisbourg." *Canadian Numismatic Journal* 21, 3 (March 1976).

Moogk, Peter N. "When Money Talks: Coinage in New France." *Proceedings of the Meeting of the French Colonial Historical Society*. Vol. 12. East Lansing, MI: Michigan State University Press, 1988. jstor.org/stable/42952181.

Moore, Christopher. "The Other Louisbourg: Trade and Merchant Enterprise in Ile Royale 1713–58." *Histoire sociale/Social History* 12, 23 (1979).

"More Bowlers Than Ever Before." *London Advertiser* (Ontario), Jul 22, 1911, 11.

"Mortgage Sale." *London Advertiser* (Ontario), September 28, 1901, 1.

Mouhot, Jean-François. *Les réfugiés acadiens en France, 1758–1785: l'impossible réintégration?* Québec: Septentrion, 2009.

"Mourn Death of Prominent Merchant." *MTr*, July 25, 1949, 2.

"Mrs. Jas. Horney Celebrates Her 93rd Birthday." *Exeter-Times Advocate* (Ontario), September 19, 1935, 7.

Murdin, Paul. *Full Meridian of Glory: Perilous Adventures in the Competition to Measure the Earth.* New York: Springer, 2009.

Murphy, Patti. "Peter McSweeney Co." *MT&T*, October 7, 1995, F2.

"N.S. Search for Buried Treasure." *Daily Gleaner* (Fredericton), July 20, 1926, 7.

"New Companies That Are Seeking Incorporation." *MDTr*, April 12, 1902, 1.

Nickell, Joe. "Investigative Files—The Secrets of Oak Island." *Skeptical Inquirer*, March/April 2000, 14–19.

North Middlesex: How It Came to Be. Parkhill, ON: Sesquicentennial Committee, 2010.

"Not Mohan's Remains." *London Advertiser* (Ontario), October 23, 1906, 1.

"Nouvelles de Moncton." *Le Moniteur Acadien* (Shediac, NB), August 28, 1884, 2.

"Obituary—Mrs. Mary A. Mohan, London." *The Catholic Record* (London, ON), September 14, 1901, 8.

"Official Closing of the London Club's Season." *Daily Free Press* (London, ON), October 10, 1901, 6.

Orr, Brenda. "Greater Moncton's Water System—Labor Problems, Delays Marked Early Development." *MT&T*, January 11, 1989, 11.

Orr, Brenda. "Moncton Area's Water Problems Date Back More Than a Century." *MT&T*, January 9, 1989, 15.

"Oscar Wilde Explains." *MDTi*, October 18, 1882, 2.

"Oscar Wilde in Moncton." *MDTi*, October 13, 1882, 3.

"Overcome in Hot Spell, John Weld Succumbs." *Globe* (Toronto), September 16, 1931, 3.

"Paid the Fine." *MDTr*, February 20, 1889, 3.

Paine, Ralph Delahaye. *The Book of Buried Treasure.* London: William Heinemann, 1911.

Parcasio, Marjun "Finders Keepers? A Historical Survey of Lost and Abandoned Property and the Law." *Law Now* (Edmonton), January 6, 2014.

"A Partial Eclipse of the Sun." *MDTr*, May 28, 1900, 4.

Perrin, Warren A. *Acadian Redemption: From Beausoleil Broussard to the Queen's Royal Proclamation.* Opelousas, Louisiana: Andrepont Publishing, 2005.

Perry, Charles. "Labour of Love." *MT&T*, September 3, 1988, 17.

"Persistent Treasure Seekers—An Ontario Man's Search for Hidden Millions." *MDTi*, September 25, 1901, 1.

"Personal Intelligence." *MDTi*, July 11, 1899, 4.

"The Petitcodiac Bore." *MDTr*, April 11, 1899, 2.

Picard, Ernest, and Louis Jouan. *L'artillerie française au XVIIIe siècle.* Paris: Berger-Levrault, 1906.

Pichon, Thomas. *Lettres et mémoires pour servir à l'histoire naturelle, civile et politique du Cap Breton.* The Haugue: Gosse, 1760.

Pincombe, C Alexander. "The History of Monckton Township (CA. 1700–1875)." Master's thesis, University of New Brunswick, 1970.

Pincombe, C. Alexander, and Edward W. Larracey. *Resurgo: The History of Moncton.* Vol. 1. Moncton: City of Moncton, 1990.

Poe, Edgar Allen. "The Gold Bug." *Dollar Newspaper* (Philadelphia, PA), June 28, 1843, 1,4.

Powell, James, and Bank of Canada. *A History of the Canadian Dollar.* 2005.

Pritchard, James. *Anatomy of a Naval Disaster: The 1746 French Expedition to North America.* Montreal-Kingston: McGill-Queen's University Press, 2014.

Pritchard, James S. *In Search of Empire: The French in the Americas, 1670–1730.* Cambridge, UK: Cambridge University Press, 2004.

"Prohibition—Lecture by J. W. Simpson." *The Listowel Banner* (ON), November 17, 1876, 8.

"Queen's Birthday Races." *MDTr*, May 23, 1890, 3.

Raddall, Thomas Head. *Halifax, Warden of the North.* Garden City, NY, Doubleday, 1965.

Raymond, W. O. *The River St. John, Its Physical Features Legends and History From 1604 to 1784.* Saint John, NB: Strathmore 1910.

"Recollections of the Olden Time." *MDTi*, December 11, 1889, 1–15.

"Relic Hunt at Louisbourg Cape Breton." *MTr*, March 1, 1912, 3.

Rennie, Neil. *Treasure Neverland: Real and Imaginary Pirates.* Oxford: Oxford University Press, 2013.

"Returns to Woodstock." *Toronto World*, April 24, 1918, 2.

Robb, W. F. "Golden Hoard Buried Beneath Irishtown Reservoir, Is Belief." *MTr*, August 12, 1950, 12.

Robichaud, Louis J. "Premier's Tribute." *MTr*, May 24, 1961, 2.

Rogoff, Kenneth S. "The Curse of Cash," in *The Curse of Cash.* Princeton, NJ: Princeton University Press, 2017.

Rosch, Eleanor. "Cognitive reference points." *Cognitive Psychology* 7, 4 (1975): 532–47.

Sarty, Roger, and Doug Knight. *Saint John Fortifications, 1630–1956.* Fredericton: Goose Lane Editions, 2003.

Sclanders, Ian. "Another Story of a Treasure Hunt For Gold Now Thought Buried Beneath a Moncton Reservoir." *Telegraph-Journal* (Saint John, NB), July 24, 1937, 1, 5.

"Scott Act." *MDTi*, October 9, 1886, 4.

"Scott Act." *MDTi*, September 13, 1899, 4.

"Scott Act Cases." *MDTi*, October 18, 1890, 4.

"A Search for Buried Treasure." *MDTr*, September 25, 1901, 7.

"Searching for Treasure Around the Old Fort." *MTr*, June 1, 1912, 4.

Sears, Wallie. "Fort Folly Indians Revive Ste. Anne Celebration." *MT&T*, 1984, 19.

"Seekers After Buried Treasure." *Daily Telegraph* (Saint John, NB), August 13, 1880, 1.

"Senator McSweeney At Home." *MDTr*, July 22, 1899, 4.

Shortt, Adam. *Documents Relating to Canadian Currency, Exchange and Finance During the French Period—II.* Ottawa: Acland, 1925.

Simpson, J. J. Wesley. *The Microcosmic Health Pamphlet; Or the Wilford Hall Revolution With a Supplement by J. J. Wesley Simpson, Esq.* Toronto: Simpson Publishing, 1890.

Singh, Simon. *The Code Book.* New York: Doubleday, 1999.

"Skeleton May Not Be That of Donohue." *MTr*, October 8, 1906, 8.

"Skeleton That of 'Paddy' Donahue." *MTr*, October 6, 1906, 1.

Snow, Edward Rowe. "Red-Taped Pirate Gold." *Life*, July 21, 1952, 37–40.

Snow, Edward Rowe. *True Tales of Pirates and Their Gold.* New York: Dodd, Mead, 1953.

"Some Facts About the River Tides." *MDTi*, October 4, 1909, 1.

Soucoup, Dan. "Acadian Gold Rush at Hall's Creek Marsh." *MT&T*, July 29, 2000, H5.

Soucoup, Dan. *Looking Back: From the Pages of the Times & Transcript.* Halifax: Maritime Lines, 2002.

Soucoup, Dan. "Search for Buried Gold Piques Readers' Interest." *MT&T*, March 25, 2003.

Stevenson, Robert Louis. *Treasure Island.* New York: Cassell, 1883.

"Still on the Hunt." *MDTi*, September 25, 1899, 4.

Storm, Alex. *Seaweed and Gold: With the Great Louisbourg Treasure of 1758.* Louisbourg, NS: True Canadian Treasure Hunting Adventures, 2011.

"Stray Gossip From Both City and Country." *MDTr*, October 10, 1896, 4.

"Stray Gossip From Both City and Country." *MDTr*, October 5, 1899, 4.

"Successful Farming." *MDTr*, September 14, 1899, 4.

Sullivan, Randall. *The Curse of Oak Island: The Story of the World's Longest Treasure Hunt.* New York: First Grove Atlantic, 2018.

Taroni, Franco, Silvia Bozza, Alex Biedermann, et al. *Data Analysis in Forensic Science: A Bayesian Decision Perspective.* Hoboken, NJ: John Wiley & Sons, 2010.

"Temperance Lecture." *Free Press* (Acton, ON), March 8, 1877, 3.

"This Afternoon's Dispatches." *Guelph Mercury and Advertiser* (Ontario), Februrary 9, 1880, 1.

Thomson, Aly. "Looters Likely to Be Scouring Sunken Treasures off Nova Scotia, Experts Warn." *The Globe and Mail* (Toronto), April 9, 2019. theglobeandmail.com/canada/article-looters-likely-scouring-sunken-treasures-off-nova-scotia-experts-warn-2/.

"Town Council." *MDTi*, September 29, 1877, 4.

"Town Council." *MDTi*, October 11, 1879, 3.

"Treasure Hunt On Near City—Boulders Bearing Inscription Lead to Search for Buried Gold." *MTr*, May 23, 1924, 1.

"Treasure Hunting Offers Inducement In New Brunswick." *Brandon Daily Sun* (Brandon, Manitoba), January 15, 1938, 3.

"The Treasure Seeker's Dream." *MDTi*, October 17, 1901, 1.

"The Treasure Seekers." *MDTi*, October 30, 1901, 4.

Twain, Mark. *The Adventures of Tom Sawyer.* Hartford, CT: American, 1876.

"Wallace." *The Listowel Banner* (ON), October 20, 1876, 8.

"Water in the Town." *MDTi*, October 21, 1878, 4.

Webster, John Clarence. *A History of Shediac, New Brunswick*. Published by the author, 1928.

Webster, John Clarence. *The Forts of Chignecto*. Published by the author, 1930.

Webster, John Clarence. *The Life of Thomas Pichon, "The Spy of Beausejour," An Account of His Career in Europe and America*. Halifax: Public Archives of Nova Scotia, 1937.

"Wedding Bells—Mohan Smith." *The Catholic Record* (London, ON), 1895, 8.

"West. County Court—Bishop Junior Sentenced to a Month in Jail." *MDTr*, March 6, 1897, 4.

"Westmorland County Court." *Daily Telegraph* (Saint John, NB), December 4, 1899, 1.

Whitcomb, Edward A. *A Short History of New Brunswick*. Ottawa: From Sea to Sea, 2010.

Widdifield, C. H. "A Barrel of Gold," in *Picturesque Prince Edward County*, edited by H. M. Merrill. Picton, ON: Gazette Book and Job Printing House, 1892.

"Windgold Guessing Contest." *The Farmer's Advocate and Home Journal* (Winnipeg), September 1, 1909, 1209.

"A Woman Who Talked Magistrate and Lawyers Down." *MDTr*, May 30, 1903, 10.

"A Young Girl's Trials." *Daily Telegraph* (Saint John, NB), October 5, 1895, 6.

Zacks, Richard. *The Pirate Hunter: The True Story of Captain Kidd*. London: Hachette, 2003.

Zahradnikova, Barbora, Sona Duchovicova, and Peter Schreiber. "Facial Composite Systems: Review." *Artificial Intelligence Review: An International Science and Engineering Journal* 49, 1 (2018): 131–52.

Index